THE LANGUAGE OF JOKES IN THE DIGITAL AGE

In this accessible book, Delia Chiaro provides a fresh overview of the language of jokes in a globalized and digitalized world. The book shows how, while on the one hand the lingua-cultural nuts and bolts of jokes have remained unchanged over time, on the other, the time-space compression brought about by modern technology has generated new settings and new ways of joking and playing with language. *The Language of Jokes in the Digital Age* covers a wide range of settings from social networks, emails and memes, to more traditional fields of film and TV (especially sitcoms and game shows) and advertising. Chiaro's consideration of the increasingly virtual context of jokes delights with both up-to-date examples and frequent reference to the most central theories of comedy.

This lively book will be essential reading for any student or researcher working in the area of language and humour and will be of interest to those in language and media and sociolinguistics.

Delia Chiaro is currently Professor of English Language and Translation at the University of Bologna's Department of Interpreting and Translation and President of the International Society of Humor Studies. She has published widely on a number of intercultural issues regarding humour and has given numerous keynote lectures at international conferences around the world. A member of the Editorial Boards of the Mouton journal *Humor: International Journal of Humor Research* and the John Benjamins journal *The Israeli Journal of Humor Research: An International Journal*, Chiaro is also Associate Editor of the "Topics in Humor" book series for John Benjamins.

THE LANGUAGE OF JOKES IN THE DIGITAL AGE

#like #share #lol

Delia Chiaro

LONDON AND NEW YORK

First published 2018
by Routledge
2 Park Square, Milton Park, Abingdon, Oxon OX14 4RN

and by Routledge
711 Third Avenue, New York, NY 10017

Routledge is an imprint of the Taylor & Francis Group, an informa business

© 2018 Delia Chiaro

The right of Delia Chiaro to be identified as author of this work has been asserted by her in accordance with sections 77 and 78 of the Copyright, Designs and Patents Act 1988.

All rights reserved. No part of this book may be reprinted or reproduced or utilised in any form or by any electronic, mechanical, or other means, now known or hereafter invented, including photocopying and recording, or in any information storage or retrieval system, without permission in writing from the publishers.

Trademark notice: Product or corporate names may be trademarks or registered trademarks, and are used only for identification and explanation without intent to infringe.

British Library Cataloguing-in-Publication Data
A catalogue record for this book is available from the British Library

Library of Congress Cataloging-in-Publication Data
A catalog record for this title has been requested

ISBN: 978-0-415-83518-3 (hbk)
ISBN: 978-0-415-83519-0 (pbk)
ISBN: 978-1-315-14634-8 (ebk)

Typeset in Times New Roman
by Swales & Willis, Exeter, Devon, UK

In memory of Christie Davies,
A great scholar and a true friend.

CONTENTS

List of figures ix
Acknowledgements x

    Introduction 1
1 The language of jokes: several years on 6
2 The language of jokes goes global 35
3 The language of jokes and gender 70
4 The language of jokes online 121
    Closing remarks 156

References *158*
Index *164*

FIGURES

1.1	Ping-pong-punning below the line (part 1)	11
1.2	Ping-pong-punning below the line (part 2)	13
1.3	A traditional joke in the form of a meme and conveyed as a tweet	20
1.4	Intertextual humour online	20
3.1	Examples of the term "giggling" emerging as an unsuitable impulse to display publicly	71
3.2	Examples of the terms "children", "schoolchild", "childish" and "childlike" collocated with the term "giggle"	72
3.3	Example of the adjective "cheap" collocated with the term "giggle"	72
3.4	Examples of the terms "woman", "woman's" and "women" as collocates of the term "giggle	72
3.5	Examples of the terms "girls", "girlish", "schoolgirl" and "girly" as collocates of the term "giggle"	73
3.6	Examples of "man", "boys" and "father" as collocates of the term "giggle	73
3.7	Examples of some collocations of the term "cackle"	74
3.8	Examples of some collocations of the term "guffaw"	75
3.9	Source: http://9gag.com/gag/6854629/-when-women-pack-vs-when-men-pack-true-or-not	101
3.10	Source: https://plus.google.com/108531052526575991056/posts/WnjH2b4xXjc	102
3.11	Source: http://cavemancircus.com/2012/02/09/the-female-vs-male-dictionary/	103
3.12	Source: https://ellebeaver.com/2014/05/13/human-brain-analysis-men-vs-women-with-jack-uppal-a-breakdown/.	104
3.13	Source: http://community.dipolog.com/media/male-vs-female-brain.226/	104

3.14	Source: http://mylipsissealed.blogspot.it/2010_06_25_archive.html	104
3.15	Women and men's remote controls	111
4.1	Ping-pong-punning below the line ("muesli")	127
4.2	Ping-pong-punning below the line ("nuts")	128
4.3	Ping-pong-punning below the line: Brexit portmanteaux 1	129
4.4	Ping-pong-punning below the line: Brexit portmanteaux 2	130
4.5	Ping-pong-punning below the line: Brexit portmanteaux 2	130
4.6	Ping-pong-punning below the line ("confectionary")	132
4.7	Ping-pong-punning below the line	133
4.8	Ping-pong-punning below the line ("Bake off")	135
4.9	Examples of "hashtaggery"	136
4.10	Manipulation of an image macro	140
4.11	Sharing "deep purple"	141
4.12	Queen Elizabeth II photobombing Australian hockey players' selfie	143
4.13	A selection of internet memes that parody Italian hand gestures	146
4.14	A selection of internet memes that compare "human" body parts to "Italian" body parts	147
4.15	A selection of internet memes regarding Italian military	148
4.16	Countryballs	149
4.17	A selection of lolcat memes	150
4.18	An example of osmotic meme transference	153

ACKNOWLEDGEMENTS

While writing this book, life got seriously in the way on more than one occasion. That is because I wrote it at a crossroads in my life. Looking after the children was gradually being replaced by looking after the elderly, not an amusing task. As Bette Davis famously said, "Growing old isn't for sissies". Neither is looking after the elderly as it gives you a glimpse into what is yet to come. A good sense of humour really helps. Writing was often sandwiched between teaching, flying around Europe and generally running around like a headless chicken, but I got there in the end.

I would like to thank many people who have contributed both directly and indirectly to this book.

First, my thanks go to the crew at Routledge. I am especially indebted to Louisa Semlyen and Laura Sandford – thank you for your endless patience and for not giving up on me. Thank you also to all the people in London and Oxford involved in the actual production of the book, especially Editorial Assistant Hannah Rowe for being at hand with her ever-ready promptness. Thank you also to proofreader Kay Hawkins and to Rachel Singleton in Exeter. Back in Italy, thank you to Piero Conficoni for assistance regarding IT glitches and anything concerning number and size of pixels.

Thanks also to Giuseppe Balirano, Giuseppe De Bonis, Janet Bing, Federico Gaspari, Giselinde Kuipers, Moira Marsh, Don Kulick and Will Noonan for responding to my frequent demands and providing insightful comments whenever I asked. I owe my gratitude also to my nerdy students, Marco Bruno, Giovanni Laghi and Vito La Banca for their attempts at introducing me to millennials' humour. All in vain guys, I still don't get it.

Thank you to all "The Graun" BTL contributors who I first admired from afar on Wednesdays ("Rhikdays") until I finally had the courage to join in the fray. You are too many to mention, but among the punning leaders thank you most of all Eidos3, Daleaway, Scottish Wildpuss and the one and only king of the castle AnglophileDe.

Special thanks go to Jessica Milner Davis for always being there with sound advice and to the late Christie Davies for his help and guidance, but especially for making me laugh with his endless tirades and for throwing political correctness to the four winds. Christie, you will be sorely missed. I know that nobody is indispensable, but you will be irreplaceable to humour scholars around the world. Thanks to Debra Aarons, my brilliant friend, for her meticulous editing and endless support. I am so glad you didn't do law, Debra, and that you stuck to linguistics instead. Thank you for being there at the antipodes. Do you ever sleep?

My gratitude also to Nikita Lobanov and Anthony Mitzel, my eastern and western political correspondents and experts on everything, but especially humour, preceded by the word "ALT". Thank you Chiara for putting up with my rants.

Finally, yet most importantly, comes my family. Thanks to my brother Joe (*molto famoso*) for providing me with an endless supply of scatological humour from his source of UK tabloids (the names of which I had best not mention) and his fixation on that childhood joke regarding two flies that still makes him giggle. And of course, a big thank you goes to my husband Pippo and our three daughters Jessica Jane, Rebecca Rose and Clarissa Clare for their endless care and support.

INTRODUCTION

At this moment in time, many people inhabit two worlds. One is the world as we know it, the "real" world that we inhabit and that physically surrounds us. The world that we can touch and feel. The other is a more distant world in the material sense, namely the world online with which we engage via technology. While these two worlds are very separate, there is also a huge amount of overlap between them. With each day that passes, we are able to carry out more and more everyday functions that were once restricted to the real world, online. Many of these functions are commercial in nature like shopping, calling a cab or ordering a meal, but others belong to the sphere of interaction in which, among other things, we can convey our feelings, attitudes and emotions. Undeniably, the virtual world overseen by the internet is, at least for the present, limited to sight and sound – the world online is, in effect, one that is language driven and mediated by an alphanumeric keyboard. In other words, if in reality immediate interaction involves speech and hearing, online it principally revolves around writing and reading. So, while we straddle both domains doing some things in one sphere and others in another, or doing some of both in either, communicating with other individuals is a constant feature of one and the other. And it would seem, at least intuitively, that a substantial amount of this communication and more generally of content online is humorous in its intent.

While I write this introduction, wherever I turn, cybernetically speaking, it would seem that the language of jokes surrounds me. Each time I check my mobile phone, I expect to receive at least one witty message via WhatsApp, or *Messenger* and if I venture onto social media, I find innumerable examples of humour that people post and share on diverse platforms. Suffice it for someone in the public eye to show his or her true colours by means of a verbal gaffe and a Twitter storm will surely follow – a hurricane that will certainly contain a fair amount of verbal irony and comic imagery. This vast amount of verbal and non-verbal play is reminiscent of my childhood. Those halcyon days that seemed only to be interrupted by fits of playground giggling at another child's performance of a joke or of a silly, often "rude" gesture, gradually to be replaced in puberty and adolescence by the more daring, but equally amusing content of salacious wit and laughter provoking games like consequences. Who could have imagined that in less than half a century that that playground silliness would be replicated in a virtual space where grown-ups could engage in ludic comity for the entire (real) world to see?

In April 2017, a well-known American airline had overbooked its seats. One passenger, a surgeon, refuses to give up his seat and is violently dragged off the carrier by airline officials. Another passenger films the incident on her phone, posts the video online and within minutes, the newsworthy incident becomes public knowledge. Within very little time, the internet is buzzing with parodies and humorous memes regarding the incident. "Fly the friendly skies", reads a parody of an ad for the airline carrier with a close up of the bleeding face of the doctor who was dragged off the plane, and another reads "Not enough seating, prepare for a beating". One of the scores of parodic videos states, "If you weren't afraid to fly before you will be afraid to fly now. We put the hospital in hospitality". Anything and everything can now be made public in real time, and anything and everything can be ridiculed soon after. In addition, humorous material online related to disastrous incidents such as the one involving the surgeon dragged off an aircraft, rather than diminishing the impact of the actual incident, adds to its gravity.

We are living in turbulent times – pun intended. On 29 March 2017, as British Prime Minister Theresa May triggered Article 50, the first step towards the UK's withdrawal from the European Union, both old and new media announced the news, often in a style that was entrenched in humour. The very lexicon of this socio-economic divorce is bursting with witty portmanteaux such as Brexit(ers), Bremain(ers) and Bremoaners – not to mention the more sensational term "Brexshit". Old media, such as newspapers, as is traditional in Britain, adopted puns for their headlines. Broadsheets opted for quite sophisticated visual wordplay with maps of the EU – *The Guardian* front page sported a colourful jigsaw of Europe with the piece of the puzzle where the UK should be, missing and *The i* chose a cut-out map of Europe with scissors that were cutting out the UK. As for the tabloids, *The Sun*'s headline read "Dover & Out" and *The Daily Express*, "Dear EU we're leaving you". These same newspaper headlines in the online version of the newspapers activated wordplay from members of the public who responded with numerous remarks. "I was expecting 'bye-ee' from *The Sun*" posted a reader of *The Guardian* online, "Or EUR DUMPED" wrote another, followed by, "We've been fuck Dover" and "Surely Ben Dover?"[1] BTL – "below the line" – is the space where readers can post comments immediately beneath articles in online newspapers, and in these spaces for free comments, wordplay abounds as readers let off steam. And, as is to be expected, there can be a lot of anger underlying much political humour posted BTL.

The hoi polloi may not be able to do much about the political strategies of those who govern them, but jokes provide a safety valve for them to highlight the erring ways of their leaders. Furthermore, in a joke they can say what they like, after all, they are "only joking". Or are they? And the internet has provided a playground, a place to share silliness, that often contains more than a grain of truth about those who govern the planet.

In addition, as I write, Donald Trump, as the 45th President of the USA, is being continually held as the target of hundreds, if not thousands, of parodies on social media platforms. These parodies come in many forms. They may be visual parodies in the form of static illustrations or image macros or memes that may consist of a combination of visual and verbal play or else they may be in the form of gifs and video-clips in which users ridicule President Trump and his governing entourage. Meanwhile, Trump's supporters retaliate with equally sharp and witty repertoire. Behind the painted smile of these invisible online comedians, repeatedly, they are making a serious point.

The overall feeling is that humour is most at home online. I really cannot remember the last time anyone actually told me a joke. But day and night family and friends literally bombard me with a wide selection of humorous repertoire albeit strictly online arriving in real time on my smartphone. There is so much witty banter occurring online that actually collecting a valid sample is a daunting task. While we can easily access hundreds of websites dedicated to jokes, capturing spontaneous repartee from naturally occurring conversation, posts and tweets would involve complex data mining from the truly huge amount of material that the World Wide Web contains. Kuipers (2006) suggests that it was in 2001 in the wake of 9/11 that verbal/visual disaster jokes spread over the internet and gained ascendency over face-to-face joke-telling. As I was writing this introduction in the summer of 2017, memetic videos regarding the imminent UK elections were literally flooding my smartphone. No one told me a joke in this regard face to face. It would appear that now more than ever, the medium has indeed become the message. A message that can be shared across geographic boundaries and without necessarily revealing our true identity.

This book sets out to demonstrate that the language of jokes in terms of words and syntax is yet to change. Puns are still puns. Satire is still satire and parody created by the populace gives vent to their feelings about politicians by whom they are represented as well as regarding socio-economic issues that are beyond their control. In this sense, welcome to Ancient Greece. What has changed instead is that we have shifted from slow humour to fast humour. Without going as far as claiming that we are dealing today with McHumour (without a "u" perhaps?), it is however true that we live in a fast-moving world online that tires very quickly of yesterday's news. The relevance of Jonathan Swift's *A Modest Proposal* still rings true in the 21st century despite our cultural and historical distance from the "Irish problem". The question is, will we still be able to engage with the glut of irony in its many forms that exist in both old and new media regarding current socio-political issues 200 years from now? Of course, we could argue that Swift was a great writer and incomparable to the stand-up comedians, anchor men and bloggers and vloggers of today. Above all, *scripta manet* – literally "writing remains". What will remain of online content? Or indeed of so much improvised comedy in both old(er) and new media. One thing is for certain, just as graffiti was the scrawl of the wild yet represented much common sense, online humour is similar. It gives voice to those who normally have no voice. The World Wide Web is a free-for-all where humour abounds. Moreover, so much of this humour is protest. Serious subjects like globalization and climate change, inefficient leaders and corruption are satirized and ironized. Joking allows the man and woman in the street to let off steam. "Save water – bathe with a friend", read a graffito in the seventies, while another read "The Death is an anagram of Ted Heath". Today there are hundreds of internet memes supporting a friendly environment, like the image macro of an angry toddler shaking his wrist saying, "I'm not telling you again, I'm going green". As for politics, memes are having a heyday ridiculing in particular the 45th President of the United States, but simultaneously not sparing any other head of state. Will this accumulation of humour change things? Probably not but, as Davies asserts (personal communication), it definitely takes the temperature of a society at a given moment more than serious discourse could ever hope to do.

This book sets out to look at the language of jokes – and more widely of humour – especially through three matters that define this moment in time, namely translation, gender and all that is socially transient.

Those who are part of an English-speaking community are unlikely to be aware that the rest of the world depends on translation. To an Italian, a Greek or a Chinese person, news, advertising, a large amount of literature, film, TV and, of course, the content of the World Wide Web are received through translation. Alternatively, from someone who has couched their message in a variety of international English and thus quite diverse from more traditional geographical or social varieties. It follows that a lot of humour on both old and new media travels by means of translation which is why I have dedicated a chapter to humour in translation where humour that is originally in English plays a leading role. How many Brits or Americans can name a Croatian comedian? Very few, although I am sure most sentient Croatians have heard of Mr Bean and John Oliver.

Gender is another key term today. The fact that so much humour on the internet is gender oriented reflects society's beliefs and attitudes. Whether women and men come from different planets or simply from different postcodes is the object of much play and inanity on the web. Absurdity that echoes patriarchal attitudes, but which also, slowly and surely, mirrors a changing society.

Which brings us to silliness. A vast quantity of stuff with which we engage on our smartphones is indeed silly in nature. Whether we are looking at a dog behaving like a human or at the repetitive movement of a well-known personality encased in a gif, this material is hardly comparable to an essay on quantum physics.

As with gendered humour, perhaps our engagement with silliness also says something about society. Certainly, I would hazard a guess that in a doctor's waiting room or in a railway carriage people are more likely to be looking at their smartphones than reading a book. And much of what we are engaging with online is transient. We live in a translated, many gendered world that hinges on the temporary. Menus are written on blackboards in chalk; commodities are bought and quickly consumed to be replaced by newer ones. Today's meme is quickly lost within a mountain of other memes that we receive. Online humour is dedicated to the here and now. Fast humour that is here today and gone tomorrow.

I have dedicated my academic life to the study of humour and I am delighted to see that so many comedians today have taken it upon themselves to talk more sense than many (most?) political leaders. Just like Swift, what they say leaves one thinking about how serious matters actually are. Their irony is clever and highly charged but alas, they will not change the world. But they do make us feel good and that we are not alone with our feelings – at least for a short while. Yet not all comedians have late-night TV shows; most remain unknown. They are the scores of comedians who hide behind a pseudonym as they create new memes and share them with others online. They too are the voice of the populace.

The more I read about humour and the more I study it, the more aware I become of how little I know about it. And if my colleagues at work snigger at this humour scholar, in the belief that humour is unworthy of scholarship and that, seeing as we all laugh, they know all there is to know on the subject, my answer is that we all possess a heart but most of us would be unable to diagnose an anomaly. More than ever am I convinced of how serious humour truly is. And I dedicate this book to all the colleagues who over the years have openly laughed at this little humour scholar. After all, as they say, she who laughs last laughs longest – or simply hasn't seen the latest news, or maybe didn't get the joke.

Note

1 Examples from the thread following article by Chris Johnson "The difference 44 years make: how the UK press said goodbye to Europe". Available at: www.theguardian.com/politics/2017/mar/29/the-difference-44-years-make-how-the-uk-press-said-goodbye-to-europe. Published and retrieved 29 March 2017.

1
THE LANGUAGE OF JOKES
Several years on

In 1992, I wrote *The Language of Jokes: Analysing Verbal Play*, a book that I look back on with fondness. This book, like many first publications, was the result of a dissertation, the subject of which, jokes, was meant to be a provocation and a way of highlighting my being different from my fellow postgraduate applied linguists who preferred to tackle aspects of language that were supposedly of more pith and moment. Jokes set out to amuse and thus, presumably, were not worthy of serious consideration, a premise that I wished wholeheartedly to challenge. Moreover, if Wittgenstein could claim that "A serious and good philosophical work could be written consisting entirely of jokes", then surely the subject was worth pursuing in its own right. Therefore, with the tacit support of one of the world's greatest philosophers I went on to dedicate much time and effort both to the subject of jokes and, by extension, to humour in general. Today, more than two decades on, I cannot help but smile at my former naivety. Older and wiser, my attempt at creating a taxonomy in *The Language of Jokes* now makes me wince, especially in the face of so many of my betters who had also produced their own classifications – not to mention those who were still to do so. As far as taxonomies went, I was in the company of those devised by scholars such as Richard Alexander 1997; Walter Nash 1985; Walter Redfern 1984; Graeme Ritchie 2004 and many others. Recently, linguist Debra Aarons, also inspired by Wittgenstein's well-known remark, produced a book in which she illustrates how "many crucial concepts of linguistics" are illustrated entirely through jokes (2012: 1) simultaneously demonstrating how, on a technical level, jokes exploit every possible option available in a language to humorous ends. However, in *The Language of Jokes in the Digital Age*, I will be dealing neither with taxonomies nor with detailed analyses of verbal humour. Neither will I attempt to insert a joke or a gag into a linguistic category or to explain its underlying mechanisms as I had done previously. Instead, my aim is to look at jokes on a wider, macroscopic level and examine their place in contemporary society.

The question that I set out to address in this book is whether the language of jokes has changed since the 1990s. If it is true that the past is a foreign country, so much has changed and so rapidly between the close of the 20th century and the first two decades of the 21st that the answer at first sight must surely be yes, jokes have indeed changed. After all, like everything else in life, change simply happens; it is inevitable. As we become older, along with the world that surrounds us, we change; similarly, both as individuals and as members of a wider society, our language and our tastes change too. It therefore makes perfect sense that jokes and especially the language in which they are couched should change along with everything else. If language has changed since the 1990s, which it has, then it must follow that the language in which the jokes are cast has also changed. The geopolitical changes that have occurred since the fall of the Berlin wall in 1989, coupled with the onset of digitalized communication that allows us to interact in real time with people on the other side of the planet, have had a considerable effect in all areas of life. Massive shifts in population have rendered inner cities multilingual with an increasing number of bilingual and bicultural residents, while, in the meantime, English has become a truly global language. Not only has English strengthened its position as a vehicular language in the traditional areas of science, technology, commerce and trade, but it has also firmly established itself as the foremost language of emails, texting and, above all, social networking. It is becoming increasingly clear that the English language dominates both the real and the virtual world of the World Wide Web. Furthermore, technology now plays a significant role in our daily lives. For instance, there has been a significant shift in the way we use mobile phones. If at first we used mobiles in the same way as we used landline phones, i.e. to speak to someone at a distance albeit while we were on the move, now speaking on a mobile has been largely replaced by texting and above all, instant messaging. It would appear that texting, sort of speech in writing, has replaced much oral communication via mobile technology. It may well be that it is mainly the elderly who use mobile phones to actually speak to someone, while younger people prefer to text. In fact, the use of texting via "smart" phones that are in fact, actually pocket-sized computers, highlights several language changes as this modality relies on the use of short cuts where acronyms replace words and emoji and emoticons can replace whole sentences. Texting, sending emails, posting messages on social media – these are all means of communicating that privilege reading and writing rather than speech and listening. So, it would seem that such virtual communication has restored a certain status to the written word that was seemingly lost previously with the prominence of landline telephony and media such as TV and radio. What I aim to examine in this volume is whether these changes have had any effect on jokes, and if so, in what way. The answer to my quest may well turn out to be surprising.

Jokes and humorous discourse

Although the title of this book refers to the language of *jokes*, discussion will not be limited to the joke form alone. While being perfectly aware that jokes may well be the most studied form of verbal humour by linguists, psychologists, philosophers and many other kinds of researchers, in all likelihood jokes are the least common form of verbal humour. It is more likely that instances of verbal humour occur in books, articles and newspaper headlines, as good lines in film, theatre and television, or as quips, asides and wisecracks in everyday conversation rather than within the framework of the joke form proper. Furthermore, in the 21st century, a joke is likely to be embedded in a virtual post, in a tweet or else circulated by means of a smartphone via instant messaging. Most probably, the reason why the joke has traditionally been the most researched form of verbal humour is simply the ease of collectability. Apart from collections of jokes in book form and those performed by professional comedians, there are entire websites dedicated to jokes. In fact, googling the word "jokes" alone results in 257 million hits, compared to 4.97 million for "quips" and a mere 199,000 for "witty asides".[1] This volume instead sets out to explore diverse areas of verbal humour, which while including jokes, will not exclude other forms of non-serious discourse ranging from witticisms and one-liners to "ping-pong-punning", i.e. sequences of semantically related puns produced by different participants in a conversation (Chiaro 1992: 113), and to internet memes and beyond. What follows are some operational definitions that aim to put some order in the intricate web that embraces what I shall loosely label "humorous discourse".

Humour

Jokes and humour are natural companions. However, while we all know what humour is, the concept itself is not only difficult to pin down, but also to unequivocally define. It is unlikely that there is or has ever been an eminent philosopher or intellectual who has not attempted to produce a definition of humour (for an extensive overview, see Attardo 1994). As with other complex concepts such as intelligence, identity and art, humour is multi-faceted and consequently yields a multitude of definitions, in keeping with its intricate nature. To wit: according to psychologist Rod Martin, humour "may be viewed as a form of mental play comprising cognitive, emotional, social and expressive components" (2007). Another way of conceptualizing humour is found in one of the most prominent theories of humour, Incongruity Theory, which follows in the tradition of a set of ideas long ago proposed by the philosophers, Aristotle and Kant. Additionally, this theory incorporates a cognitive aspect in the production and reception of humour. Incongruity Theory is based upon the ability to recognize incongruity, or what Koestler called "bisociation" (1964). The recognition of incongruity is certainly fundamental to the processing of humour, although not all that is incongruous is necessarily funny.

Laughter, too, although it may be a response to a playful stimulus, is not an essential manifestation of either understanding or appreciating a humorous stimulus because it can reflect emotions other than humour (Chafe 2007; Glenn and Holt 2013; Provine 2000). For example, Provine claims that it is quite common to laugh because of nervousness or anxiety, although it would appear that most laughter simply punctuates natural breaks in the conversation (Provine 1996). Consequently, psychologists of humour have adopted various labels for the emotional reaction to a humorous stimulus. McGhee labels it as simply the "humor response" (1971); Ruch, however, linking the response to some kind of pleasure or amusement adopts the term "exhilaration" (1993a) while Martin prefers the word "mirth" (2007). Even though laughter and smiling may be visible responses to an amusing stimulus, notably, all three labels avoid including the display of physical reactions as the sine qua non of humour appreciation, recognizing that humour can exist in the absence of such reactions. Furthermore, linguist Wallace Chafe points out that the terms "mirth" and "exhilaration" are limited as they are restricted to euphoria and pleasure alone, which themselves may not be the essential reaction to humour, neither do they describe other emotional reactions to humorous stimuli. Chafe therefore opts for the expression the "feeling of non-seriousness" to describe the sensation that everyone recognizes but cannot be unequivocally described (2007: 1). This raises the question of what "non-seriousness" actually refers to and what we mean when we use terms such as "amusing" and "funny". Something can be "funny ha-ha" in that it is amusing, but it can also be "funny peculiar" in the sense of odd and strange – incongruous. Thus, we come full circle as we return to the importance of the role of incongruity, apparently an essential feature of humour that additionally evokes the recognition of a playful frame, one of non-seriousness.

To complicate matters further, we should be wary of confusing the notion of humour with *sense of* humour. Unlike humour per se, sense of humour is linked to characteristics of an individual's personality, and different people have a different sense of humour; in other words, we are not all amused by the same things or to the same degree. However, not even a person with a very good sense of humour is likely to be in a permanent state of light-heartedness. Appreciating a humorous stimulus depends on a combination of both an individual's personality and their frame of mind in a certain situation and at a certain moment in time (see Ruch 1993b).

Openness towards humour is considered to be a positive personality trait. For example, a person looking for a partner on a dating site will tend to seek someone with "a good sense of humour", and there is research that shows that "a good sense of humour" can enhance marital relationships (Hall 2013; Lauer and Lauer 1986; Ziv 1988, 2010). So, as well as involving cognition and emotion, humour also exerts a variety of social functions. Amongst its assorted purposes, humour can, for example, serve as a societal gelling agent by enhancing affiliation amongst people; it may alleviate tension in stressful or awkward situations; it can be a coping strategy. In this view, whatever its function at a given moment, the fact remains that humour leads to beneficial effects on people's minds and bodies. Humour may not necessarily allow us to live longer, but it will certainly allow us to live better (Martin 2007: 332), bearing in mind, however, that just as it can calm and appease, humour also has the power to offend, criticize and control. In this regard, Billig (2005) suggests that ridicule, an aggressive form of humour, may well play a part in maintaining social order.

As is obvious, humour also functions as a major form of expression, manifested in entertainment contexts such as film, television sitcoms, theatrical performances and stand-up comedy as well as in literary works and the visual arts. The use of humour is prominent in marketing, advertising and newspaper headlines. Importantly and noticeably, a significant new location for humour is the World Wide Web rife with entire sites devoted not only to jokes, but also to comic video clips and memes. However, what is interesting about much humorous material online is that so much of it is actually produced by users themselves. During the first decade of the 21st century, comic PowerPoint presentations frequently travelled from laptop to laptop in the form of email attachments. Gradually these comic PowerPoints were generally replaced by amusing video clips, cartoons, memes and witty chain text messages that are spread (hence the adjective "viral") by means of smartphones, tablets and other mobile devices – the name of the popular instant messenger WhatsApp is in itself a play on words.

It is thanks to the technology involved in Web 2.0 that people may now actively engage with internet content. If at first we had to make do with witty PowerPoint attachments, now we can create and upload our own clips, gifs, selfies, etc. For example, YouTube hosts countless videos uploaded by members of the public. Anyone can produce and post a homemade video on YouTube, just as they may post a scene they themselves have extracted from a professionally made film or a TV series or even create a compilation of different scenes by a certain actor or on a particular topic. And much of what people upload on YouTube appears to be actually humorous in intent (see Shifman 2011). Of course, these compilations beg a number of questions. They are not only divorced from the contexts in which they first appeared, but they are consumed in a different era and this must surely have an effect of the way they are received.

Similarly, the Facebook platform also allows users to upload and share things with others, and undoubtedly here too, much of what is created, uploaded and shared is humorous (Baym 1995; John 2012; Shifman 2007, 2013). The pattern seems to be that first I, as an individual, find something funny online that may make me laugh or smile. Second, as I am alone with my laughter, I decide to share that same object of amusement with others, many of whom will display a "like" and possibly forward the message to others who will in turn do likewise. So by forwarding, sharing and stimulating "likes" in others, we somehow create a new form of collective online laughter.

Back to reality. Finally, and above all, humour is everywhere in our everyday lives in the form of witticisms that typically pepper many routine interactions. Apart from jokes themselves, which I will discuss later, much verbal humour occurs quite randomly within regular conversation. Unlike jokes that disrupt ongoing interaction and are performed by those who tell them, witty remarks occur casually, intertwined naturally, in ongoing discourse. Witty repartee occurs in a wide assortment of interactions, ranging for example, from a public speaker trying to warm up and connect with an audience, to an anxious patient at the doctor's wishing to make light of a possibly serious symptom. On the internet, an updated form of ping-pong-punning can be found on forums regarding any subject whatsoever in which one participant will break away from the discourse at hand by creating a pun that will be elaborated upon by another participant who will produce a new pun connected to the first. Next, another participant will join in with another related pun, another participant with another and so on. An example of ping-pong-punning online is illustrated in Figure 1.1, which shows a series

FIGURE 1.1 Ping-pong-punning below the line (part 1)

of screen shots taken from a thread in *The Guardian* following an article reporting a change in the recipe for the shell of a traditional item of confectionary in the UK, namely Cadbury's creme eggs.[2]

Someone triggers a long sequence of puns by posting the comment "I bet it's all been masterminded by *un oeuf* in marketing" and is followed by 15 comments by different participants all containing egg-related puns, with only one commentator appearing and punning twice in the same thread. What is especially interesting about ping-pong-punning such as this is the richness and the variety of linguistic repertoire that is displayed by participants. As we have seen, the session kicks off with an instance of translation-based target-language oriented wordplay (Delabastita 2005: 166). In fact, while the pun pivots on two French words, *un oeuf*, it can only work as such in English where it roughly sound like "an oaf". This quip is immediately followed by an accidental-but-on-purpose reference to "yolks" instead of "jokes" that is in turn followed by an allusion to "foul play" and another to not wishing to "shell out" for this new chocolate egg. The fourth poster claims not to be "eggstatic" about the change while the next person feels "ovoid". An interesting meta-joke then occurs with "Not another pun-fest" contradicted by the same participant in the second line of her post with another instance of translation-based wordplay with "Unoeuf already". Puns including "eggistential angst" and "egging on" follow and while someone attempts to say something serious – well unpunny at least – accusing the journalist who wrote the article of poor spelling, the complainant's seriousness is ignored and is told that journalists' heads are likely to be "scrambled". There is a first attempt to close the thread with someone accusing someone else of having "poached" all his or her puns. The response is an offer to provide others preceded by "shell I . . ." followed by a totally nonsensical threat of being "emboiled in a scrambled with that Pundemonium". Next we have the accusation, "This thread is a total yolk" followed by the authoritative "Albumen and women out there need to give it a rest". Purely nonsensical (but fun), this thread is a performance of wit and talent. Interestingly, as in real life sessions of ping-pong-punning, there is something extremely performative about this outburst of "pundemonia". It is evident that each contributor is trying to match, if not outdo the previous one. Moreover, a significant difference emerges between a session of ping-pong-punning in real life and similar banter online. In real life, ping-pong-punning consists of a battle of wits in which, as the name suggests, like the sport itself, speed is as essential as precision. In real life, ping-pong-punning occurs in real time and puns come in fast with little time to think of a riposte in between one utterance and the next. If we examine the timeline of the banter in Figure 1.1, we find that very often quite a long time lapses between one post and its punning response. In other words, we no longer see the immediacy of the real life version of banter as contributors have all the time in the world to think of and construct responses. Although when someone reads the thread, the result is like being privy to similar conversational play in real life, in effect the thread is far more constructed and less immediate than is its real life counterpart. Although the medium in which this performance occurs is immediate, at the same time content remains static and (can remain) eternally available. Online ping-pong-punning is more similar to a drawn out game of chess than ping-pong.

Figure 1.2 illustrates a similar instance of ping-pong-punning extracted from the same thread but visible further down within the timeline of the text. Although readers see content of a thread vertically, the timeline is actually haphazard in the sense that contributions occur quite randomly and at any time. In other words, a contributor may respond to another contributor at any point at any time within a thread. Consequently, responses depend on both when the contributor actually sees ambiguity worth punning about, coupled with the time to create and then post a response.

Again, we find several instances of punning around the term "egg", i.e. "political-correct-egg-ness"; "eggcellent", "eggsactly", "eggsporting", "eggsample" and "eggsaggerating". As earlier, someone attempts to call the participants to order by implying that their wordplay does not involve true punning. "Did you read about puns in a text book and not really understand?" asks one participant, but the comment is basically brushed off with a "can you go over the main points again", which causes another participant to punningly react with a "Dairy me".

Evidently, wherever we turn, including serious online newspapers, we are likely to find instances of verbal humour outside the joke form proper.

el0villano   12 Jan 2015 20:32
it's political correct-egg-ness gone mad..........

LeftOverIdeas ↪ el0villano   13 Jan 2015 12:24
Did you read about puns in a textbook and not really understand?

barnetbarney ↪ el0villano   13 Jan 2015 14:02
Corr-egg-ness
FTFY

el0villano ↪ LeftOverIdeas   13 Jan 2015 14:12
can you go over the main points again.......?

SmithfieldBuilding ↪ el0villano   13 Jan 2015 14:14
Dairy me

FranklyS ↪ el0villano   13 Jan 2015 18:34
Eggsactly.
I would never consider the Cadbury's Creme Egg to be eggcellent, it's not to my taste, but this is yet another eggsample of the US eggsporting it's particular brand of capitalism to the detriment of quality, and I don't think I am eggsaggerating the seriousness of this issue!

FIGURE 1.2 Ping-pong-punning below the line (part 2)

The joke form

Most probably, the joke form is the part of verbal humour that has been most widely researched. Chafe remarks that scholars show a preference towards studying jokes and favour them to other forms of verbal humour. In fact, he goes as far as comparing jokes to fruit flies that "provide a relatively simple model for genetic studies because of their small size, the ease of raising them in a laboratory, their short life-cycle, and their possession of only four pairs of chromosomes" (2007: 99). As well as being easily collectible, jokes are simple, self-contained units stripped of what Chafe calls the "messiness" of off-the-cuff occurrences of non-seriousness entwined within serious discourse. Furthermore, joke forms and formats are also predictable – think of categories such as knock-knock jokes, elephant jokes, lightbulb jokes, etc. In all these cases, the structure is simple, repetitive, immediately recognizable and hence easily collectible.

Narratively speaking, joke-telling is comparable to storytelling. First, as with the traditional narrative structure of stories, many jokes tend to fit into a limited number of storylines. For example, in the same way that fairy tales favour actions occurring three times (as in *Goldilocks and the Three Bears*; *Rumpelstiltskin*; *Three Billy Goats Gruff*, etc.) so do many jokes such as garden-path jokes, Irish jokes, etc. (Chiaro 1992: 49–58). Second, a story will be typically set apart and detached from the main flow of the ongoing discourse. A story told during a conversation, at a dinner party for example, will characteristically interrupt the general flow to be "performed" by whomever tells it. Moreover, one story will typically lead to another on a similar subject, perhaps told by another speaker. People who tell jokes behave in a similar fashion. A joke will interrupt ongoing conversation and will often be followed by another or more jokes that will be linked to it in some way either in content or in terms of belonging to the same genre (Norrick 2000). A single joke may even generate an entire joke-capping session in which participants tell a string of jokes interconnected by subject matter (Chiaro 1992: 105–17). A modernized version of joke-capping sessions are the sequences of puns made by different participants on internet forums, online threads. etc. (see Figures 1.1 and 1.2, and Chapter 4 in this volume).

Last, similarly to storytelling, joke-telling lies half way between performance and conversation. Jokes typically occur within a frame in which surrounding interaction remains on hold throughout its presentation. The joke teller will characteristically interrupt the flow of the interaction, take the floor and narrate a joke (Sacks 1974, 1978). In place of "Once upon a time. . ." or "Long, long ago. . ." we may find something like, "There was an Englishman, a Scotsman and an Irishman" or a variation on the three participants. In other words, when someone tells a joke, she or he will perform it detached from the rest of the ongoing communication. In terms of Goffman's (1981) analysis of social settings, the joke teller literally performs front stage.

Philosopher Simon Critchley asserts that time freezes during the interval of a joke in that "we undergo a particular experience of duration through repetition and digression, of time literally being stretched out like an elastic band" (2002: 7). While it is well-known that timing is essential in joke-telling – controlling pauses and hesitations, for example, are vital assets of a good comedian – much of the success of a joke lies in the contrast between the extension of time during the build-up of the joke, the setting, and the swiftness and surprise of the final punch.

The General Theory of Verbal Humour

Raskin's Semantic Script Theory (1984) is the first articulated and developed theory of verbal humour. Attardo and Raskin further expanded and developed Semantic Script Theory into the General Theory of Verbal Humour (GTVH; 1991). According to the GTVH, script opposition is an essential component of verbal humour. Attardo and Raskin argue that any single occurrence of verbal humour, i.e. any humorous script, must necessarily consist of two overlapping scripts, one of which is apparent and at the same time shields another, less noticeable, script that is not immediately discernible. These two scripts must be in opposition to each other in order for humour to result. The joke below illustrates the mechanism of script opposition in verbal humour:

> *Girlfriend:* "Darling, will you give me a ring on our wedding day?"
> *Boyfriend:* "Sure, what is your number?"[3]

The girl who is asking her boyfriend for a ring on her wedding day clearly desires a band of gold for the third finger of her left hand. However, the boyfriend's reply reveals that the primary script, in which his girlfriend requests a ring, is in opposition with a secondary script that only becomes clear when we see the boyfriend's response. By asking for her telephone number, it is clear that her boyfriend has interpreted the request "give me a ring" for "give me a phone call/call me" on [their] wedding day. The boy deliberately or accidentally misinterprets his girlfriend's request because the script allows him to do so in that it contains two perfectly overlapping scripts. The joke is a poor one because the girl clearly states that the ring is for their ("our") wedding day and that they will be getting married. The incongruity lies totally in her boyfriend's response. The humour – or attempt at humour – occurs because the overlapping scripts are also in contrast with one another. The boy's response highlights the (slight) incongruity of his girlfriend's utterance by ignoring the reference to their wedding day. Still, the joke is an example of simultaneous overlap and opposition in a single script. These, according to Raskin and Attardo constitute the essential features of verbal humour.

However, this is clearly a sexist joke that portrays women as being primed and possibly desperate to marry, with men doing their utmost to avoid falling into the wedding trap by deliberately misunderstanding requests. Similar chauvinistic jokes will be discussed in more detail in Chapter 3.

Attardo develops the GTVH further to speculate that all jokes can be broken down into six mechanisms known as "Knowledge Resources" (1994). The first

Knowledge Resource (KR) that is essential in a joke is language (LA). Jokes consist of words and the LA Resource refers to how words/language are/is used to create humour.

> Why did the cookie cry?
> Because its mother was a wafer so long.
> *Shultz and Pilon 1973*

If "was a wafer" did not sound like "was away for" there would be no joke – it is language that makes the joke possible. Thus, LA is the lowest common denominator in a verbal joke. The second KR is Narrative Strategy (NA) or the way a joke is structured – the NA may be a long twisted "garden-path" style structure, a riddle, a question and answer format, a limerick, etc. Third, all jokes must have a target (TA) or a butt. Typical targets are people belonging to certain ethnic groups (e.g. Belgians in French jokes; Irishmen in English jokes, etc.); mothers-in-law; tightfisted people (e.g. the Scots), politicians, etc. The fourth KR is Situation (SI) and refers to what the joke is actually about, while Logical Mechanisms, the fifth KR, point to the incongruity present in the script. Jokes are often set against a background of improbable places and odd situations; everyone knows that cookies do not cry and they certainly do not have wafers for mothers, but for the duration of the joke, disbelief is suspended. The final KR is Script Opposition (SO).

The essential mechanism of the GTVH account of verbal humour creation is to highlight the binary perspective created by the overlap of opposing scripts. Another linguistic theory known as conceptual blending presents us with an equally useful set of ideas to study verbal humour. Conceptual blending consists of a "basic mental operation" by which we make sense of things by selecting from existing knowledge we already possess in order to create new meaning (Fauconnier and Turner 2002). If we examine a joke as an example of conceptual blending, rather than seeing it as an incongruity created by two separate opposing scripts co-existing within a single script, as dictated by the GTVH, we come up with an amalgam of meaning (see also Bing and Scheibman 2014). Where the GTVH sees a joke as exposing hidden incongruity, conceptual blending sees jokes more in terms of a fluid osmosis of meaning.

Form and content

Attardo's 1994 KRs highlight the interplay that exists between form and content in a joke. In all probability, SO is the most vital KR for both the creation and the recognition of verbal humour. Yet sometimes, we simply do not "get" a joke. Not getting a joke may be due to any number of reasons including limited knowledge of the language to lacking the relevant world knowledge necessary to understand what is supposedly humorous.

Nevertheless, we usually know when someone is telling us a joke as people are likely to introduce it with an expression such as "Have you heard the one about", "Listen to this joke" or other words to alert us to some new aspect of the discourse. Even if the speaker does not signal the arrival of a joke, its form and content will set it apart from serious discourse. A joke is distinguished by its narrative features, notably the implementation of a target and of situations typical to other jokes. The surprise we get when the "hidden" script is revealed in the punchline is generated by a combination of inappropriateness and unexpectedness that may give us pleasure, a gleeful reaction or at the very least recognition that its purpose was humorous. According to Raskin (1984), jokes break the bona fide rules of communication thus warning recipients to take them lightly. In fact, the makers of jokes deliberately break Gricean maxims (Grice 1975). A joke is pure invention thus untrue and ambiguous thus unclear. These features of a joke fly in the face of the maxims of quality and manner. Many jokes use repetition and lead recipients up lengthy garden paths so that the features of brevity and conciseness are markedly absent, flouting the maxims of both quantity and manner. Finally, jokesters also regularly violate the maxim of relation by ignoring relevance to any preceding discourse.

However, outside the joke form, verbally expressed humour may be less easily recognizable. We may not always be aware that we are privy to humorous discourse when verbal humour is embedded within serious discourse. In fact, when it is unclear whether the speaker is being serious or whether s/he is joking, maxims are broken in a more treacherous manner. Several expressions in English underscore the indefiniteness of non-seriousness – "You must be joking", "Are you joking?" and "I'm being perfectly serious" are all utterances that suggest that the speaker is walking the fine line between serious and non-serious discourse. It is certainly troublesome to distinguish an ironic remark from a serious one if the speaker is wearing a deadpan expression, unless there are contextual clues, including one's knowledge of the speaker.

Finally, jokes allow us to talk about many subjects that would be taboo outside the play frame of non-serious discourse. In most cultures that we know of, death, sex and religion are topics normally handled with care and delicacy in everyday interactions with others. The ambiguity of non-serious discourse allows us to defy social convention and play with forbidden subjects, as we are safe within an area in which anything goes precisely because we are *only* or *just* joking. And this, of course, begs the question of whether we are ever indeed "just" or "only" joking.

Verbal ambiguity

Puns and punning are the essence of verbal ambiguity, even though this is not readily acknowledged (see Aarons 2012 and Chiaro 1992).

> Jokes about German sausages are the Wurst.
>
> Broken pencils are pointless.
>
> Two fish are in a tank. One turns to the other and asks, "How do you drive this thing?"

Traditionally, there has been much debate about jokes that play on language alone and those that play on world or encyclopaedic knowledge (e.g. Hockett 1960), but this dichotomy is surely a false one. All jokes play on language by virtue of the fact that they are made up of and consist of language itself. The three jokes above exemplify basic puns that do all indeed play on words, but they are also pointing at something in the real world. Therefore, while these rudimentary one-liners are manipulating language, at the same time there is no escaping that they also denote aspects of reality. However, leaving aside puns *sensu stricto*, i.e. in words with more than one meaning such as homonyms, homophones, homographs and polysemes, the term pun can be stretched to encompass double entendre based upon diverse forms of linguistic ambiguity beyond lexis (see Chiaro 1992).

> I didn't like my beard at first. Then it grew on me.

If something or someone grows on me, it means that I gradually accept and find this pleasurable. However, the expression "to grow on someone" also has a literal meaning that goes towards creating either the necessary SO and overlap or the conceptual blending for the script to work as a joke. Interestingly, it is the literal meaning, i.e. that beards grow on people that is less evident than the idiomatic, metaphorical meaning. In other words, it is the hidden script that refers to the growth of facial hair. Strictly speaking, this utterance is not a pun; but it does have two readings that would classify it as punning or paronomastic in essence.

According to Cicero there are "two types of wit, one employed upon facts, the other upon words" (*De Oratore* II, LIX, 239–40) (1965: 337) so, unlike the examples discussed so far, superficially the following joke simply plays on facts:

> Two snowmen are standing next to each other in a yard. One says to the other, "Funny, I smell carrots too".

So far so good. We all know that snowmen traditionally have carrots for noses. However, what happens when a reference becomes highly specific in some way? Many jokes rely on highly specific subject matter that will not be accessible to all recipients. The jokes that follow are extremely complex. Knowing that snowmen have carrots for noses is a pretty basic piece of world knowledge; connecting Mahatma Gandhi or a Scottish football team to a song from the musical *Mary Poppins* requires very specific types of encyclopaedic knowledge.

Because he walked barefoot most of the time, Mahatma Gandhi had several calluses on his feet. He also ate very little, which made him rather frail, and with his odd diet, he suffered from bad breath. He was a super callused fragile mystic hexed by halitosis.

Super Caley go ballistic, Celtic are atrocious
Headline in The Sun, February 2000

The punchline of the Mahatma Gandhi joke does not consist of an exact pun but of an expression which, when recited quickly, sounds like "supercalifragilisticexpialidocious", the title of a well-known song from the 1964 Disney musical *Mary Poppins*. Gandhi's predilection for bare feet may well have caused calluses – hence rendering him "super callused" while his continual fasting may have made him "fragile" as well as causing "halitosis". Thus "super callused fragile mystic hexed by halitosis" cleverly sounds like "supercalifragilisticexpialidocious" while containing several elements that describe the Indian politician. Similarly, the headline reported in *The Sun* newspaper plays on the same song title. In the case of the headline, the trope is a *homeoteuleton* or a word with the same or similar ending as another (in this case the ("morpheme") "-ocious" in the word "atrocious").

Language and culture are inextricably linked so that those not familiar with the song will not see or get either joke, and, of course, there is the rub. Over and above the song, the Mahatma Gandhi joke relies on fairly basic general knowledge – although a higher level of knowledge with respect to knowing that snowmen's noses are made with carrots – but in order to get the headline, the reader requires extremely specific knowledge. The headline, in fact, is a very precise reference to Scottish football when Inverness Caledonian Thistle's (aka Caley) had beaten Glasgow's Celtic 3–1 in the third round of the Scottish Cup football competition.[4] This is an obscure reference to those unacquainted with Scottish football tournaments and above all to those with no historical knowledge of them. At the time of writing, the same wordplay appears in numerous internet memes targeting 45th President of the USA, Donald Trump. The basic meme features a close up of President Trump's face accompanied by the caption "SUPER, CALLOUS, FRAGILE, RACIST, EXTRA, BRAGGADOCIOUS" in upper case. The meme went viral and mutated in its journey across millions of smartphones. For example, Matt Lieberman tweeted the meme and comments, "If you say it fast enough, Trump's really quite atrocious" thus parodying the lyrics of the original song.[5] T-shirts and mugs boast variations on the theme such as "Super Callous Fragile Bigot Extra Braggadocious" and "Super Callous Fragile Racist not my nazi Potus". Furthermore, users have generated a variety of memes featuring Julie Andrews in the persona of Mary Poppins and Trump disguised as the chimney sweep from the eponymous film with a similar caption.

In all these examples, the recipient must be able to make a number of complex cognitive connections. In a sense, jokes like these are similar to crossword puzzles – they require working out. While crossword puzzles take time to solve,

FIGURE 1.3 A traditional joke in the form of a meme and conveyed as a tweet

FIGURE 1.4 Intertextual humour online

jokes are immediate. Both ideally end in a feeling of satisfaction at having resolved a conundrum. In a polysemiotic text, such as an internet meme, the puzzle becomes more complex as recognition of the purely visual elements in the meme provides further meaning to its verbal content. Cicero encapsulated the central idea of verbally expressed humour most succinctly when he said, "a witty saying has its point sometimes in facts, sometimes in words, though people are most particularly amused whenever laughter is excited by the union of the two" (II, LXI, 248) (1965: 383).

Joke structure

According to Norrick, jokes are "typically narrative in form" (2000: 169–70). Excluding formulaic jokes such as "knock-knock" and riddle jokes, Norrick follows in Hockett's (1960) footsteps by proposing that jokes are made up of a three-step structure consisting of a "build-up" that is their main body, a "pivot" around which "dual meaning potential revolves" and closure with a "punchline". He goes on to suggest that Hockett's notion of pivot not only conforms to Attardo and Raskin's GTVH in the sense that it provides overlap and opposition and hence dual meaning potential, but that it also fits in with Koestler's notion of bisociation. As Norrick argues, humour arises from the perception of a single event "in two self-consistent but habitually incompatible frames of reference"; hence, cognitively, the receiver of a joke is not only linked to its associative context but is simultaneously bisociated within its frames of reference. Bisociation theory thus synthesizes and subsumes several other theories such as those of Bateson (1953), Bergson (1900), Freud (1905) and Fry (1963). The joke that follows illustrates a typical structure consisting of a build-up, a pivot, closure and a punchline:

> An aeroplane was about to crash, there were five famous passengers on board but only four parachutes left. The first passenger said, "I'm Kobe Bryant, the best NBA basketball player. The Lakers need me. I can't afford to die". So he took the first pack and left the plane.
> The second passenger, Hillary Clinton said, "I am the wife of the former president of the US. I am also the Secretary of State. For the sake of international stability, I need a parachute". She took the second parachute and jumped out of the plane.
> The third passenger, President Barack Obama said, "I'm President of the United States of America. Our country needs intelligent solutions, and as a former Harvard Law School professor, I am the only person who can offer those solutions. Americans can't afford for me to die". So he quickly grabbed the pack next to him and jumped out of the plane.
> The fourth passenger was the Pope and he turned to the fifth passenger, a Rabbi and said, "I am old and frail so I don't have many years left. As a good Catholic, I will sacrifice my life and let you have the last parachute".

The Rabbi turned to him and said "Thank you but it's really OK ... there are enough parachutes for both of us. America's most intelligent President has just taken my Tallit bag".[6]

The text opens with a problematic situation – a plane with five well-known passengers on board is about to crash, but there are only four parachutes. Each of the first three passengers puts forward an argument as to why they, rather than someone else, should get to use a parachute. The structure consists of three identical iterations, with relevant substitutions.

1. The first/second/third passenger + NAME
2. Said, "I AM + THE REASON FOR THEIR IMPORTANCE ON THE PLANET"
3. So he/she quickly grabbed the pack next to him/her and jumped out of the plane.

The build-up consists of the introduction of the three passengers, with the situation of a lacking parachute as the pivot. The change in structure and closure occurs with passenger four who, instead of arguing his case for a parachute, offers it to the fifth passenger, who in turn provides the punchline of the joke. This is a complex joke as it breaks with the norm of three people in a joke where the third provides the punchline. However, jokes do not need to be lengthy in order to have a narrative structure. As Norrick points out, one-liners can also exhibit narrative structure:

> A panhandler came up to me today and said he hadn't had a bite in weeks so I bit him.
>
> *Norrick 2000: 171*

This one-liner consists of three episodes each narrated in chronological order couched within three clauses in the past tense. There is a build-up, "A panhandler came up to me today and said he" a pivot providing ambiguity "<u>hadn't had a bite</u> in weeks" followed by the final punchline "so I bit him". The content is highly compressed, but lends itself to expansion into a lengthier narration, something that would be tricky in the case of short formulaic jokes of the Q and A, riddle or "knock-knock" type:

> Q. Why did the banana go to the Doctor? A. Because it was not peeling well.

While being short and succinct, unlike one-liners, short formulaic joke types like the above lack cohesive links that create narrative flow. Drawing on a predictable formula is an important part of joke construction and appreciation, the longer structure of the aeroplane joke above is also formulaic albeit drawn out at length. The aeroplane joke contains background information followed by three episodes each concluding with a sentence that opens with a conclusive "so" which provides cohesion while allowing the story to develop. Similarly, the one-liner about the panhandler consists of three interlocked clauses recounting three events thus creating a storyline. In order to transform the banana joke into a one-liner with narrative structure, we simply set up a situation containing the pivot "a banana", add the conjunction "and" for cohesion, and place the punchline into an utterance:

> A banana went to the doctor and said "Doctor, Doctor I'm not peeling well".

The repetition of "Doctor" also references the joke to the tradition of (formulaic) "Doctor, Doctor" jokes:

> "Doctor, Doctor my sister here keeps thinking she's invisible!" "What sister?"

> "Doctor, Doctor everyone keeps throwing me in the garbage". "Don't talk rubbish!"

> "Doctor, Doctor, I've got amnesia". "Just go home and try to forget about it".

Of course, these one-liners could be easily lengthened and restructured to become lengthier narratives, but they would no longer fall into the same cycle of jokes.

> A guy suffering from a miserable cold begs his doctor for relief. The doctor prescribes pills. But after a week, the guy's still sick. So the doctor gives him a shot. But that doesn't help his condition either. "Okay, this is what I want you to do", says the doctor on the third visit. "Go home and take a hot bath. Then throw open all the windows and stand in the draught". "I'll get pneumonia!" protests the patient. "I know. That I can cure".[7]

Humouring the patient as in the one-liners is maintained in this longer joke, but it is clearly a different joke in terms of structure.

Joke targets

As we have seen so far, jokes work on the element of surprise in the punchline, a punchline that, ideally, makes us feel good and laugh. It has been proposed that this feel-good emotion derives from our physical or social distance from the target of the joke. According to the philosopher Hobbes, we tend to laugh at others' misfortunes, feel superior and partake of what he called the "sudden glory" (1991: 43) of our superiority over the target of the joke. This is a way of expressing what is known as the Superiority Theory of Humour. Superiority Theory can be traced back as far as the Ancient Greeks with Plato reporting, "when we laugh at the ridiculous qualities of our friends we mix pleasure with pain" (1975: 50) and Aristotle claiming that comedy imitates "persons who are inferior" (1970: 23). Freud considered many jokes to be "tendentious", arousing feelings that could be considered conflictual, aggressive and superior (1905). Indeed, slipping on a banana skin or receiving a custard pie in the face are examples of exploiting the rudimentary elements of comedy. We can enjoy these things from the safety of a spectator; in other words, we might find them funny or enjoyable as long as we are not the victim. Our response therefore emerges from a position of superiority. We feel good because we feel superior to the victim. Hundreds of jokes focus upon some kind of underdog or loser. There are stupidity jokes that attribute lack of intelligence to an outsider; someone who comes from a different part of the country; otherwise the stupid person may be a woman with blonde hair (from Essex in UK jokes), a dictator or an engineering student. We also find underdogs in sex jokes that focus on someone sexually inexperienced or lacking in sexual knowledge, a cuckold, a gay man or a lesbian. Furthermore, in the category of sick jokes the target may be babies, disabled people, rape victims or the subjects of fatalities or disasters.

The work of Christie Davies has been largely dedicated to the study of jokes and their targets (Davies 1990, 1998, 2002, 2011). His research explores diverse categories of jokes collected around the world and provides extensive social and historical reasoning as to why a certain group of people becomes the butt of a joke cycle. Amongst the categories of jokes examined by Davies, we find ethnic jokes, stupidity jokes, those about canny people, about politicians, religion and sex, as well as disaster jokes. Emerging from Davies' work is that time after time the punchline involves the stupidity of the person involved. This narrative operates over and above the target proper, in other words, whether the jokes sets out to ridicule a politician, an Italian soldier or a mother-in-law. A brief overview of the most common joke targets appears below, with reference to the work of Davies for exhaustive historical and social whys and wherefores.

The stupid underdog

The inhabitants of locations known as "Fooltowns" (Davies 1998) have provided material for jokes stretching too far back for memory. Over the centuries, city-dwellers have typically scoffed at their rustic, peasant neighbours for their simplicity, so that just as the Ancient Egyptians made fun of the Nubians, present day inhabitants of England's metropolitan areas ridicule people from Essex – especially the girls. Every centre has its own periphery – its own foolish country yokel. The English have the Irish; North Americans have the Poles; the French the Belgians. The list is endless: Davies provides a comprehensive table of who considers whom stupid (and canny, see below) in several countries around the world (1998: 2–3). The question to be posed is this: what exactly are we doing when we make fun of the different other? Davies argues that certain types of ethnic humour, particularly those in which the outsider is in some way depicted as an underdog or inferior by the hegemonic majority, arise from feelings of economic or sexual fear in the minds of a consolidated and well-established group that they then direct against the new peripheral group entering their society.

Thus, it is hardly surprising that migrants are the butt of jokes in many cultures. In Italy, for example, a country which until recently had a strong tradition of outward migration but little or no internal flow of migrants, the *meridionali*, namely southerners who left the poor towns and villages of the South to seek employment in the affluent cities of the North, became the butt of such jokes. The trait of stupidity in Italian jokes is frequently pinned onto the *carabinieri*, one of the country's police forces, a profession which has traditionally been heavily populated by southerners in search of easily available employment. Today, however, while *carabinieri* jokes continue to flourish, those about stupid southerners in general have been replaced by those regarding manual workers from Asia, Africa and Eastern Europe. Thus, from peripheral migrants, Italians themselves have now shifted to inhabit the centre and consequently permit themselves the newly acquired privilege of becoming the perpetrators of jokes in which new arrivals become the target.

Entire professions can be the butt of stupidity jokes. Davies examines jokes in which engineers, orthopaedic surgeons and the Marines are targeted, as well as aristocrats, dictators, lawyers and bankers. Clearly, in many cases these jokes allow people to vent negative feelings towards a certain category of person from the safety of "it's just a joke":

> Why is the Tory party known as the cream of society? Because it's rich and thick and full of clots.

> How many Conservatives does it take to screw in a lightbulb? None, they only screw the poor.

> Tony and Cherie are at a restaurant. The waiter tells them tonight's special is chicken almandine and fresh fish. "The chicken sounds good, I'll have that", Cherie says. The waiter nods: "And the vegetable?" he asks. "Oh, he'll have the fish", Cherie replies.

The first two jokes make fun of the UK Conservative party. The first is traditional (see Chiaro 1992: 104) linking party members to a ruling class élite that is seen in the second lightbulb joke as working against the interests of the lower classes. The third joke makes fun of ex-Labour Prime Minister Tony Blair and his wife, Queen's Counsel Cherie Booth. What the three jokes have in common is a desire to criticize British politics and politicians over and above their specific political affiliations.

Canny jokes

According to Davies, stupidity jokes are the largest category of jokes that occur in different countries, and although the target may vary, the jokes are universal. Alongside jokes about imbeciles, plenty of popular jokes are about crafty, stingy, canny people. While many countries have their own national misers to joke about, such as the Genoese in Italy and the Armenians in Greece, the Scots and the Jews appear to be the international butts of canny jokes.

> A Scotsman, an Englishman and an Australian were in a bar and had just started on a new round of drinks when a fly landed in each glass of beer. The Englishman took his out on the blade of his Swiss Army knife. The Australian blew his away in a cloud of froth. The Scotsman lifted his one up carefully by the wings and held it above his glass. "Go on, spit it oot, ye wee devil" he growled.

Davies argues that canny jokes are the flipside of stupidity jokes and observes several similarities between the two categories arguing that in both, the contrast adopted is that "between things mental and physical, whether of the body or of the earth ... between mind and matter" (2011: 21). The butt of stupidity jokes are often those whose occupations are associated with material things, for instance, those concerning the soil (labourers, country bumpkins, etc.), while the butt of canny jokes are interested in material or financial gain (misers, lawyers, bankers, etc.). "There is an interesting asymmetry between the two sets of jokes in that stupidity is always laughable but intelligence is funny only when it is linked to the morally dubious acquisition of rewards" (Davies *ibid.*). The joke below provides a good example of this argument.

> A Scotsman has a prostitute give him oral sex. He is about to ejaculate and shouts "Swallow and I'll give you an extra buck!" The prostitute gulps and answers, "What did you say?" The Scot answers, "Nothing".
>
> *Adapted from Davies 2011: 96*

While the tight-fisted Scotsman is undoubtedly targeted, so is the guileless prostitute, although in the end, canniness is rewarded as the Scotsman trumps the woman financially.

Sex

According to the *Oxford Dictionary*, dirty jokes are "concerned with sex in a lewd or obscene way" or, as the *Urban Dictionary* puts it dirty jokes are "to do with disgusting acts of sexual innuendo or other things people might find grotesque".[8] Yet despite dirty jokes being grotesque and obscene, the very fact of their being "jokes" renders their "lewd" content laughable. Freud, on the other hand, saw dirty jokes as being powered by libidinal impulses from which we derive illicit pleasure (Martin 2007).

As Lord Chesterfield famously said about sexual intercourse, "the pleasure is momentary, the position ridiculous, and the expense damnable". If Chesterfield's attribution of the ridiculousness of the positions the human body adopts when engaging in sexual activity is general, then it is hardly surprising that jokes about sex abound. More than any other joke category, jokes about sex remind us of the fact that although we are human, we have the bodies of animals. Furthermore, indelicate jokes concerning sexual acts exemplify transgression from the etiquette of social discourse in which we tend to avoid such subjects. In that sense, jokes about sex are an adult version of scatological playground jokes and songs dealing with nudity, defecation, flatulence and urination – aspects of life that are kept backstage in society. Should someone break wind in a lift, they would be flouting a social norm that would be seen by some as disgusting and by others as funny, or possibly a mixture of both. Typical schoolchild humour includes taunts like "Look up, look down, your pants are falling down!" and the more mischievous "Why fart and waste when you can burp and taste?" Children joke about what they know to be unmentionable and so do grown-ups. By doing or saying the unmentionable, we set ourselves up to be laughed at as disgust becomes entwined with pleasure.

With examples stretching from the literary works of authors such as Aesop, Kafka, Swift and Orwell to Gary Larson's *Far Side* cartoons, philosopher Simon Critchley provides us with examples of satire in which animals take on human features (2002: 31). However, Critchley argues that while the animal who becomes human is endearing and amusing, when the reverse happens and the human becomes a beast, the effect is one of repugnance. Jokes about sex may well remind us of the animal within us, if, as argued by Critchley humour functions by "exploiting the gap between being a body and having a body" (2002: 42), which could explain our mixed feelings of laughter mingled with disgust.

Although by definition a dirty joke is about some kind of sexual activity, at the same time it may also be targeting someone's stupidity. Examining Donald McGill's traditional "naughty" seaside postcards, we see that they are mainly based on saucy double-entendres that usually involve an element of stupidity. A typical postcard features a bespectacled, intellectual-looking man sitting under a tree next to a voluptuous woman in a short, tight dress. The man, who is reading *Kim* asks the woman if she likes Kipling, to which she replies "I don't know, you naughty boy, I've never been Kippled".[9] As Aarons points out (2012: 95), there is also something inherently (and, I would like to add, mysteriously) funny about the word "Kipling". Had the gentleman been reading Browning and had he subsequently asked the woman if she liked Browning to which she replied, "I don't know, I've never been browned" it would no longer have been remotely funny.

As we can see, the joke has a double target; the stupid woman who has never heard of Kipling but also the naïve man who does not take advantage of the woman's (supposed) availability and is therefore considered equally stupid (see Chapter 3 for a lengthy discussion of humour and gender). As is shown in the example below, many jokes involving sex, as well as being salacious, simultaneously target someone stupid or canny.

    Q. Why don't Essex girls use vibrators?
    A. They chip their teeth.

In his pioneering work on conversation analysis, Harvey Sacks describes the structural complexities of the following dirty joke:

> KEN: You wanna hear muh – eh ma sister told me a story last night ... There – There was these three *girls*. And they were all *sisters*. And they were all married to three brothers ... So, first of all, that night, theya're – on their honeymoon – uh, the mother-in-law says – (to 'em) well why don'tch all spend the night here 'an then you can go on yer honeymoon in the *mor*ning. First night th' mother walks up th' first door and she hears this uuuuuuuuuhh!! Second door it's HHOOOHH! Third door it is *no*thing. She stands there for about *twu*nny five minutes waitin for sumpna happen – nuthin. Next morning she talks t' first daughter and she sz – wh how come ya – how come ya went YEEEEEEAAHAGGH last night 'n daughter sez Well it *tickled* mommy 'n second girl how come ya screamed. O mommy it hurts hh third girl walks up to her – why didn' ya *say* anything last night. W*you* tol me it was always impolite t' talk with my mouth full.
>
> Sacks 1978

Although Sacks was mostly concerned with the structure and performance of the joke and its effect on the listeners present, its content pivots round the sexual ingenuity of the three brides and especially the third. The dirty joke is considered as such because it hints at the practice of fellatio. The joke targets (a) the sexually naïve and inexperienced daughter – someone unknowing and surprised at what is happening and (b) the daughter's literal adherence to her mother's rules that make her appear even more foolish. Therefore, although this is a dirty joke, it is a stupidity joke too. Whether we are dealing with a naïve bride or a nosey mother, a canny Scotsman or a stupid prostitute, a dim-witted woman or a self-absorbed gentleman, the sexual element in these jokes takes second place to the idea of someone either taking or not taking advantage of someone else. This is clearly illustrated in jokes about cuckoldry in which the adulterer is the "clever" or canny person who gets away with doing what is wrong and getting one up on his or her partner.

> David was seconds away from receiving a vasectomy when his brother and sister-in-law barged in holding their new-born baby. "Stop! You can't do this!" exclaimed the brother. "And why not?" asked David.
> "Don't you want to have a beautiful baby someday? Like my wife and I have here?" David said nothing.
> The brother grew impatient, "C'mon David, I want a nephew. David, make me an uncle".
> David couldn't take it anymore. He gave his sister-in-law an apologetic look and asked his brother, "You're sure you want a nephew?" "Yes", the brother replied. "It would be an honour". "Well congratulations, you're holding him".

Again, the joke pivots around a sexual relationship that is regarded as taboo in society. Although the sexual element is not overtly mentioned – the recipient has to work it out – the target is the cuckolded brother and his non-knowingness. According to Susan Sontag, the comic is "essentially a theory of non-knowing, or pretending not to know, or partial knowing" (2004: 92). Jokes about sex, and especially those about cuckoldry, as well as being tendentious, satisfy the notion of partial knowing.

> Giuseppi walks into work, and he says, "Ey, Tony! You know who's-a George Washington?" Tony says, "No, Giuseppi, who's-a George Washington?"
> He says, "Hah! George-a Washington the first-a President of-a United States. I'm-a go to night school, learn all about-a United States, and become-a US-a citizen".
> A couple of days later, Giuseppi walks into work and says, "Ey, Tony! You know who's-a Abraham Lincoln?" Tony says, "No, Giuseppi, who's-a Abraham Lincoln?"
> He says, "Hah! Abraham-a Lincoln is-a sixteenth President of-a United States. I'm-a go to night school, learn all about-a United States, and become-a US-a citizen".
> A guy in the back of the shop yells, "Yo, Giuseppi . . . you know who Fishlips Lorenzo is?" He says, "No. Who's-a Fishlips Lorenzo is?" The guy yells, "That's the guy who's bangin' your wife while yo're in night school".

In a party at a luxurious villa, the host says to his playboy guest, "See the women in this room? Except for my mother and my sister I've been to bed with them all". The irritated playboy retorts, "Well then, that means that between the pair of us we have been to bed with them all".

These two jokes targeting Italians are both very different yet are both based on "partial knowing". The joke about Giuseppe is a joke playing on the target's ignorance of his wife's infidelity. While Giuseppe is at night school where he is learning about the USA in order to become a citizen, another Italian is cuckolding him. Education is often seen as a prime value for migrants and Giuseppe is proud that he is going to school and using his head to learn about history. Yet Fishlips Lorenzo, someone who obviously does not go to school, who does not use his head but uses his body and physical strength to "bang" Giuseppe's wife gets the upper hand. What Giuseppe learns and "knows" from school is negatively compensated by the goings on that he does not know about in his own home. Furthermore, this partial knowing is common knowledge to Tony, the third party who informs Giuseppe. Giuseppe is the target because of his partial or total lack of knowledge. It is a stupidity joke.

The second joke is an Italian joke that I have translated into English that also plays on ignorance/stupidity and partial knowing. Above all, the joke plays upon a value that was once common in Italy regarding the purity of men's mothers and sisters and the fact that through their sexuality, sons and brothers could become cuckolds as much as they could through their wives' infidelity. Therefore, while the host proudly boasts about his sexual conquests, the playboy outplays him by confronting him with what was previously unknown information regarding his mother and sister. Thus, the flipside of jokes that align sex with stupidity are jokes that play on sex and canniness.

> When a man asked his widower father why he had married a young nymphomaniac whom he could never satisfy, instead of a woman his own age, the old man said, "Son, I'd rather have ten percent of a good business than a hundred percent interest in a bankrupt one".

The canny widower turns an apparently disadvantageous sexual partnership to his advantage by comparing it to the small yet permanent interests gained by investing in a flourishing business paralleled to no gains in a bankrupt one. So here too, success in matters of the mind and finance outstrip manual and/or bodily, i.e. sexual, concerns.

In mainstream western culture, jokes based on sex generally display an adherence to heteronormative societal rules and attitudes. Although cuckolded males are often the target, jokes highlight women's promiscuity while there are entire categories of jokes that ridicule gay men, lesbians and of course, blondes (see Chapter 3).

Religion

Jokes about religion were extremely common in music hall culture in the UK which, until the post-war period, focused on the greed and hypocrisy of clerics (Brown 2006: 128). Similarly, in Roman Catholic Italy, many jokes target nuns and the issue of chastity, while in English jokes, Irish priests are often depicted as being drunk. Rather like jokes about sex, those about religion are a delicate subject matter. In talking about Jewish jokes, Davies discusses the historical and social reasons for this tradition that is strengthened and perpetuated by Jews themselves who in their jokes target themselves as well as other religious groups (2011).

> An Irish priest is driving down to New York and gets stopped for speeding in Connecticut. The state trooper smells alcohol on the priest's breath and then sees an empty wine bottle on the floor of the car. He says, "Sir, have you been drinking?" "Just water" says the priest, fingers crossed. The trooper says, "Then why do I smell wine?" The priest looks at the bottle and says, "Good Lord! He's done it again!"

Is this joke about religion or is it another canny joke? The crafty priest uses his wits to disentangle himself from a tricky situation, but clearly, the joke touches subject matter that might cause offence to some as it could be seen as blasphemous. Jokes about religion, rather like those involving politicians, allow people to react against authority albeit only within a verbal play frame. For example, the allegations of sexual abuse regarding Catholic priests around the world spawned hundreds of jokes on the internet, yet it is notable that when Conan O'Brien made the following remark on his talk show, it was ill-received by the Catholic League:

> The Pope let two 11-year-old boys ride in the pope mobile with him. Afterwards the Vatican told the Pope "that's not the kind of publicity we're looking for".[10]

The child abuse scandal in the Catholic Church is naturally a sensitive subject. Indeed the suggestion that all priests are paedophiles is as absurd as the one that claims all blonde-haired women are stupid and promiscuous. However, some people may take offence at the suggestion that the head of the Catholic Church could be perceived as a paedophile. On the other hand, publicly joking about something as serious as the child abuse scandal resists the strictures of typical mainstream media discourse and is liberating in this way, despite being simultaneously shocking. Perhaps this is the strongest effect such humour could evoke. Humour is, after all, in the ears of the beholder.

Disasters

Within minutes of a major disaster, the death of a well-known personality or a scandal involving someone famous, despite being in what many people would consider bad taste, jokes based on the calamity begin circulating the internet. Disaster jokes have long been around, but since the internet has replaced the playground and the pub, they are disseminated closer to the event and more quickly than in the past. Opie and Opie (1959) report a playground joke about serial killer John Christie:

> Q. If John Christie had two sons what would he call them?
> A. Ropem and Chokem.

During the 1940s and 1950s, John Christie was responsible for strangling and raping eight women and then hiding their corpses in a house in London. It seems likely that researchers Opie and Opie censored the playground joke about the murderer as the original response; "*Rapem* and Chokem" may have been considered too racy for a book published in the fifties. After Christie's execution, several sources report another playground joke regarding Christie's last request that was "A cup of tea and a couple of tarts". It is difficult to say how jokes such as these originate. Kuipers (2006) argues that they probably stem from an instance of wordplay in a conversation about the negative incident that is subsequently developed and expanded into the form of a joke, after which it is quickly disseminated.

With regard to the spread of disaster jokes, Oring (1992) provides a number of hypotheses as to the reason for the popularity of these kinds of jokes. With particular references to the spate of question and answer jokes that arose following the explosion of the space shuttle Challenger disaster in 1987, Oring argues that the very "unspeakability" of the disaster that "may conjoin an unspeakable, and hence incongruous, universe of discourse to a speakable one" is unique to the joke form (1992: 23). The space shuttle explosion and later the death of Princess Diana and the events of 9/11 all received huge media coverage imbued with a rhetoric of tragedy and mourning. Oring asks himself if joke cycles about disasters are not a rebellion and claims convincingly that such cycles may well be an insurgence against public discourse and the conventionalization of media discourse surrounding disasters.

Suspending disbelief

Like other fictional works such as novels, plays and films, jokes work on the notion of suspension of disbelief. Those participating in the performance of a joke, whether the joke is narrative or formulaic in nature, put reality on hold throughout its enactment and enter what Bateson (1953) defines as a "play frame" in which we, the listeners, adhere to an unwritten pact. We temporarily enter a sort of time freeze in which rules of reality stand still for the duration of the joke (Critchley 2002: 7). If we consider just two of the examples examined so far, it would be extremely unlikely that the President of the United States, his Secretary of State and the Pope would be travelling aboard the same aeroplane, and it is even more improbable that a banana can speak, let alone walk into a surgery and converse with a Doctor. Yet, of course, it is these very implausible circumstances that signal the fact that we are entering a play frame, in this case, joke territory. In addition, a number of joke categories work around a series of mechanisms that defy all common sense and logic. Attardo, for instance, chooses to examine the category of "lightbulb jokes" (1994: 70–8) both in terms of the way in which they are constructed and in how they build up the recipients' expectations.

> How many Californians does it take to screw in a lightbulb? Ten. One to screw it in and nine to enjoy the experience.

Although it is clear that screwing in a lightbulb is a simple operation that can be carried out by a single person, "lightbulb jokes" set out to target and ridicule different categories of people by asking, for example, "How many X, Y, Z (e.g. lawyers/ teachers/feminists/blondes, etc.) does it take to screw in a lightbulb?" The answer will usually be a number higher than one, followed by an explanation for the high number of people involved. This explanation will play on a stereotypical feature of the targeted group. Whenever we are questioned about the number of people of a certain category required to screw in a lightbulb, based on our past experience of the trope, we automatically know that we are in the realm of non-seriousness and we will expect a facetious (but often very acute) answer to be delivered. In fact, jokes allow us to suspend our disbelief in terms of illogical mechanisms, such as those involving a large number of people to carry out a simple task. In jokes, animals and objects often take on human attributes and adopt human behaviour. "Bartender" jokes, for example, typically involve anthropomorphized animals or objects entering a bar and making requests.

> Three pieces of string walk into a bar. The bartender says, "Sorry, we don't serve strings here!" They go outside and one of the strings messes up his hair and ties himself up. He walks back inside and the bartender says, "Aren't you one of those strings I just got rid of?" The string says, "I'm a frayed knot!"

> A duck walks into a bar, and asks the bartender, "Got any duck food?" The bartender just shakes his head and says, "Nope". The duck leaves. The next evening, the duck comes back and asks the bartender, "Got any duck food?" Again, the bartender shakes his head and says "Nuh-uh" and again, the duck leaves. The next day, the duck comes back again. The duck asks, "Got any duck food?" The bartender just shakes his head yet again and says, "Nope". Anyway, after a couple of weeks of slowly simmering irritation, the bartender finally snaps when the duck comes in, and screams at the unfortunate bird, "I swear that if you ask me for duck food again I'll nail your feet to the floor!" Startled, the duck leaves without saying another word. The next evening the duck still comes in but instead asks, "Got any nails?" Mildly surprised, the bartender replies "No". A short pause follows. "Got any duck food?"

> Two dragons walk into a bar. Dragon One: "It's hot in here". Dragon Two: "Shut your mouth!"

Alongside anthropomorphism, jokes typically take place in far-fetched settings. Heaven, Hell, desert islands, cannibal cauldrons, firing squads and, as we have seen, falling aeroplanes with a combination of famous passengers are typical joke situations. This is why, as we shall discover further on, joking about the here and now outside the joke form, may be doubly ambiguous and raise questions regarding whether the joker is to be taken seriously or not.

Notes

1 Sources: www.google.co.uk/#q=Jokes; www.google.co.uk/#q=witty+asides and www.google.co.uk/#q=quips. All retrieved 22 November 2014.
2 Comments following an article by Adam Gabbatt, "Shellshock! Cadbury comes clean on Creme Egg chocolate change", featured in *The Guardian* 12 January 2015 and available at: www.theguardian.com/business/2015/jan/12/shellshock-cadbury-comes-clean-on-creme-egg-chocolate-change. Retrieved 7 July 2016.
3 Joke retrieved from Gag Universe available at: www.gaguniverse.com/joke-1142-girlfriend-darling-will-you-give. Retrieved 7 December 2015.
4 Scott Murray, "The Joy of Six: great football headlines", *The Guardian* 12 December 2008. Available at: www.theguardian.com/sport/blog/2008/dec/12/joy-of-six-headlines. Retrieved 25 November 2014.

5   Although I was unable to trace the original meme, I would like to thank Matt Lieberman from UCLA for allowing me to use his original tweet with the meme that is available at: https://twitter.com/social_brains/status/781501429420883968. Retrieved 27 February 2017.
6   An updated version of the joke is as follows: The first passenger said, "I am Steph Curry, the best NBA basketball player. The warriors and my millions of fans need me, and I can't afford to die". So he took the first pack and left the plane. The second passenger, Donald Trump, said, "I am the newly elected US President, and I am the smartest President in American history, so my people don't want me to die". He took the second pack and jumped out of the plane. The third passenger, the Pope, said to the fourth passenger, a 10-year-old schoolboy, "My son, I am old and don't have many years left, you have more years ahead so I will sacrifice my life and let you have the last parachute". The little boy said, "That's okay, Your Holiness, there's a parachute left for you. America's smartest President took my schoolbag". Available at: www.reddit.com/r/Jokes/comments/5c2j2a/an_airplane_was_about_to_crash_there_were_4/. Retrieved 27 February 2017. The joke is extremely memetic as it is replicated in dozens of versions including an Italian version featuring Obama, Putin, Berlusconi and as always, the Pope.
7   Joke available at *Reader's Digest*: www.rd.com/jokes/doctor/. Retrieved 10 August 2016.
8   See www.oxforddictionaries.com/it/definizione/inglese/dirty and www.urbandictionary.com/define.php?term=dirty%20jokes. Retrieved 2 June 2016.
9   Description of a postcard on view at the Donald McGill Museum in Ryde (Isle of Wight, UK): http://saucyseasidepostcards.com/. Retrieved 16 February 2015.
10 The remark occurred on *Conan* (TBS) 14 April 2014: www.catholicleague.org/conan-hits-belt/. Retrieved 23 February 2015.

2
THE LANGUAGE OF JOKES GOES GLOBAL

From the 20th century onwards, performed humour, previously restricted to the stage and the radio, could now also be enjoyed on screen. Beginning at the turn of the 20th century with the establishment of the "silver-screen", a medium for showing a wide range of comic films, by the 1950s, after the advent of television, an assortment of comedic products became available in people's homes too. In western countries, at the start of the 21st century, a further change occurred in the production and consumption of entertainment as a series of new and "smart" screens started to spread many varieties of audiovisual products, including, of course, different forms of comedy. At the time of writing, people are able to watch comedies, sitcoms and a spectrum of comic audiovisual material via laptops, tablets and mobile phones, yet significantly, none of these technologies has replaced or destroyed its predecessors. Just as the advent of films did not eradicate books and in turn, TV did not supplant the cinema, smart screens are not replacing TV. All happily co-exist, although it does appear that the way people consume screen products is indeed changing.

Initially with the arrival of DVD technology and subsequently with the availability of media streaming and commercial providers such as Netflix and Amazon, we can now watch films and TV products whenever and wherever we like. While the performance of humour remains constant, in essence such performances do, however, seem to be appearing in new places being differently consumed and diffused through communities of viewers.

It goes without saying that thanks to a number of user generated sites online such as YouTube, millions of audiovisual texts are now easily available, not only in their original fullness, but also, and above all, in the form of clips, compilations and in "greatest hits" formats. Weitz sees the internet as an "apparent goldmine of humour related performance" (2017) but wonders whether being able to control the performance by skipping, repeating and pausing, changes the viewer's response.

Not only that, but compilations made up of clips from a comedian's different performances may also affect response. Clips by their very nature are divorced from the whole in which they originally occurred, not to mention their historical context. In other words, a user who uploads a favourite comic clip provides something that is partly original; it is his or her favourite part of a film perhaps. However, this clip can be seen and revisited repeatedly by others, yet at the same time, it will remain devoid of its original context.

Just as the general public can now make and post its own materials aimed at entertaining others online, they have also become protagonists on TV. Towards the end of the 20th century, television shows began, on an increasingly large scale, to spotlight not only well-known personalities, but also members of the public. While mainstream game shows, talent shows and cookery programmes have been a traditional part of TV schedules, contemporary versions of these shows now embrace a much wider variety of genres and sub-genres. So-called lifestyle TV now includes, for example, programmes based on self and home improvement as well as dozens of contest shows. These programmes show ordinary people and/or well-known personalities who may be involved in hunting for property, choosing a partner, planning a wedding, or undertaking a "reality" challenge such as trying to survive on a desert island. A prominent feature of these programmes is that their participants convey the impression of naturalness, spontaneity and, of course, "being real". While the primary focus of these shows ranges from the quest for the right wedding dress, or looking ten years younger to baking the perfect sponge cake, a typical episode is sure to contain a fair amount of light-hearted banter as well as instances of diverse types of verbally expressed humour. The humour may manifest itself in the programme presenter's wordplay directed at the home audience; it might take the form of joking, teasing or sarcastic remarks made by a participant aimed at other participants in the programme. This humour often serves as a way of involving audiences emotionally with the contestants and creating a sense of familiarity with them. Whatever the humorous remark and whoever it is aimed at, it is likely that viewers tune into these shows to watch participants' performance (humorous or otherwise), as much, if not more than because of their interest in their subject matter of the programme itself.

However, a fact often overlooked by English speakers who have the privilege of watching programmes produced in English with English-speaking audiences in mind, is that speakers of other languages around the world are likely to consume many of the same programmes, albeit through translation. In other words, in order for these products to travel from culture to culture, first they have to undergo a number of changes brought about through the necessary process of translation. This shift from one language to another is likely to cause radical divergence from the original discourse and particularly the humorous aspects of that discourse.

In fact, many more screen products are translated from English into other languages than vice versa simply because of the strength of the English language and North American media systems that generate the bulk of audiovisual productions. For example, while TV programmes like *Britain's Got Talent*, *MasterChef* and

Location, Location, Location are broadcast in Italy either in their dubbed versions or accompanied by subtitles, their reciprocal Italian equivalents, *Italia's Got Talent*, *MasterChef Italia* and *Cambio Casa Finalmente!* – literally, "I'm finally changing house!" – are not broadcast in the UK or in the USA. The same is true of programmes in other languages too. Broadly speaking, with the exception of Scandinavian noir detective series that are regularly translated and subtitled for UK audiences, as far as TV is concerned English language speaking products have the lion's share.[1]

Over and above lifestyle/reality TV, the power of English-speaking and especially North American based media is such that English language movies and sitcoms are internationally well-known, as are English-speaking comics, such as Amy Schumer, the Wayans brothers and John Oliver. However, while their international fame can also be explained by the fact that their recorded performances undergo the process of translation, the same cannot be said for comic products and comedians from non-English-speaking countries. Popular comedians such as Italian Maurizio Crozza, Spanish Dani Rovira, French Raymond Devos, Russian Evghenij Petrosian and German anchorman Harald Schmidt are unlikely to be known outside their countries of origin. A custard pie may well be a custard pie, but there is a huge imbalance in the availability of geographical and lingua-cultural sources of screen products. Discussing the homogenization of young people's tastes and what they consume in a globalized world, Dutch sociologist Marieke de Mooij (1998) argues that despite the fact that youngsters around the world dress in a similar way (e.g. in terms of brands of jeans, trainers, etc.) and enjoy the same kind of junk foods, their tastes in music differ significantly. Indeed, alongside international pop mega-stars, each country has its own musical celebrities that are rarely, if ever, successful elsewhere. The same is true for the personalities in other media, and screen comedy is no exception. Thus, as with pop music, the globalization of audiovisual comedy is largely one-directional, emanating from the USA and to a lesser extent, the UK.

Humour in unscripted TV entertainment

"Scripted" comedy refers to a comedic script that has been written with performance in mind. Such comedy contains lines that the actors have studied, learnt, rehearsed and finally performed. Sitcoms are scripted and the scripts are performed by actors. On the other hand, "unscripted" programmes, such as those in the various lifestyle formats, including talent shows, contests and so on, are considered to display spontaneity and improvisation, especially because of the presence of members of the public. Yet this is unlikely: for people appearing completely unprompted on TV, ignorance of content and lack of structure in their performances might prove risky. So, before filming, at the very least, talk show guests will have an idea of the questions the host is going to ask them and contestants in cookery competitions are likely to know beforehand what they are going to bake. Thus, the difference between scripted and non-scripted TV is not especially clear-cut.

As illustrations of such blurring, there is a spread of possibilities. First, the presenters of "unscripted" programmes, who are usually TV personalities in their own right, are likely to make use of humour. However, the type of jocularity that presenters adopt will, of course, vary not only from person to person but also according to the recipients of the discourse. For instance, a TV chef alone on a set explaining a recipe to a remote audience may have a different comic style from a trio of chefs judging a cookery contest, bantering both amongst themselves and with competitors. Even so, it is unlikely that so-called spontaneous discourse is off-the-cuff; a certain amount of scripting is bound to be involved. Although there is nothing to stop competitors themselves making witty remarks or jokes, the extent to which these remarks are spontaneous and unscripted remains a mystery. Second, participants in many "unscripted" formats may be the butt of humour and laughed *at* because of their shortcomings. It may be the case that this last use of humour is unprompted; however, it may indeed be possible that initiators of such jocularity are prepared to make remarks to exploit the shortcomings of participants to humorous ends.

The role that humour plays can be identified in an overview of different types of non-serious discourse adopted by players within some randomly chosen popular cookery, talent and lifestyle formats.

Presenting with humour

While audiences may expect humour to be part of the discourse of the host of a variety show or a chat show, they can now expect it to be part of the talk of presenters in more disparate programmes too. In fact, many presenters of lifestyle, talent and reality shows make use of humour. For example, cookery programmes of the 21st century are not restricted to recipes but also provide comic relief. Rossato (2009) provides an extensive account of the history of televised cookery programmes in the UK since the 1940s, arguing that a significant change in these shows over time lies in the way that their content has shifted from the merely instructional towards a more entertaining stance. If from the seventies to the nineties TV chefs such as Delia Smith and Madhur Jaffrey appeared before an audience to explain how to create a dish, which is exactly what they did and nothing more, today's TV chefs seem also to be there to entertain and to amuse. Successful celebrity chefs like Jamie Oliver and Nigella Lawson try to create an intimate relationship with their audiences and frequently stray from the task of simply illustrating the dynamics of a recipe. And as they stray, they use humour.

The importance of hosts to a TV programme is due both to their skills in the subject at hand (e.g. cookery, dancing, singing, etc.) and to what Langer (1981) has defined as television's "personality system" which "works directly to construct and foreground intimacy and immediacy". While the movie star system of the more distant past placed personalities beyond the reach of the public, both in terms of their physical distance on the big screen and in real life, television constructs an aura of familiarity by bringing personalities into people's homes on a regular daily or weekly basis. TV personalities typically enter domestic environments and act within a similar environment recreated on screen, such as the living room with sofas and chairs typical of the chat show or a kitchen especially created on the set. Nowadays, however, cookery programmes are often recorded in authentic locales and part of the attraction of many of these shows are the chefs themselves. For example, Nigella Lawson has recorded programmes from what appears to be her London home and many of super-chef Jamie Oliver's shows are recorded in either his home or those of his friends. Thus, personalities enter viewers' households in replicated (and envy inducing) home environments while also (seemingly) allowing viewers to share in their private lives. Audiences see personalities in close-up shots so that they are able to witness their reactions and emotions as the presenters apparently engage with them informally. Langer highlights how the barriers that exist between the personality and the public seemingly break down. Jamie and Nigella have both developed distinctive TV behaviours. Jamie's casual ordinariness and Nigella's sensuality exemplify what Langer described as "playing" oneself (1981: 335), a factor that renders them familiar to audiences.

Both Nigella and Jamie create a bond with viewers through their warm and friendly chitchat that includes a fair amount of humorous discourse (Chiaro 2013). In fact, while explaining how to prepare their dishes, the two chefs will typically pepper their instructions (pun intended) with witty banter. Much of Nigella's humour consists of gentle unassuming mockery. Nigella has a curvaceous figure and highlights her love of food with declarations like, "I might give myself a modest portion" [of a freshly prepared kedgeree]; the "modest portion" turns out to be quite generous. She also plays on her carefully contrived sexual allure. As she adds hot chilli pepper to a dish, she tells viewers that: "I always like to go just a little too far I suppose". Moreover, she sometimes attempts an even more allusive style of humour – while she is preparing a spatchcock she declares, "I like a bit of dismemberment in the evening".[2] The credits at the end of each episode of *Nigella Bites* feature Nigella dressed in her nightwear raiding her fridge during the night and sensuously eating a snack. While playing on her sensuality and abundant curves, Nigella does not take herself seriously and the late night invasions of her refrigerator are very much tongue-in-cheek and self-mocking, contributing to the warm, not too serious TV persona she has created.

Jamie Oliver, on the other hand, is stylistically less subtle than Nigella. For example, when peeling onions makes him cry, he complains of "Me old sinuses!" and he exploits traditional Cockney expressions like "the old caramello is bubbling away like the clappers",[3] creating a relaxed and humorous atmosphere. Nigella and Jamie, as many other celebrity chefs, are funny and charming; and it could well be that audiences watch them as much, if not more, for entertainment purposes as for their recipes.

Comedy duo Mel Giedroyc and Sue Perkins, the presenters of *The Great British Bake Off*, a contest to find Britain's best baker, have also created their own TV personalities, playing themselves by making ample use of humour.[4] In each episode, amateur bakers compete against each other in a set of baking challenges judged by cookery writer Mary Berry and celebrity chef Paul Hollywood while the duo provide comic relief, interacting not only with the audience but also with each other, the judges and the contestants. Mel and Sue are especially dedicated to creating rudimentary puns pertaining to cakes and baking. For example, typical *Bake Off* puns include, "How do you make a Swiss roll? Push Roger Federer down a hill" (Series 5, Episode 1) and greeting contestants who are about to bake a Madeira cake with "Right m'dearas" (Series 6, Episode 1). In the same vein, in an episode in which competitors were asked to make puddings, they were told to expect their "just desserts" (Season 5, Episode 4). Again, in a 2015 spin-off in which comedians competed against one another to raise money for charity, Mel opens the programme with a pun about the contestants making an "effort to make some dough".[5] The couple's punning repartee has become such an important part of the show, that at the start of an episode in which the contestants are about to make bread, the duo are seen (pretending to be) thinking up gags. Mel visibly acts out her thinking and says, "Bohemian Bap-sidy?" with which Sue pretends to judge the pun approvingly, "That's good".

However, not all the duo's puns are perceived to be innocent causing several viewers to complain to the BBC about their "smutty jokes" in which they refer to [cakes'] "soggy bottoms" and "cracks", to "hot buns" and to a cake tin looking like a "piles cushion". In an episode in which contestants were baking tarts (Series 5, Episode 5) Sue asks one of the participants "What's your version of a tart?" then turns to the camera and quizzically raises her eyebrows. Later in the episode, Mel asks a female participant whether she is a pie or a tart. The contestant answers that she is a tart to which Mel answers, "So am I" and they both break into giggles. Are these puns innocent or deliberately saucy?

Winner of the third series John Whaite (2014) defends the duo's banter claiming that punning is part of British comic tradition, arguing that when Judge Mary Berry complimented him on his "lovely sausage" he "almost fell off [his] my stool" but she was merely commenting on his bake. Although Whaite's exact response was: "Steady on Mary", the rejoinder did not make the cut. As Mary's remark was not endorsed with a rebuttal, it remains ambiguous and not necessarily lewd. To quote political cartoonist Martin Rowson (2014):

> But there lies the true beauty of cheap sexual innuendo: it's both subversive and deniable: the double meaning, the code cementing the conspiracy of laughter between jester and jestee, means any filth detected by anyone choosing not to get the joke exists solely in the filthy minds of the complainant.

Therefore, when Sue tells contestants attempting to bake Berry's cherry cake that they "have got two hours to pop Mary's cherry [pause] in the oven", the interpretation of the remark remains entirely in the mind of the viewer. Certainly, this kind of innuendo is within the British comic tradition from cheeky seaside postcards (see Chapter 1) to the *Carry On* tradition and, as Rowson points out, it is not altogether divorced from the kind of innuendo adopted by Lawrence Sterne in *Tristram Shandy*, a book that is well part of Britain's literary heritage.

Andrew Zimmern, the presenter of *Bizarre Foods with Andrew Zimmern*,[6] exemplifies a very different way of using humour when presenting. Zimmern allows himself to be laughed at, albeit benevolently, by audiences as he travels the world and presents cuisines that are perceived as being disgusting according to the common imaginary. Zimmern will typically present a local dish that might consist of some kind of insect or the unlikely body part of an animal. After showing audiences how the dish is sourced and prepared, he will then proceed to eat it. So, while for many viewers the very contents of the dish itself may raise a horrified smile, as Zimmern slowly chews, savours and swallows beetles, white worms from the larvae of crickets or bull's testicles, his facial expressions are likely to provoke laughter and amusement – especially when the food is not to his taste. However, the incongruity of Zimmern's expressions of ecstasy as he tastes a foodstuff that is unlikely to be found on a regular diet, are sufficient to create humour.

How Clean is Your House is another of many UK TV lifestyle makeover programmes that includes humorous discourse.[7] Each episode presents experienced cleaners Kim Woodburn and Aggie MacKenzie who visit an exceptionally filthy and unkempt home. After inspecting the premises for dirt and grime, Woodburn and MacKenzie reprimand the owners for their slovenly habits, offer practical advice on how to carry out household tasks, and with the help of a team of professional cleaners, proceed to clean the premises to utmost perfection. However, if on one level, this "before and after" format is instructive, especially in terms of tips regarding how to set about a variety of household tasks, on another level the programme is also funny. Apart from the shock/amusement factor arising from viewing the extreme living conditions of the occupants of the households, each episode is also a sort of humorous cautionary tale in which the participants and television audiences are engaged by and in laughter (Chiaro 2016a).

Actor Paul Copley provides whimsical, often alliterative voiceover narration for each episode. Typically, the show begins with an overview of someone's filthy household with the camera focusing on piles of rubbish and debris, accompanied by music from a horror movie. Kim and Aggie first quickly inspect the household and then change into their cleaning uniforms while yellow and black barricade tape reading "Grime investigation" is placed around the offending property together with a "Caution – Cleaning in progress" placard. Copley continues the tongue-in-cheek mode with witty comments (see Chiaro 2016a). In the episode concerning the "Crossword Lady", a well-spoken woman whose central London flat is in a total mess because she prefers doing crosswords to cleaning, Copley's voiceover says:

> Rosie Loveland is a crossword fanatic but when it comes to cleaning, **she hasn't got a clue**. With over 3,000 books, she spends all her time pondering over puzzles rather than **solving her hygiene problems** . . . Rosie is obsessed with words but **cleaning is clearly not in her vocabulary**.

Like Mel and Sue of the *Bake Off*, Copley takes words and expressions from the semantic field related to the specificity of each episode and spins out as many connected puns as possible. For example, in the "crossword lady" episode, when Kim arrives in a black cab, Copley asserts that, "Kim's got the knowledge" playing on the name of the rigorous training that London taxi drivers go through in order to get their badge known as "The Knowledge". The wordplay continues with remarks noting how Kim and Aggie are "puzzled by the boudoir of books", are about to face a "cleaning conundrum" as they stop Rosie reading "dirty books". In addition, Rosie, who was "clueless" about cleaning, finds a "solution to 24 years' muck" when Kim and Aggie make a "clean sweep". Unlike Mel and Sue's risqué remarks, the closest to innuendo in the episode are Copley's references to "dirty books". It seems unlikely that Copley's voiceover has not been carefully thought out, written down and rehearsed at length in order to get the essential timing right. The same must also be true of Mel and Sue who are able to come up with numerous cheeky and fitting puns in each episode of the *Bake Off*. The concept of "unscriptedness" definitely needs to be stretched somewhat when applied to these sorts of shows.

Another type of humour in *How Clean is Your House* involves the use of foreign words and accents for comic effect. An episode involving the untidy house of Frenchwoman Veronique allows Copley to indulge in some cross-language wordplay. In a camp voice, Copley declares, "When it comes to hunting out the dirt, Kim and Aggie are a *tour de force*", as they get the "*enfant terrible*" to say "*au revoir*" to clutter. The joking continues as the "*crème de la crème of cleaning*" are in an apartment that has lost its "*panache*", which by the end of the episode is pronounced "*c'est magnifique*" while the "slovenly kitchen that used to be a terrible sight to behold, is now a place for one of Veronique's *soirées. Vive la différence*". The *Bake Off* presenters Sue and Mel also adopt foreignness for comic purposes as in the episode on European cakes (Season 5, Episode 5). Sue parodies a Dutch accent, a Lithuanian accent (pre-empted by "I apologize to all Lithuanians") as well as a Swedish accent when the contestants bake a Swedish Princess Layer cake known as a *Prinsesstårta*.

Ant and Dec (Anthony McPartlin and Declan Donnelly) the two Geordie presenters of the talent contest *Britain's Got Talent*,[8] also "play themselves" while mainly remaining backstage watching contestants – who hope to win a place to perform before the Royal Family – sing or dance before a panel of judges. Above all, the duo encourages performers before they go on stage and then, after their performance, either congratulates or commiserates with them. The cameras focus on the duo as they provide comic relief to audiences through their reactions to each competitor's performance. Ant and Dec, behind the scenes, look into the camera, i.e. at the remote audience at home, and supply a wide range of reactions to each act. They may give a thumbs up, exaggeratedly nod their heads in approval, or in some other way display their enjoyment of the act on stage. They may, however, mimic a weak act too. In fact, much of the time the duo actually mocks the performers' shortcomings, albeit not in an unkind manner. Since they are so popular, we may conclude that audiences enjoy watching them manifestly expressing a taboo, i.e. ragging participants for their deficiencies that they will nonetheless presumably take in good humour. Part of the entertainment value of these talent shows may indeed lie in watching untalented people make fools of themselves. Audiences may well derive enjoyment from the way the duo highlight performers' lack of talent so that the result is a combination of laughing "at" the player and "with" the duo.

The teasing scold

Many lifestyle and reality formats involve a certain amount of (friendly?) scolding. From the cake that has not risen to the tone-deaf singer, judges and presenters make use of irony to tease the unfortunate object of adversity.

Bake Off judge Paul Hollywood adopts a fine line between irony and sarcasm when competitors' bakes are not quite up to scratch. In the 2015 *Comic Relief* spin-off of the show, he tells comedian Jo Brand that he "love[s] the taste of the biscuits", pauses, and then adds "the ones that aren't burnt". Again, after tasting some custard slices he says, "I think that's quite something", leading the contestant to think that he was happy with the result, but then repeats the phrase with different intonation so that, "yes it's quite something" becomes ironic.

In *How Clean is Your House*, Kim and Aggie use humour to comment on disgustingly dirty houses. In the first frames of each episode when they enter each new messy living space, they squeal and shriek in mock horror at the sight of insects, larvae and general filth. Then, when they meet the residents of the households, those who are responsible for the mess, Kim will typically reprimand them with expressions like "You dirty beggar", and "[the house is] . . . a diabolical disgrace", or "Two words come out of my mouth. 'Bone idle'". The audience knows that Kim is being serious but at the same time her chastising is all part of the pretence of the show so that the overall effect is humorous. Once the culprits get cleaning, any complaints about working, such as a woman who complained of a back problem (Series 5, Episode 1), are met with comments like "Don't start that rubbish, you've not bent that back in years". Kim's dry humour does not stop at faults in cleaning. When asked how long ago she had last washed the kitchen sink, a student answered, "I done it two months ago" to which Kim retorts, "You're not reading English are you?" On another occasion, in a shopping centre where Kim and Aggie are asking people how often they vacuum the carpet (Series 7, Episode 6), a man answers that he hoovers once a fortnight. "You live on your own, my dear?" asks Kim and when the man says that he does, she retorts, "I'm not surprised, you dirty thing". Hearing Kim's overt rudeness to the grime offenders makes good entertainment – audiences laugh at her outright as she calls the "dirt offender" a "daft apeth", "lazy beggar" and other daring epithets. These insults are taken as funny because people generally do not tell it like it is, especially in contexts where the normal rules of politeness amongst acquaintances are in play, preferring to soften their opinions of others' shortcomings. And, all other things being equal, we certainly tend to avoid being discourteous to others. In other words, the incongruity that leads to humour lies in the breaking of the rules of conventional conversational behaviour and politeness rather than in the content of *what* is said, which is, after all, not funny per se. Social norms are thwarted. The programme is therefore as entertaining for the audiences for the banter as it is for the makeovers themselves.

The kind of scolding exemplified in the talk of *Britain's Got Talent* judge, Simon Cowell, is also sharp but closer to sarcasm than Kim's acerbic comments. Like Kim, Simon entertains the public because he dares to be rude in situations in which conversational rules (and social norms) demand moderation. He tells a contestant who claims that her voice is similar to that of Whitney Houston's that "It wasn't remotely like Whitney Houston". The comment is neither ironic nor inherently humorous; the comic factor lies in its inappropriateness under the circumstances, a talent show. Audiences expect judges to be kind to weak contestants; Simon's remarks have a shock value that appears to attract viewers. He tells a tone-deaf contestant from Lithuania, "I don't know what a cat being squashed sounds like in Lithuania but I now have a pretty good idea", and a trio of singers "You sounded like three cats being dragged up the motorway". This provides amusement, further highlighted when the contestants dare to answer back. The Singing Souls, a trio of young girls who receive boos from the studio audience and who Simon asserts to be "one of the worst groups I've ever heard in my life", challenge him with "You wanna come up here and sing, Simon?" When he tells them "Here's the deal, you sing, we judge", they answer back rudely and begin to argue with the judges. Meanwhile, Ant and Dec, from behind the scenes, display their own reactions for the consumption of the remote audience, laughing and saying, amongst other things, "Now, that's attitude".[9]

The question is how far this use of humour can be considered as "only" joking? When does teasing become mockery and ridicule? If Kim and Aggie scold people responsible for poor housekeeping, while smiling as they scold them, they deride their interlocutors' shortcomings no matter how gentle they are with them. As for *Britain's Got Talent*, the show is on occasion reminiscent of a circus or an arena in which the audiences take pleasure in others' faults and delight in the grotesque. Audiences watch from afar and enjoy Cowell's humorous, rude comments that pivot on the inadequacy and inabilities of performers. In a politically correct world, it is quite paradoxical that this type of behaviour passes without righteous comment while a double entendre regarding a bun or a bottom can cause quite a stir – pun intended once more. It is tempting to agree with Billig's notion that ridicule can be seen as a tool to maintain socio-normative order. It is possible that audiences are thinking that someone who is tone deaf but wants to become a famous singer should choose a more realistic dream and that someone who lives in a filthy home should clean it up. The use of humour as a reprimand may soften the impact of impoliteness or rudeness; on the other hand, it may well reflect what audiences believe needs to be said.

Behaving badly for a laugh

The *Comic Relief* spin-offs of the *Bake Off* in which contestants are professional comedians provide extra humour. Comedian Jo Brand "misbehaves" throughout her appearance. As soon as the competition begins with something difficult for the contestants to bake, she dejectedly asks, "Anyone fancy a coffee?" Then, she accidentally misses out ingredients, forgets to flour a board and asks the audience "Have I got butter on my bum?" as she displays her derrière to the camera for a close up. In another spin-off of the series, *An Extra Slice*,[10] presented by Brand herself, she asks the studio audience, "Shall I tell you what my favourite biscuit is?" Pantomime-style the audience loudly answers "Yes!" and she replies, "The next one!" In yet another *Comic Relief*, comedian Jonathan Ross attempts to bake a cake in the shape of the Royal Albert Hall. Naturally, his cake does not resemble the famous building in the least, which is funny in itself, but the comedian does provide an ironic rebuttal to his coming last in the competition: "When people saw the first Picasso they were confused. They didn't understand Cubism. Well, that's what we're seeing right now. The shock of the new, they're encountering avant-garde baking". These examples reinforce the claim that such television programmes are more about their participants than cooking or music or home improvement.

Another personality famous for his "bad" behaviour on set is comedian and *Britain's Got Talent* judge, David Walliams. Walliams is especially funny when he openly challenges fellow judge Simon Cowell. Music and television producer Cowell plays the part of the very serious, strict judge whereas Walliams promotes unlikely performers that are, however, appreciated by the audience in the theatre. Walliams' behaviour creates the impression of a clash between the judges, facilitating tit-for-tat style banter and constant teasing between the two of them. Much to the delight of the audience, Cowell typically openly disapproves of Walliams' choices, opening the way for witty repartee. The result is undoubtedly funny irrespective of how scripted or unscripted these interactions actually are.

A lot of Walliams' comedy is based on gender-bending (see Chapter 3). He can act very camp and openly flirts with attractive male competitors, but above all Walliams gives us some credence to unscriptedness as a lot of his gags seem to be truly ad lib. When a member of a boy band blows a kiss at a female judge, Walliams demands in a camp tone, "Won't anybody blow a kiss at me?" (Season 9,

Episode 6) thus playing on the ambiguity of his sexuality. He also dabbles in innuendo, such as when he asks a male dancer "When you do the splits did you hurt yourself as you went down with quite a crack?"

Above all, Walliams is simply adroit. Following the performance of a twelve-person boy band, judge Amanda Holden asks Walliams what he is thinking, to which he replies:

> I was thinking there's something for everyone in this room isn't there? They've got the cute young one with the floppy hair, they've got the big butch one who's a car mechanic and they've got the one with glasses for the more intellectual *Guardian* reading ladies.

Walliams makes light of his (presumed) bisexuality, his facial expressions clearly display sexual interest in the members of the band and his "something for everyone" refers above all to himself. He then uses irony to stereotypically describe three of the performers as the kind of "ladies" to whom they would each appeal. Walliams' comedic style touches upon taboo because he is a male who flirts openly with other men but in a joking/not-joking way. We are not 100 per cent sure that the band appeals to "ladies" in general more than it does to Walliams himself – not to mention the fact that Walliams played a cross-dressed "lady" in an on-going sketch in the comedy series *Little Britain*.[11] His style is also reminiscent of actor Kenneth Williams who adopted a similar camp-comedic style.

Translating humour for the movies and television

In present day internationalized and transnational culture, the "traditional" screens of cinema and television broadcast swathes of humorous discourse worldwide. A glance at box office figures across Europe reveals that movies produced in the USA and distributed by the so-called "majors" far outnumber films produced in and distributed by other countries. It therefore stands to reason that audiences the world over are more likely to be familiar with North American films and actors than those of other countries. According to McCrum *et al.* (2002), at the beginning of the 20th century, the force of the US movie industry was such as to make Hollywood a significant catalyst in the growth of English as the first truly global language. In fact, Hollywood contributed to the spread of English as an early precursor to the way rock music and the internet were to do in the later part of the century. However, apart from the UK and other English-speaking countries, elsewhere in the world, these films required translation. Ironically, by the late 1920s, it was two comic actors, Stan Laurel and Oliver Hardy, who were to play a central role in kick-starting the screen translational modality of dubbing.

While the film industry was also developing in its own right in Europe, language created a seemingly insurmountable obstacle for US directors wanting to expand their market. In fact, to overcome the language barriers they saw in

Europe, producers inserted short dialogues in the relevant target languages within the English dialogues, but this soon proved to be unsatisfactory with audiences. Consequently, Paramount Pictures set up a large studio in Joinville, France, dedicated to the production of multiple-language versions of the same film. This, however, turned out to be economically unfeasible and the quality of the results was generally inferior compared to the original films.

Meanwhile, in the USA, Laurel and Hardy were already popular artists when movies that had to that point been silent switched to becoming talkies. The duo's director, Hal Roach, immediately saw opportunities in the European market but also understood the problem of language barriers. Roach decided to adopt the European technique of producing the same film in different languages with the difference that he would use the comic duo to act in the various European languages. He, too, would shoot French, Italian, Spanish and German versions of each film casting native speakers in all the secondary roles, but with the difference that the two actors would read their lines from a prompt in the different languages. The result was that Laurel and Hardy's bizarre pronunciation of the four major European languages (French, German, Italian and Spanish) added to the comic effect of their films and to their great success in the Old Continent. From this moment onwards, only a small step was required to create the practice of dubbing, as we know it today. In fact, the idea of substituting the original voice track with one in another language is generally attributed to the Austrian film producer Jakob Karol, who in 1930 realized that the technology to do this was already available (Paolinelli and Di Fortunato 2005: 45–6). At first, dubbing into European languages was carried out in the USA, but by the early thirties, each European country had begun to set up its own dubbing industry.

Traditionally, Europe was divided into two major screen translation blocks, consisting of the UK, the Benelux and Scandinavian countries, principally subtitling nations, and central and southern European countries stretching from Germany, across France and down to Spain, that were mostly dubbing nations, with Greece and Portugal opting for subtitles. Both dubbing and subtitling present advantages and disadvantages of a practical nature and of a sociolinguistic and political kind. Countries that originally favoured dubbing tended to do so for protectionist reasons seeing the establishment of dubbing in Italy and Germany as a means to inhibit English, but above all, to promote national languages (Bollettieri Bosinelli 1994). Conversely, a preference towards subtitling in Scandinavia reveals more than just an open attitude towards other languages (especially English), but a relatively inexpensive way to develop screen translation for small populations (Chiaro 2009a, 2009b). Nevertheless, the previously conventional division has dissolved with the circulation of technologies such as DVD and DVX that usually contain subtitles even in the presence of a dubbed version. Moreover, a preference for subtitling is quickly gaining ground across Europe, especially amongst younger generations of viewers, in countries traditionally seen as dubbing strongholds. Furthermore, cable and satellite TV packages such as Sky and on-demand internet streaming media such as Netflix also provide viewers with a choice of both translational modalities, while cinemas in traditional dubbing countries also offer screenings with subtitles. In addition to all this, with the spread of English and with increasing numbers of people wanting to see films and TV series as soon as they are released, there is a tendency for consumers to download products straight from the web. As more and more people access (mainly English language, but not only) audiovisual products via tablets and smartphones in real time, subtitles for downloads and streaming are often provided by fansubbers, armies of young unprofessional translators whose mission is to translate new products as soon as possible into as many languages as possible for fans around the world. Thus, fast and cost-effective subtitling has rapidly become the most common form of screen translation especially amongst young (mostly highly) educated people who have proficient English language skills.

With regard to scripted screen comedy, translation has an impact not only on the way the original source humour is conveyed, but also on how it is perceived in different parts of the world. Notoriously, translating humour is not an easy task; in fact, humour is generally considered untranslatable. Nevertheless, what we mean by the term "untranslatable" is not the translator's inability or the impossibility of translating it but rather the equivalence of the translated humour to the source text (Chiaro 2008, 2010a). Yet we only have to think of the great works of literature to see that verbally expressed humour has been translated countless times in and out of scores of languages. Obviously, these translations are not identical copies of the originals; after all, if such precise imaging were possible there would be no need for translation in the first place. Conversely, with the term "untranslatable" we refer to the extreme difficulty involved in the task coupled with the knowledge that the text may lose some of the desired effect in translation. In other words, because verbally expressed humour tends to pivot upon its source language together with highly specific cultural elements pertaining to the source culture, the lack of equivalence between the two versions is likely to be more evident than in non-humorous discourse. Furthermore, if translating humorous discourse in written form is no easy task, translating it for the screen is even more difficult owing to the fact the words uttered by actors on screen are linked to a series of images and sounds that need to be taken into account. A humorous remark in a film or a sitcom may well be bound to a visual or auditory element on which it will depend for humorous impact. Translating humour on screen is rather like translating Lewis Carroll's concrete poem, "The Mouse's Tail" in which the translator needs to deal not only with the verbal pun "tail/tale" but also with the visual pun of the words arranged in a way as to form the shape of a mouse's tail.[12] Likewise the screen translator has to juggle with different combinations of verbal, visual and acoustic features all of which are superimposed on one another to create an amusing whole (Chiaro 2009a: 143, 2010b).

Nonetheless, whether we are considering instances of humour in big screen movies or for TV sitcoms, the challenges translators face are identical.

For example, how do you translate humour based on a highly specific cultural reference? David Katan's concept of "chunking" (1999) is useful to describe typical ways in which translators deal with cultural references in general. By chunking "upwards", for example, a translator working towards Portuguese could substitute the term for a British custard tart with the word "*bol*", the generic term for "cake" or else, by chunking "downwards", she could translate it with "*pastel de nata*", the term for a typical local pastry. This is all well and good, as long as viewers cannot actually see the object on screen which, indeed, they could in a comic scene from the movie *My Big Fat Greek Wedding*.[13] Upon receiving a bundt cake from her future son-in-law's American mother, Maria, who had never seen such a cake before, is confused and in an attempt to repeat the term "Bundt" she loudly utters "A bunt? A boont? A bonk?" The Italian translators chunked downwards and chose to translate "Bundt" with the term for an Italian speciality "*cassata*". Maria thus utters "Una cassata? Una cazzata?" The translational choice is a good one because "*cazzata*" is, like "bonk", slightly taboo and therefore likely to get a laugh.[14] However, Italian viewers can actually see the tall, highly risen Bundt cake and, as a cassata is a round, white, flat cake decorated with brightly coloured glacé fruits, there is a striking mismatch between visual and verbal codes.

Over and above issues regarding culture specificity, humour anchored to a visual element on screen is likely to be one of the trickiest translational obstacles, although it is by no means the only one. How do translators deal with language variation? Accent in particular is a frequently used comic device on screen. What should translators do? Is substitution with a local variety a feasible solution? This is only one of the many complex choices facing translators of screen humour. Then there is the issue of censorship. For example, swear words are often used for comic purposes thus putting the translator in a dilemma, as what may be acceptable in the source culture may not be equally acceptable elsewhere. Last, but certainly not least, how does a translator handle visual humour that does not involve the use of verbal language? As it does not require verbal translation, could purely visual humour be considered universally amusing?

The opening scene of the classic comedy *It's a Mad, Mad, Mad, Mad World*[15] features "Smiler" Grogan (played by Jimmy Durante), an ex-convict on the run, whose car crashes in a mountainous area of California. A group of men take the seriously injured Grogan out of his car and lay him on the ground. As Grogan struggles to stay alive, very ostentatiously, he kicks a bucket. The camera zooms into the bucket, follows it as it slowly and noisily rolls down the mountainside, until it comes to a stop. At this point, Grogan flamboyantly breathes his last breath and dies. While not exactly a visual pun, this is a visual gag depending on words that remain unsaid. Even though the "bucket scene" is silent, the "joke" is obvious but only to those familiar with the English euphemism for death, i.e. "to kick the bucket" and therefore lost in translation despite the fact that no translation is required owing to the absence of dialogue.

Non-verbal humour

Visual humour

So, could it really be that words are the only obstacle to the universality of humour? Certainly, Monty Python's Ministry of Silly Walks needs no explanation and neither does Groucho Marx's chicken walk and his ever-present large cigar. Pre-code comedy on screen, i.e. before sound allowed actors to use their voices, certainly travelled the world, with comedians such as Charlie Chaplin and Buster Keaton quickly reaching international fame through purely visual comic capers that centred on how their bodies interacted with their surroundings. The body movements and facial expressions of these comics seemed to communicate more than words could ever do. However, much as their brilliant comedic skills deserved recognition, their worldwide success also says much about US control of the film industry. It should be noted that of course there were plenty of silent comedians elsewhere such as Britain's Max Wall and Richard Hearne (aka Mr Pastry) and Italy's Totò whose style of comedy was quite similar to that of their more famous counterparts yet remained confined to national borders. More recently, the silent comedy of Rowan Atkinson in the persona of Mr Bean has gained success worldwide at least partly due to the absence of words and thus the non-requirement of translation. Undoubtedly, the quasi-slapstick nature of Mr Bean's comedic style plays a big part in his success as he embodies both the underdog who typically gets into scrapes and the canny shrewdness of one trying to turn a series of everyday situations to his own advantage. Furthermore, Atkinson himself agrees that one of the reasons for Bean's success is that he is "a child in a grown man's body" and wonders:

> [w]hy the Japanese and the Chinese and people in the Mississippi Delta and Italy and Scotland, why they all understand Mr Bean. It is not just because he doesn't speak although that helps. It is because he is a child, and that is the level on which any culture can appreciate him.[16]

According to Sontag (2004), the comic involves not knowing, pretending not to know, or partial knowing and refers to the innocence of stars like Charlie Chaplin, whose helplessness and apparent "defect of understanding and childlikeness" were at the core of their humorous capacity. It is thus hardly surprising that Atkinson claims to be inspired by French comic Jacques Tati, who as actor and director tended to both disregard dialogue and to adopt a childlike stance. Furthermore, Tati, Stan Laurel, Chaplin and Bean, after getting into all sorts of "messes" often shared the facial expression of a little boy lost who has just committed a naughty deed. One of Stan Laurel's most famous photographs depicts him scratching his head with a dumbfounded expression on his face – a look also typical of comedian Michael Crawford's "Oooh!" spoken while holding a finger to his mouth after having created total havoc in most episodes of the BBC sitcom *Some Mothers Do 'Ave 'Em* (1973–78).[17]

The third episode from the TV series *Mr Bean* entitled *The Curse of Mr Bean* exemplifies several features of purely visual comedy.[18] From the moment that Mr Bean arrives at the public swimming pool the audience can see what he is thinking as he sets eyes on the kiddie slides and the super-high diving board. Bean displays an excited demeanour as he clearly wants to have a go on two inappropriate objects – a kiddie slide and a high diving board – and herein lies not only the incongruity of the situation, but also the expectations on the part of the audience of inescapable, hilarious disaster. Unable to play on the kiddie slides, he climbs up to the highest diving board only to realize that he is too scared to jump. As he makes a series of faint-hearted attempts to jump, he achieves a comic effect through his facial expressions and clumsy posture. The camera juxtaposes close-ups of Bean's terrified face with aerial shots of him lying flat on his stomach on the diving board with the pool below him as he slowly drags himself towards the edge of the board. After much procrastination, Bean ends up dangling from the edge of the diving board, legs akimbo and hanging onto the board with one hand. A young boy impatient to dive into the pool finally stomps on Bean's hand so that he falls into the water. As though this was not enough, once in the water Bean somehow loses his swimming trunks that are then retrieved by a little girl who takes them away with her. Naked, Bean tries to get out of the pool and reach the changing rooms without being noticed, only to be seen from behind by a group of female bathers – he turns towards them and they scream at the sight of his naked body. The humour in the entire sketch is achieved through a mixture of Bean's physical reactions to his various predicaments, but also his childlike responses to situations.

Acoustic humour

The persona of Mr Bean provides several examples of non-verbal acoustic humour too. At the opening ceremony of the 2012 Olympic Games in London, Bean "performs" with the London Symphony Orchestra. Silent as always, Bean engages in lots of visual gags all carried out with his signature deadpan expression. On an acoustic level, throughout the orchestra's rendition of *Chariots of Fire*, Bean continually strikes the same single piano note with one finger.[19]

Bean provides another acoustic gag for 2015 *Comic Relief* in a sketch called *Funeral*. During a funeral service, Bean blows his nose at length and very loudly. When he notices that he is annoying the other mourners, Bean blows even harder into his handkerchief and "plays" a tune with the snorting sounds he produces.[20] Once more, Bean displays conduct comparable to that of a naughty, badly behaved child using the ostentation of backstage behaviour, in Goffman's (1981) terms, in which he breaks social norms.

Verbal humour

To reiterate, verbal humour on screen faces much the same challenges in translation as it does when it occurs elsewhere such as in writing and in speech.

However, the translation of verbal humour on screen faces additional challenges, as the gag is likely to be linked to other signs on screen. Audiovisual products are polysemiotic in nature; they are the result of the intersection of different signs that make up a meaningful whole. In other words, auditory verbal signs such as dialogue and song lyrics transect a series of visual verbal signs like street signs, newspaper headlines, etc. In another dimension, these diverse verbal signs will in turn intersect with a series of purely acoustic features like music and background noises in general, as well as with a multitude of purely visual features such as settings, actors' facial expressions and body movements, etc. (see Chiaro 2009a: 143). As in the example from *My Big Fat Greek Wedding*, a verbal gag anchored to a visual element is going to be especially problematic in translation when the element in question is also culture-specific. On the other hand, even a straightforward gag that is not anchored visually to any other element on screen is automatically rendered more complex because it is performed, rather than occurring in print or an everyday conversation.

Purely linguistic orally conveyed verbal humour

A conversation in the first episode of TV series *Wayward Pines* (Fox 2015) contains a witty pun that is successfully translated for the Italian version. "What is the only fish to work in a hospital? A sturgeon" – "*Sai qual è l'unico pesce al circo? Il pesce pagliaccio*" – "Do you know the only fish in a circus? Clownfish". In the translation, a hospital is replaced by a circus to accommodate a suitable answer and retain the pun that, although different from the source pun, is still a pun.

However, wordplay translation can prove to be more arduous as in an episode of *Six Feet Under* (HBO; 2001–05), containing two examples of purely language-based wordplay. In order to translate "What do you call an Italian hooker? A pastitute" the gag undergoes a huge transformation, as it becomes "*Sai perchè le italiane prendono la pillola?*" – "Do you know why Italian women take the pill?" – "*Per sapere che giorno della settimana è*" – "So they know what day of the week it is". Surprisingly, the joke is turned into a politically incorrect ethnic underdog joke for an Italian audience. Why the translators opted for a stupidity joke is hard to say, after all, the translation is for Italian audiences yet translators opted to insult, albeit through a joke, their target audience by suggesting Italian women are stupid. There is a huge difference between the wordplay created through the "pasta"/ "prostitute" blend and carrying the concept of prostitution over to dumbness in the translation.

In the same episode (Series 4, Episode 7) Keith falls for an old joke based on a fake name when a colleague tricks him into reading the name "Heywood Jeblome" aloud. The trick lies in the fact that the fictitious name "Heywood Jeblome" should be pronounced "Hey, would you blow me?"

Keith: I don't know this person!
Javier: Well say his name right, maybe you do!
Keith: Ok, Ok! Heywood Jeblome! Heywood Jeblome!
Javier: Hehehe
Keith: What's so fucking funny?
Javier: Say it again
Keith: Heywood Jeblome!
Javier: Sure I'll blow you, K.

In the Italian translation Keith is tricked into repeating a fake Russian sounding name, Andrei Koimaski which phonologically deconstructs into "I'd go" (*"andreī"*) "with men" (*"coi maschī"*). Noticeably, the Italian translation, albeit effective, is much weaker than the English as it omits the reference to fellatio. We cannot be sure whether the translators deliberately censored the gag or whether it was the best translation possible. Nevertheless, the Italian tease remains successful (for in depth discussions on translation and bowdlerization in audiovisuals, see Bucaria 2009 and 2010).

Verbal humour is often based on the exploitation of accents; in fact, it is common for UK comedians to have pronounced regional pronunciations. Stand-up comedians such as Scottish Billy Connolly and Frankie Boyle, Irish Dara O'Briain, Liverpudlian John Bishop, Geordie Chris Ramsey and Cockney Mickey Flanagan all exploit their regional identities through the way they speak. British comedy is imbued with class and its protagonists reflect this through their use of language. The *Carry On* movies (1958–78) provide examples of the entire gamut of English accents, from Kenneth Williams' and Leslie Phillip's RP to Bernard Bresslaw's and Barbara Windsor's Cockney; these films closely echoed Britain's class system. Elsewhere, many successful comedians also rely on regional variation for their acts. In Italy, Roberto Benigni has a Tuscan accent and Checco Zalone uses Barese, while use of *argot* is usual in the performances of French comedians such as Manu Payet and Smain. This marked use of non-standard accents in comedy ties in with the suggestion that we tend to laugh at others occupying spaces in the peripheries of society (see Chapter 1). When humour is based on the way that something is said, including the ethnic and or social variety in which it is couched, being able to convey the underlying intention behind the use of a particular accent poses an enormous translational difficulty.

The 21st century has witnessed a trend to endow the voices of computer generated animated films with those of well-known transnational personalities, for example, Mike Myers gave Shrek his Scottish accent in the eponymous film, while Eddie Murphy voiced Donkey in African-American Vernacular English. Clearly, Shrek's Scottish lilt and Donkey's African-American speech that are inevitably lost in translation provide extra dimensions to those who are able to grasp the connotation of using those accents. Nonetheless, the question arises as to whether, over and above translation, foreign audiences will recognize linguistic variation in a language other than their own. If a product is subtitled, presumably recognition of difference will rely on viewers' previous knowledge of specific varieties, but in the case of dubbing, the situation is not as clear. Substituting a variety in Language A with a variety in Language B might at first be seen as a good solution, but such a choice is unlikely to convey or connote similar effects to those experienced by the audience in the target language and culture. Therefore, dubbing countries usually adopt the so-called "homogenizing convention" (Sternberg 1981) so that any social or regional peculiarity is flattened out in translation by simply replacing it with the standard variety. The result of using this strategy is that in dubbed products it is common to hear a member of a street gang in the USA speak in the same way as his lawyer, and for the audience not to be able to distinguish a Brit from an American, a Scottish from an Irish person, or a German from an Austrian. Typically, one or two characters are signified with a non-standard source variety while surrounding characters adopt the standard language. For example, it is common for male comic characters in the Italian version of comic films set in Ireland to be endowed with a high-pitched voice and a slightly effeminate inflection. This same way of speaking is generally also given to mainstream English-speaking comic actors who traditionally play the part of the nincompoop, such as Jerry Lewis and Danny Kaye.

Similarly, the clichéd variety of English adopted by Italian-Americans on screen is consistently replaced in Italian films with the accent and syntactic structures that are typical of Sicilian Italian. The negative stereotypes linked to this translational choice are evident and possibly reflect the original intention. In the animated film *Shark Tale*,[21] Robert De Niro voices mobster shark Don Vito who is surrounded by other fish thugs voiced by Italian-Americans such as Martin Scorsese thereby clearly referencing Francis Ford Coppola's *The Godfather*. In Italian, the fishy mobsters become Sicilian, strengthening a negative stereotype in US movies regarding organized crime. Within the same film, Ernie and Bernie are two Jamaican jellyfish henchmen voiced by Ziggy Marley and Doug E. Doug. Their Rasta speech is compensated in the Italian version with laid-back Roman teen-speak gobbledegook voiced by two well-known Italian personalities, pop star Tiziano Ferro and comedian Luca Laurenti. Undeniably, these films exploit an underlying truism that links Italy and Sicily to organized crime. True to this cinematic tradition, inarticulate, Italian-American, teddy-boy-styled lawyer Joe Gambino played by Joe Pesci in *My Cousin Vinny*[22] becomes Sicilian in the Italian version, while the southern brogue of the inhabitants of the small sleepy town in Alabama where the film takes place becomes an unlikely standard Italian. Clearly, this inaccuracy and non-sociolinguistic equivalence interferes with the sense of comic otherness that the audience should ideally experience.

While computer-animated graphics have taken over traditional animated movies, Nick Park's *Wallace and Gromit*[23] series of films appear in marked contrast to digital productions like *Shrek*, *Frozen*[24] and so on. In fact, these products are completely low-tech – characters are made out of plasticine and they move by means of the stop-motion animation technique[25] while the voices of the characters belong to UK actors like Michael Caine, Helena Bonham Carter and Ralph Fiennes. Comparing these two traditions of animated movie making, we might note that the glossy Hollywood veneer connected with computer-animated digitals is supplanted by a more homely effect achieved by using the voices of British celebrities that are well-known for their stereotypically upper class or working class accents. In *Chicken Run*[26] voices from both continents mix and merge when Rocky Rooster (strangely enough voiced by Australian Mel Gibson as a rooster from Rhode Island) flies into a chicken coop in northern England.

Clearly, the comic undertones conveyed through the accents in *Wallace and Gromit* are untranslatable. Nevertheless, there have been some solutions to the issue of the translatability of accents in which their comic effect is successfully retained. The Italian dubbed version of Hong Kong martial arts comedy movie *Shaolin Soccer*[27] adopted two unusual strategies so that the dub itself actually added to the humour – thus, dubbing in the sense of "doubling" the filmic quality and the audience's pleasure. Voice actors with different Italian regional accents such as Neapolitan, Sardinian, Tuscan, Sicilian, Lombard, Barese and Calabrese dubbed the original Mandarin and Cantonese-speaking actors. For some reason Italians perceive these accents as humorous per se. Furthermore, casting well-known footballers such as Damiano Tommasi, Giuseppe Pancaro, Marco Delvecchio, Siniša Mihajlović, Angelo Peruzzi and Vincent Candela as voice actors provided another winning solution.

Visually conveyed verbal humour

Possibly one of the most famous visually conveyed verbal gags on screen occurs in a scene from *A Fish Called Wanda*[28] in which unintelligent American, Otto (Kevin Kline) is in Wanda's (Jamie Lee Curtis) bedroom insulting the British in a loud voice:

> [the British] . . . counting the seconds to the . . . weekend so they can dress up as ballerinas and whip themselves into a frenzy at the . . .

when he finds a note from Archie (John Cleese) to Wanda that reads as follows:

> So see you at the flat at 4,
> It's 2B St. Trevor's Wharf E.1.
> All my love,
> Archie

Otto reads out the note aloud but manages to combine it into the preceding dialogue so that the audience hears:

[the British] ... counting the seconds to the ... weekend so they can dress up as ballerinas and whip themselves into a frenzy at the ... [reads the note that the audience can see] ... flat at 4, 2B St ... To be honest I ... er ... hate them.

Denton (1994: 31) comments on the challenge this scene poses to translators who need to manipulate the target dialogue so that it successfully integrates the note that audiences will see on screen while at the same time retaining its comic impact. It would be impossible to transpose the phonological association between the flat number "2B" and "to be" to which Otto cleverly adds "honest" into another language. The Italian repair strategy is however quite ingenious:

[c]ontano i secondi che mancano all'arrivo del fine settimana per potersi vestire come delle ballerine e andarsi ad ubriacare ... [reads] nell'appartamento Quattro al 2B ... due bi ... cchieri e poi crollano.

[literal translation: "they count the seconds till the weekend so they can dress up like ballerinas and get drunk ... in apartment 2B ... two gl ... glasses and they drop"].

What the translation does is to play on the phonological association between "2B" in Italian which reads "*due bi*" with the words "*due bicchieri*" – "two glasses". By having Otto pause after uttering the first syllable of the word "*bicchieri*" – i.e. /bI/ – the translators successfully adopt the identical strategy of the source text. While the meaning is not identical as two glasses do not reflect "to be honest", the fact that the Italian utterance links the idea of glasses containing alcohol into the stereotype of drunken Brits, a typecast that Otto is fond of repeating throughout the film, actually enhances the translation.

A common visual/graphic trope on screen concerns flower arrangements in films about funerals. In the film *Undertaking Betty*, the hearse displaying a flower arrangement that reads "Old Bag" is likely to be lost on audiences outside the UK, especially with its reference to the main character's deceased yet obnoxious mother-in-law.[29] On the other hand, the so-called "Bastard Hearse" in the BBC2 comedy sketch show *League of Gentlemen* (BBC2 1999–2002) in which the flowers spell out the word "Bastard", is likely to be understood universally. Again, in Mr Bean's *Funeral* sketch mentioned above, the comedian upsets a coffin in a church so that the flower arrangement reading "L O V E" falls over and breaks to pieces. In an inept attempt at reconstructing the arrangement, Bean puts the flowers together so that they spell the word "V O L E". Now, while foreign audiences might simply laugh at the spelling muddle that Bean has created, autochthonous audiences might also laugh at the silliness of the term "vole". While there is nothing inherently funny about the animal itself, there is something nonsensical about the choice of rodent, thus rendering the mix-up, like much of Monty Python's humour, both silly and surreal.

Culture-specific verbal humour

While not specific to cinematic/TV and audiovisuals in general, verbally expressed humour based on cultural references is problematic in translation even when the joke is based on something that one might expect to be understood globally. The animated films in the *Shrek* series, for example, are full of references to fairy tales and to other films.[30] These references act as triggers for laughter and although they are destined to remain unappreciated by non-autochthonous audiences, the films have been extremely successful worldwide. For example, in a well-known line from *Shrek*, Donkey says:

> Now I'm a flying talking donkey! You might have seen a housefly, maybe even a superfly, but I bet you ain't never seen a donkeyfly! Ha, ha!

This, to an English-speaking audience, would be a clear reference to the Walt Disney classic *Dumbo* the flying elephant.[31] Lord Farquaard (the "bad guy" in the *Shrek* series whose name is a salacious pun for adult viewers) chants "Run, run as fast as you can. You can't catch me, I'm the Gingerbread Man", as he amputates the biscuit's leg. This, and references to "the Muffin Man who lives on Drury Lane" are extremely Anglo-centric references to traditional English nursery rhymes. Yet, although it is clear that "Every film is a foreign film, foreign to some audience somewhere – and not simply in terms of language" (Egoyan and Balfour 2004: 21), the kind of "foreignness" in question appears to be specific to a dominant English-speaking culture alone. Given such specificity, it is surprising that the film was so successful at a global level. These culture-specific references may well be outweighed by the strength, colour and vibrancy of the visuals, the music and the storyline.

Lingua-cultural wordplay is extremely complex to translate. Take for example a complex wordplay based on a cultural reference from the TV series *Six Feet Under*. After discussing surrogate parenting with his life partner Keith, David Fisher has a dream in which he finds himself in a farmyard where there is a sign reading "Eggs for Sale" (Series 5, Episode 2). In this surreal dream scene, Keith appears dressed in dungarees and driving a tractor. When he gets down from the vehicle, he approaches David and says, "I am the egg man" to which David asks "goo goo g'joob?" The entire exchange is lifted verbatim from the Beatles' song "I am the Walrus" (*Magical Mystery Tour*, 1968) yet in the Italian translation it is lost because while Keith says "*Sono l'uomo delle uova*" (literally: "I am the egg man"), the phrase bears no relation to the Beatles' song. In fact, in place of the well-known chorus of "goo goo g'joob", Keith replies "*Cosa vuoi da me?*" ("What do you want from me?"). However, this (non)-joke is likely to go by unnoticed in translation as it occurs within a bizarre dream sequence in which nothing makes much sense anyway, but this may not always be the case.

Lingua-culturally based verbal humour

Humour is most culture-specific when language and culture are combined to create a comic effect (see Chapter 1). In the film *Lock, Stock and Two Smoking Barrels*, many characters have Cockney accents and adopt London market trading banter to this end.[32] Unlike the simple use of regional varieties discussed earlier, and over and above accent and morpho-syntactic features that distinguish it from the standard variety, Cockney repartee depends on a combination of rhymes, assonances and culture-specific references. The film opens with the scene of a street trader attracting his customers with quick-firing monologue typical of the capital's market "barrow boys":

> Right let's sort the buyers from the spyers, the needy from the greedy, the ones who trust me from the ones who don't cos if you can't see value here today you're not up here shopping, you're up here shoplifting. You see these goods? Never seen daylight, moonlight, Israelites, Fanny by the gaslight. Take a bag, come on. I took a bag home last night cost more than ten pound, I can tell you. Anyone like jewellery? Look at that one. Handmade in Italy, hand-stolen in Stepney. It's as long as my arm, I wish it was as long as something else. Don't think because these boxes are sealed up, they're empty. The only one who sells empty boxes is the undertaker and by the look of some of you lot here today, I'd make more money with me measuring tape.

Rhymes, assonance, couplets and repetitions are plentiful and present a significant translational challenge. How is a translator to carry out the task of translating the rhymes of "buyers/spyers" not to mention the crescendo of references that begin with "Never seen daylight, moonlight" that follows with "Israelites" that blends into "Fanny by the Gaslight", a British film from the 1940s. The banter is nonsensical yet cleverly amusing. The trader puns on the term "bag" playing on its slang meaning in the UK of an ugly woman whom he presumably paid for sex as she "cost [him] more than ten pound" the very price he is asking for the stolen bags he is selling. The replication of "hand" with "made" and then with "stolen" complicate matters further and highlight the extreme culture specificity of the banter. The closing joke about the coffins contains an implicit insult to his customers when he claims that he would "make more money with me measuring tape".

Verbal/visual humour

Verbal humour with a visual anchor

Verbal humour with a visual anchor takes translational difficulty up a notch. In a scene from the film *Philomena*,[33] the two main characters are travelling in a car when Philomena (Judi Dench) is first seen fiddling with the contents of her handbag that include a packet of Tunes – a brand of throat lozenges sold in the UK. After asking Martin (Steve Coogan) what kind of car he is driving, to which he answers that it is a BMW, Philomena offers him a Tune. Audiences can see Philomena unwrapping the packet of sweets as she asks "Would you like a Tune, Martin?" to which he jokingly replies, "If I hum it, will you play it?" but Philomena obviously does not get the joke and insistently asks him, "No would you like a Tune?" Martin lets it go, thanks her, takes a Tune out of the packet, unwraps it and pops it in his mouth. In the Italian version, the routine containing the joke is omitted. Although the packet of sweets with the label reading "Tunes" can be clearly seen on the product's wrapping, it can only have meaning to an autochthonous audience. The verbal exchange in the Italian dubbed version is limited to an exchange about the nationality of the car. Philomena's offer of a lozenge is substituted with her asking Martin if he likes "them" ("them" referring to German cars), and the pun on the word "tune" in the source text is replaced with "I prefer English cars". Philomena then replies that she was talking about sweets. As a consequence, the Italian translation is rather nonsensical, and certainly not funny, but supposedly an Italian audience would not pay particular attention to an old lady rummaging in her bag for sweets. In other words, while a UK audience is going to match Philomena's fiddling with a packet of sweets to her utterances, it is likely that Italians would pay no particular attention to them at all.

Product placement can certainly cause added difficulties in translation. In an episode of the US TV series *The Sopranos*, leading character Tony (James Gandolfini) sends his analyst a gift basket containing a packet of Tide washing powder with a tag reading "Thinking of you, your Prince of Tide". Even if non-English-speaking audiences understand the reference to the 1991 film *The Prince of Tides*[34] about the relationship between an analyst (Barbra Streisand) and her patient (Nick Nolte), the brand name of the detergent varies around the world. In France, Germany and Italy the product goes by the name of *Dash*, in Latin America, it is called *Ace* and in Poland *Vizir*, thus any attempt to tie the name of the brand of washing powder to the remark would create a strong dissonance between the visuals and the storyline.

Translation as a humorous device

Translation itself as a humorous device is by no means a novelty. Before the advent of the internet, tourists would send amusing attempts at translations that they came across in their travels around the world to newspapers that would publish them for the amusement of their readers. However, with the ubiquity of smartphones and the tendency for people to be continuously connected to each other via this technology, today when travellers spot an amusing translational error, they are likely to photograph it and post it on a social networking site.

In fact, googling the term "failed translations" produces 96.9 million hits and searches for similar translations into English from specific languages generate millions of hits too.[35] Failed translations are indeed the object of humour as we can see from title pages such as "35 Hilarious Chinese Translation Fails" and "When translations go wrong – 13 of the funniest English fails".[36] These websites include oriental menus presenting dishes such as "Fries pulls out rotten child" and "Crap Stick" as well as unfortunate road signs such as "Slip and fall down carefully". Restauranteurs and hoteliers are an excellent source of material as they are especially prone to accidentally amusing their clients by producing signs such as, "Guests are encouraged to take advantage of the chamber maid" translated from Japanese or by including a dish called "Chocolate Puke" on a menu in a restaurant in China. Once someone spots and posts the error on the web, it will be shared and forwarded to others, who in turn will share with others in an endless chain of sharing. If the error is especially spicy – pun intended – the screen-shot may go viral and "trend" on various social networks.

Usually, translational faux pas are the result of the work of amateur translators who will typically presume that English lexis and syntax work in the same way as they do in their own language.

> Every room has excellent facilities for your private parts. In winter, every room is on heat. Each room has a balcony offering views of outstanding obscenity! You will not be disturbed by traffic noise, since the road between the hotel and the lake is used only by pederasts.

Similar mistranslations have been around for decades and are funny because they sound nonsensical. Relying on their limited knowledge of English, these non-professional translators are misled by false friends that lead them to produce texts that are ludicrous to English speakers in that specific context.[37] So on one level, failed translations are amusing because we laugh at the inadequacies of the person who produced them while we laugh with the person who discovered the blunder. On another level, however, the bloopers are also amusing because of their taboo-laden inappropriateness. These translations accidentally enter into areas of distastefulness. The Spanish hotelier-cum-translator speaks of "private parts"; [being] "on heat"; "obscenity" and "pederasts" – all misplaced and misused words that seem to be too wrong to be true. Here too there is an element of Sontag's partial knowing. The recipient knows that sexual offenders are unlikely to populate the hotel lake or that vomitus will not be on the menu at mealtimes, but the architect of the translations has ventured into tricky territory where he or she has seriously slipped up, thus creating some racy incongruity.

Gulas and Weinberg's (2010) discussion of global advertising explores the dangers of how ignoring subtle differences in language and culture can change a serious message into a comic one and vice versa. Again, the internet is bursting with examples of products, such as the Chinese "Soup for Sluts", Ghanaian "Pee

Cola" and Italian "Fagottini" – "little faggots". None of these product names are funny in their source languages, but the inherent taboo elements they contain in English render them funny to English speakers. All the translational faux pas, attempts to translate or to "sound English" that go sadly wrong are translation-based and involuntary, but as Delabastita (2005) points out, although they may appear to be bilingual, they are, in effect, monolingual as they will only be seen as transgressing by those au fait with English.

However, if we consider translation in a wider sense, it can also be taken to describe the speech of someone speaking in a language other than their own. When we speak in a language that is not our mother tongue we are, in a sense, presenting a translated version of ourselves. Although we may not necessarily make language errors or faux pas, our otherness and difference with native speakers of the language is likely to emerge, amongst other things, through our pronunciation. This otherness and difference reflected through speech has traditionally been used as the butt of ridicule – a negative form of humour but nevertheless humour. Interference of the articulatory habits of one group of speakers from one language to another is a well-known source of humour. *The Italian Man Who Goes to Malta*, a comic video clip available on YouTube, exemplifies a sort of ridicule that makes fun of foreign, in this case Italian, accents. The video features an Italian in Malta whose hackneyed Italian causes others to constantly misunderstand what he is trying to say:

> One day an Italian man went to a restaurant in Malta and wanted two pieces of toast, and the waiter gives him one, and the Italian man says, "I want two piece". The waiter says, "Go to the toilet". The Man says, "You no understand I want two piece on my plate", then the waiter says, "You better not piss on the plate you son of a bitch!" The man says, "I did not even know him and he calls me a Son of a Beach?" Then he goes to a bigger restaurant and finds himself with a spoon and a knife but no fork. He says, "I want a fock"; the waiter says "Everybody wants to fuck" and he says, "You no understand I want to fock on the table" and the waiter says "You better not fuck on the table you son of a bitch!" Then later he goes to a hotel and in bed, he doesn't have a sheet. "Call the manager and tell him I wanna sheet!" says the Italian man. The other guy says "Go to the toilet" and the Italian man says, "You no understand I wanna sheet in my bed!" and the other guy says, "You better not shit in the bed you son of a bitch!" The Italian man goes to the check-out corner and the check-out man says "Peace on you" and the Italian man says "PISS ON YOU TOO, YOU SON OF A BEACH! I'M GOING BACK TO ITALY!"

The difficulty of Italian speakers to distinguish between the sounds /I/ and /i:/; and to articulate the /ɔ:/ sound in the word "fork" creates a series of problems for the Italian in Malta. Rather like the translational gaffes described previously, the text works on a series of words that the Italian man mispronounces and inadvertently "translates" into what are taboo terms in English, so that the term "piece" is perceived as "piss"; the term "fork" as "fuck" and "sheet" as "shit". The story ends with him feeling insulted by the check-out person who wishes him "Peace on you", which he misinterprets as "piss on you". However, accent apart, the numerous videos available on YouTube recounting the tale also use visuals to ridicule Italianness. In what claims to be the "original animated version", the story is presented by Luigi, an unkempt, swarthy, moustachioed cartoon character wearing an Italian football shirt out of which we see the hairs on his chest emerging. There is a picture of the Tower of Pisa on the wall behind him. Luigi has a very strong (and improbable) Italian accent.[38] Several live enactments of the story are also available in which the actors adopt an exaggeratedly "Italian" accent that deliberately amplifies the phonological features that cause the confusion. *The Italian Man Who Goes to Malta* is an example of an internet meme (see Chapter 4).

Especially on screen, such cultural stereotypes are a common source of humour and through the use of visual elements, the ridicule is not limited to verbal language alone. When Tom and Jerry disembark from a cruise ship in Naples in the classic cartoon feature *Neapolitan Mouse*, they are met by a swarthy moustachioed, local mouse in the backstreets of Naples to the sound of mandolins playing "Santa Lucia".[39] In Disney's *Lady and the Tramp*, audiences see the two enamoured dogs sitting at a table covered with a red and white chequered tablecloth as they eat spaghetti served by a rotund Italian waiter while the background music is provided by the sound of a mandolin.[40] Global advertising also frequently targets Italian men for being Latin lovers. The 2015 Superbowl commercial for the FIAT 500X features an elderly Italian who accidentally drops his last Viagra pill just as a mature woman sexily beckons him towards the bed upon which she lies, scantily dressed.[41] Instead of landing in his mouth, the blue pill falls and travels along pipes and over the rooftops of a stereotypical Italian town until it lands in the petrol tank of a FIAT 500X. The car suddenly swells and becomes larger and more potent-looking as the voiceover claims, "The All New Fiat 500X. Bigger. More Powerful. And Ready for Action", as the car receives admiring and sexually laden glances from women passing by. The commercial then cuts to a scene of the man who dropped the pill lying on the bed snoring loudly as his frustrated wife looks on drumming her fingers. Latin lovers and sexually active elderly Italians are also lampooned in campaigns such as those of Bertolli oils and spreads (see Chiaro 2004) and more recently, the Mutti tomato sauce campaigns that play on street behaviour such as cat-calling and wolf whistling. One Mutti ad features four pasta shapes calling out to (harassing?) a bottle of Mutti sauce as it/she voluptuously walks past them. They call out to her, yell "Redhead" then follow her.[42] This example of politically incorrect street behaviour (that occurs not only in Italy), is successfully exploited by the Mutti copywriters to comic effect. However, although Italian characters are frequently teased on screen, other cultures are not exempt from this mockery. In the 1991 Disney cartoon feature, *Beauty and the*

Beast, the French candlestick named Lumière is not only connoted by accent but also through his sexual proficiency as he continually makes advances towards the curvaceous feather duster, Babette, who is, predictably, also French. These sexually driven French characters support Davies' claim (2011: 76–112) that in the Anglo-Saxon common imaginary, the French are recognized for their abundant and varied sex life that is the subject of copious jokes.[43] *Beauty and the Beast* also ridicules the British through the characterization of the humanized teapot, Mrs Potts, and the clock, Cogsworth, who is inflexible, fussy and always punctual.

Certainly laughing at and making fun of the outsider is a given, yet interestingly, taking command of language and playing with words seems to appeal to exiles, émigrés and to those who in some way either cross the lines between languages and cultures, or else fall through its cracks. Not only do writers such as Ionesco, Nabokov, Beckett and Joyce, but also comedians like the Marx Brothers and more recently Margaret Cho and John Oliver, to mention just a few, all write or perform through a language variety which is not completely their own. It is almost as though these writers and comedians find it impossible to be entirely serious in their non-native tongues. Nabokov apparently wanted to call his memoirs "Crime and Puns", while according to Brophy, Joyce wrote *Finnegan's Wake* while "in the grips of compunsion" or as Redfern puts it, Joyce's "translingual pun disappears up its own Erse" (Redfern 1984: 164–70).

The émigré and all that is transcultural are certainly a mark of the present moment. Right now society is in a constant state of flux. People today easily, constantly shift and change social position in terms of where we live, where we work, our hair, our faces, our bodies – even our sexual orientation – in what Bauman famously labelled "liquid society". The world as we know it is in a constant state of translation, albeit not in the sense of Jakobson's famous but restricted definition of "translation proper", i.e. interlingual translation concerning the transfer of language from Language A to Language B, but in a much wider, polysemiotic sense (Jakobson 1959). As pointed out earlier, those whose mother tongue is English may not be aware of the fact that we live in a verbally translated world. Much of the textual content on the web appears in a variety of English that is the result of translation from other languages. Often this variety of English is neither a lingua franca nor even international English but some sort of odd sounding translationese. Beckett famously said that "In the beginning there was the pun" and we can safely add that the pun was untranslatable. Of course, there are a number of strategies available to translators who have to deal with the thorny area of verbal humour. Ideally, the translator will try to match wordplay in the source language with an instance of similar wordplay in the target language, but of course, this is an arduous task. As jokes play on either linguistic or cultural incongruity or a combination of both, it is unlikely that two languages will possess the same lingua-cultural inconsistencies to create an instance of wordplay that will be an identical of the original. Thus, instead, translators might substitute wordplay in Language A with a completely different example of wordplay in Language B, doing their best to retain some element of the source joke. Another common strategy is for translators to compensate for an untranslatable joke in Language A by inserting an occurrence of wordplay in Language B elsewhere in the text where it might fit in better in the target language. Of course, translators may even omit the wordplay altogether (for a detailed discussion of translational strategies, see Chiaro 2017). To examine this more thoroughly, if the recipient requires a translation it probably means that he or she is not proficient in the source language in the first place, therefore unlikely to be aware of the substitution or omission. In other words, although the target language result may not be what was originally intended, it is important that in terms of response, the recipient recognizes the humorous function of the text. Better still, if the translation is nevertheless funny, then the aim has been achieved – formal equivalence is relatively unimportant, while functional equivalence is fundamental (see Chiaro 2008).

When we convey a joke or a pun in another language, we run the risk that it will fall flat. We can indeed substitute the stupid Irishman, Pole, Belgian or *carabiniere* with a stupid other; the canny Scot with a canny other of our own, but only as long as we steer clear of paronomasia, highly specific cultural references or a combination of both. However, given that translation is impossible, and that "not finding the same thing funny as anyone else finds funny is of course a common immigrant experience" (Phillips 2001), nonetheless so many exiled writers have achieved exactly this, namely rendering humour liquid, and bi and/or trans-lingual by using translation itself as a comic device. As illustrated in depth by Delabastita (2005), translation of Shakespeare is a prime example of this sort of cross-language play. For example, in a famous translation scene from *King Henry V*, French Princess Katherine's pronunciation of innocent household words such as "foot" and "gown" are turned into the bawdy taboo French terms "*foutre*" and "*con*". This is no different to what happens today in viral videos such as *The Italian Man Who Goes to Malta*. As we saw, the Italian gets into trouble when he asks a waitress for a "fuck (fork) on the table"; and a "shit (sheet) on the bed"; or indeed *The French Man Who Goes to Malta* who asks for "a big cock" instead of "a big Coke".[44] According to Freud, what comes between "fear and sex" is "Fünf" and nothing more. These jokes depend on phonemic features and articulatory habits being carried over from one language to another and serving to rationalize the comic pun.

Simplistic as it may sound, when two or more languages come together on screen, the situation will tend to involve either conflict or confusion (see Chiaro 2016b). There are scores of multilingual films and TV products set against a background of war, unrest, danger, poverty and anxiety. Clearly, this is a parallel with reality – trenches, prisoner of war camps, dismal war-torn peripheries and sweatshops often act as settings for films in which polylingualism simply underscores angst and torment. Vice versa, the home of mix-up and confusion is surely the comedy. A single linguistic misunderstanding – almost inevitable if two people do not speak the same language – and the farce, and subsequently the laughter, begins.

We find some of cinema's first trans-lingual mix-ups in the Marx Brothers movies. Sam Wood's 1935 comedy *A Night at the Opera* is a film totally based on migration, part of which takes place on a ship sailing from Italy to New York in which the Marx Brothers are stowaways. The film highlights both the inevitability and the problematics of translation, but above all, as discussed at length by Cronin (2004: 55–63), it pivots upon translation's humorous potential. The very famous contract scene features Driftwood (Groucho) reading a legal contract to the illiterate Fiorello – Chico Marx in his persona of a rustic Italian. The scene is a parody of legal language in English, but it also shows how translation is as much intralingual (i.e. involving different varieties or registers of the same language) as it is interlingual. In other words, legalese may be as impenetrable to native speakers of English as it is to many foreigners. Driftwood puns away on the legal term "party" in a language which is not Fiorello's, telling him to "pay particular attention to this first clause because it's most important . . . the party of the first part shall be known in this contract as the party of the first part". By the time Driftwood and Chico arrive at the "party of the ninth part" the contract is in shreds. The scene culminates in a cross-language pun where the legalese term "a sanity clause" intersects with Fiorello's misunderstanding of both legalese and English so that Chico "translates" what he hears into what he knows namely that "there ain't no such thing as Santa Claus".

However, cross-language humour need not always be so exact. Adenoid Hynkel's speech in Chaplin's *The Great Dictator* (1940) consists entirely of what Sternberg labelled "vehicular promiscuity" (1981); what Sherzer calls "mock-language" (2002) and Cronin labels "pseudo-language" (2004). At the Rally of the Sons and Daughters of the Double Cross, Hynkel's rant is actually pure twaddle, yet the abundant use of words such as "*Wienerschnitzel*" and "*Sauerkraut*" give it a German flavour. But what is most convincing about Hynkel's speech is that it is accompanied by a voiced-over interpretation in English which, in serious contrast with Hynkel's gibberish, further adds to the comic effect of the scene. The interpreter drastically reduces the content of Hynkel's discourse – which is already garbage – therefore displaying the scope of being able to tamper with the original message through translation and the possible untruth of much translation:

> *Hynkel:* "und nach der Tsuden".
> *Off screen interpreter:* "The Jews".
> *Hynkel:* "unbelievte Sauerkraut mit der Juden".
> *Interpreter:* "His Excellency has just referred to the Jewish people".

The voiceover provided by the interpreter demonstrates how translation has the power to censor and by default, to lie. In Italian, there is a saying "*Traduttore traditore*" – literally "translator traitor". One can never be certain of the validity and truth of a translation but has to trust the translator and rely on their honest rendition. There are countless books and films regarding espionage where the double agent is bilingual – a term that derives from the Latin *bilinguis*, literally "split" or "double" tongued, rather like a serpent, hardly the most endearing and trustworthy of creatures. In another famous scene from the same film, Hynkel rages against Italian dictator Napoloni calling him "Napaloni, de Grosse Peanut, de Cheesy Ravioli" and at one point the couple duel armed with German sausages and spaghetti. Naturally, comedy is a genre in which much typecasting and stereotyping tends to occur. However, it is worth noting how, at least as far as Italian and German stereotyping is concerned, the traditional food of Hynkel and Napaloni's respective cultures become worthy of mockery.

The Marx Brothers also use mock language in *A Night at the Opera*, when the brothers are rumbled as stowaways and they take on the identity of three Russian aviators in order to get off the ship in New York. Unluckily for the stowaways the real aviators happen to be famous and were scheduled to give a speech at the City Hall. As the brothers set out to impersonate the Russian aviators, Driftwood/Groucho acts as the interpreter, although the language he is translating from is clearly not Russian but gobbledygook. Yet the officials listening to the "interpreter" take what Driftwood is saying as bona fide. The Mayor of New York only doubts the aviators when he notices that Harpo's false beard is coming off, at which point he accuses them of being phoneys. Unperturbed, interpreter Driftwood converses with Harpo in balderdash relaying to the mayor that his guests are insulted, and offended walks away saying, "Of course you know this means war".

UK comedian Catherine Tate also uses mock language in a well-known sketch from the BBC's *The Catherine Tate Show* in which she plays the part of a secretary who claims to be able to interpret into English from seven different languages.[45] At an important board meeting, it soon becomes clear that she can neither speak nor understand any of the languages of the delegates present. Tate reads the nametag and country of affiliation of each foreign delegate sitting around the table and then babbles in sounds that resemble the perception of the language in question according to the collective imaginary. She achieves a comic effect by reproducing hackneyed sounds and gesticulations of each language she preposterously "translates". For example, Tate inflates the nasal sounds of French, repeats the Spanish silent dental fricative in her Spanish, and produces a series of high-pitched squeaks to articulate her Chinese "translation". The sketch is deliberately politically incorrect and highlights the typical way we mock and parody those different from ourselves. As we know in comedy, anything goes. According to Sherzer, this is a way in which the dominant group in a society ridicules the non-dominant language group using "mock" language based on code-switching: "usually one that is characteristic of groups low on the political-economic and social hierarchy of a community – is inserted into the discourse of the dominant language of the same society, in a purposely parodic form" (2002: 93–4). Sherzer asserts that idioms like *hasta la vista baby* and *no problema* illustrate a way in which non-Hispanic Americans actually mock Spanish speakers.

There are countless examples of cross-language humour in film, on TV and, of course, on the web. The well-known interpreting scene in Benigni's *La Vita è Bella* in which Guido, played by Benigni deliberately mistranslates what the SS Kapò is saying and Tom Hanks' Krakozhia speaking Victor Navorski in *The Terminal*, who deliberately mistranslates in order to avoid the arrest of a fellow migrant illustrate how humour and translation can thrive on cross-linguistic misunderstanding (see Chiaro 2016b).[46]

Possibly the most extreme form of translation as a source of humour can be seen in the movies by Sacha Baron Cohen (see Cronin 2004: 72–80). Beginning with the title of the film that he directed and stars in, *Borat! Cultural Learning for Make Benefit Glorious Nation of Kazakhstan*, the exploiting of translation for humorous purposes emerges very clearly. The title reads like a mistranslation, and when we insert the DVD we read that we are watching "pre record Moviedisc for purpose domestic viewing of movie film" and that "sellingpirating of moviedisc will result in punishment by crushing". Now, Sacha Baron Cohen is a native speaker of English who plays the part of Borat Sagdajev, a Kazakh journalist. Cohen speaks neither Kazakh nor Russian, yet we see the use of a sort of Cyrillic in the opening credits. At the start of the movie, we are in Romania, where people speak Romanian, yet we are told that we are in Kazakhi territory. Borat is accompanied by Azamat Bagatov who speaks Armenian, yet conversation between Bagatov and Borat (who actually uses Hebrew here) must be mutually unintelligible, while the subtitles provided are inaccurate. As Cronin points out, the use of languages in this film underscores the limits of intercultural understanding. For viewers who are familiar with none of the languages involved, the speech is simply that of the unintelligible "other". While this may be very amusing, the fact that anything not linguistically recognized as belonging to the centre is of little importance should make us think. Is the underlying message that is being conveyed that otherness is of no importance within a dominant language and culture?

Finally, Quentin Tarantino's *Inglourious Basterds* (2009) is a film that highlights the importance of being able to speak more languages than one during a conflict. During the Second World War, being a polyglot in Europe could save your life. SS Colonel Hans Landa, played by Christoph Waltz, uses his polylinguistic ability to treacherous ends. However, in one of the funniest – and cleverest – scenes in the film, US soldier Aldo Raine, played by Brad Pitt, and his associates attempt to pass as Italians before Landa. Brad Pitt's accent is atrocious, but even more of a giveaway is the mismatch between their incorrect use of Italian gesticulation coupled with the wrong verbal language. How were they to know that Landa's Italian was native speaker like?[47] Audiences laugh at the linguistic incompetence of the Americans while simultaneously fearing Landa's treachery.

Notes

1. Scandinavian "noir" is a TV and filmic genre based on Scandinavian crime fiction. Examples include the Danish TV series *Forbrydelsen* (2007–12) later adapted in the USA as *The Killing* (2011–14) and Swedish Stieg Larsson's bestseller *The Girl with the Dragon Tattoo* adapted into a movie.
2. Examples from Nigella Lawson, 2002. *Nigella Bites*. Channel Four DVD.
3. Jamie Oliver. 2004. *Pukka Tukka: An Essential Guide to Cooking*. Video Collection International DVD.
4. *The Great British Bake Off*, 2010 to 2016, distributed by BBC Worldwide.
5. The 2015 *Great Comic Relief Bake Off*.
6. *Bizarre Foods with Andrew Zimmern* was produced by Travel Channel USA and broadcast from 2006 to the present.
7. *How Clean is Your House* was produced by Channel 4 and first broadcast from 2003 to 2009.
8. *Britain's Got Talent* broadcast on ITV3 from 2007 to present.
9. Scene available at: www.youtube.com/watch?v=BfWTxg72JpM. Retrieved 3 November 2015.
10. *An Extra Slice*, BBC2, 2014 to 2016. The show follows what happened in the previous episode of the *Bake Off* and shows unseen footage.
11. *Little Britain* was a BBC television series broadcast between 2003 and 2005. One of David Walliams' persona in the series was Emily Howard whose repeated catchphrase was "I'm a lady and I do lady's things" hence the undeliberate link with his remark about the band on the talent show. See Chapter 3 for further discussion.
12. See *The Lewis Carroll Society of North America* at: www.lewiscarroll.org/tag/the-mouses-tale/. Retrieved 14 July 2015.
13. *My Big Fat Greek Wedding*, released in 2002 and directed by Joel Zwick.
14. Depending on the context, the word *cazzata* can mean "bullshit" or "fuck up"; in either case, it derives from the word *cazzo*, a vulgar term for "penis".
15. Directed by Stanley Kramer and released in 1963. The scene described is available at: www.youtube.com/watch?v=w00Kab17aeI. Retrieved 11 January 2017. I would like to thank Graeme Ritchie for drawing my attention to this gag.
16. Quoted from an online interview with Rowan Atkinson (21 August 2007). Available at: http://moviehole.net/200711633dvd-interview-rowan-atkinson. Retrieved 3 August 2015.
17. Images of Stan Laurel and Michael Crawford adopting the above-mentioned poses are respectively available at: https://classicmoviehubblog.wordpress.com/tag/stan-laurel/ and www.doyouremember.co.uk/memory/some-mothers-do-ave-em. Both retrieved 6 August 2015.
18. Originally aired 1 January 1991.
19. Mr Bean at the opening ceremony of the 2012 Olympics in London. Available at: www.dailymotion.com/video/xti810_mr-bean-at-2012-olympics-opening-ceremony_fun. Retrieved 3 August 2015.
20. Mr Bean at *Comic Relief 2015*, available at: www.dailymotion.com/video/x2jkcpx. Retrieved 3 August 2015.
21. *Shark Tale*, released in 2004, was directed by Bibo Bergeron, Vicky Jenson and Rob Letterman.
22. *My Cousin Vinny*, released in 1992, was directed by Jonathan Lynn.
23. The *Wallace and Gromit* series consists of animated films directed by Nick Parks between 1999 and 2011.
24. *Frozen* was released in 2013 and directed by Jennifer Lee and Chris Buck.
25. This technique involves the physical manipulation of an object so that it seems to move on its own. The object is moved a bit at a time and photographed with each small movement so that put together into a single sequence the individual frames create the illusion of movement.

26 *Chicken Run*, released in 2000, and directed by Peter Lord and Nick Parks.
27 *Shaolin Soccer* was released in 2000 and directed by Stephen Chow.
28 *A Fish Called Wanda* was a British and US co-production, released in 1988 and directed by Charles Crichton.
29 *Undertaking Betty* (aka *Plots with a View*) was released in 2002 and directed by Nick Hurran.
30 *Shrek* was released in 2001 and directed by Andrew Adamson and Vicky Jenson; *Shrek II* was released in 2004 and directed by Andrew Adamson, Kelly Adamson and Conrad Vernon; *Shrek III* was released in 2007 and directed by Chris Mikker and Roman Hui.
31 *Dumbo* was released in 1941 and directed by Ben Sharpsteen.
32 *Lock, Stock and Two Smoking Barrels* was released in 1998 and directed by Guy Ritchie.
33 The film *Philomena* was released and directed by Stephen Frears.
34 Directed by Barbra Streisand.
35 See www.google.it/search?q=I+remember+the+corned+beef&ie=utf-8&oe=utf-8&client=firefox-b&gfe_rd=cr&ei=Yop3WOSUEcHCXsT0rKAN#q=+failed+translation+. Retrieved 12 January 2017.
36 See www.boredpanda.com/funny-chinese-translation-fails/ and www.mirror.co.uk/news/weird-news/translations-go-wrong---13-3700064. Both retrieved 12 January 2017.
37 False friends are words in two languages that are very similar yet have very different meanings in each language. For example, an English speaker might think that the Spanish word *embarazada* has the same meaning as the English word "embarrassed", but, in fact, *embarazada* means *pregnant*.
38 *The Italian Man Who Went to Malta* – (official animated version) available at: www.youtube.com/watch?v=YjXGywPzkw0. Retrieved 17 January 2017.
39 *Neapolitan Mouse* was directed by William Hanna and Joseph Barbera, USA, 1954.
40 *Lady and the Tramp* was directed by Clyde Geronimi and Wilfred Jackson, USA, 1955.
41 Video available at: www.youtube.com/watch?v=YAcLViTHDOo. Retrieved 19 January 2017.
42 Video available at: www.youtube.com/watch?v=fcoR75dX5rM&list=PLOqQ75wVRdqf3p1wI_zMzt-oI48X6aeZ4. Retrieved 19 January 2017.
43 *Beauty and the Beast* was directed by Gary Trousdale and Kirk Wise, USA, 1991.
44 Video available at: www.youtube.com/watch?v=PFkzSfRFiMU. Retrieved 23 January 2017.
45 *The Catherine Tate Show*. 2005. UK/BBC2, Directed by Gordon Anderson. Sketch available at www.youtube.com/watch?v=QNKn5ykP9PU. Retrieved 23 January 2017.
46 *La Vita è Bella* 1997, directed by Roberto Benigni. *The Terminal* 2004, directed by Steven Spielberg.
47 Scene available at: www.youtube.com/watch?v=OxEY3DRJUFs. Retrieved 23 January 2017.

3
THE LANGUAGE OF JOKES AND GENDER

A major concern marking the first two decades of the 21st century is an ongoing debate about crucial issues pertaining to gender. Following in the wake of Women's Studies and Feminist Theory, intellectual debate regarding gender has expanded to include studies in masculinity and, additionally, the wide gamut of sexualities. The traditional binary opposition between male and female genders is now complemented by LGBTQI while society is slowly but surely moving towards attitudes that are inclusive of all genders and nuances of sexuality. In fact, gender has now begun to be accepted as a social and cultural construct that, as first argued by Judith Butler (1990), is as much about performance as about fixed behaviour that is the natural result of chromosomes and physical characteristics. However, gender is wherever we turn, and the fact remains that for an individual filling in a form, applying for a job or a mortgage, or participating in a survey – alongside name and date of birth, the applicant's gender is required. Everything we do implicates gender – from how we speak and move to how we dress – so it follows that the way we "do" humour, the way we accept humour and even our sense of humour may, in some way, be marked in terms of gender.

Since the mid-1990s, the internet has grown exponentially to occupy the prominent place it does in almost every area of life. Apart from the ubiquity of social networks such as Facebook, Twitter, Instagram, Pinterest, etc., the internet is also the source of answers to any query one might have. It has become the norm to find directions, go shopping and even find a partner online. Therefore, it should come as no surprise to find that the internet is also a massive source of humorous materials and is, furthermore, a "major player in the production and distribution of humor, in general, and humor about gender, in particular" (Shifman 2007). If, as argued by Billig (2005), comedic texts bring into play dominant ideologies and cultural codes, an investigation of online humour should provide an up-to-date perspective on what Shifman and Lemish consider to be "highly charged issues such as gender and sexuality" (2010).

This chapter will first focus on instances of verbally expressed humour targeting gender that can be found on the internet with particular attention to humour that "goes viral" by means of social media. This will be followed by a discussion of gender-related humour that is politically "charged". Charged humour is very much in the limelight within the genre of stand-up comedy where the stage has become a place for women comedians to voice and challenge all number of social givens. Finally, I will examine comedy that plays with the fluidity of gender.

Male, female, humour and laughter

Starting from the binary biological distinction between male and female, let us attempt to understand how similar or how different these categories might be in terms of humour styles. With regard to gender, it is worth exploring whether the same things amuse both males and females and whether the way in which they perform humour might vary too. Given that humour is closely connected to laughter, a good starting point could be to explore whether males and females laugh in the same way.

At first sight, the most obvious difference could be that the quality of laughter differs in the two sexes in terms of sound if only because males generally have deeper voices than females, but what does the word "generally" tell us in any meaningful way? Presumably, some females have longer and slacker vocal chords than do most males and thus produce huskier laughter, just as there will be males with tighter vocal chords and the high-pitched voices normally associated with females.

However, in English, there are a number of laughter words, i.e. words that indicate a type of laugh, that instinctively seem to be more associated with one gender rather than with another. For example, "giggle" (Figures 3.1 to 3.6) and "cackle" (Figure 3.7) appear to connote females rather than males, while "guffaw"

| F9X 3056 | and was surprised to see Britta covering her mouth to stifle a | giggle | . The Doctor was standing with his hands behind his back. |

| AMC 606 | , Wendy pulled the banister away from the wall. Stifling a | giggle | , she hazarded a guess that the wardrobe would be full of |

BPB 385	Committee? What is British Committee?' She suppresses a hysterical	giggle	. 'You must know who they are. You know,
BPA 2146	cackle, and fell fractionally forward. Forster suppressed a nervous	giggle	. They reached the main deck, dropping down in a defensive
C8A 1890	. 'Tall and dark . . . ' Jennifer stifled an impulse to	giggle	. A tall, dark stranger — that was what fortune-tellers always
C8T 1461	at the same time. I had an almost irresistible impulse to	giggle	. I know it was only a reaction to shock but it

| FEE 3052 | and You. Good Old Mavis, I thought, suppressing a | giggle | ; she takes her defeats like a lady. I said ' |

| H8J 2090 | own?' He sounded so hard done-by that Claudia wanted to | giggle | , a feeling she sternly repressed. Give in to it and |

| F9X 3766 | n't hit the island', Ace tried to stifle an inappropriate | giggle | , 'I guess it'll just sink into the brains. |

| HW8 1608 | ?' I put on my stern voice so I wouldn't | giggle | . 'She kicked him — in the place which is most |

FIGURE 3.1 Examples of the term "giggling" emerging as an unsuitable impulse to display publicly

72 The language of jokes and gender

APW 3003	the same thing, my lord'. They stiffened. To	giggle	would be childish, and spoil it all. 'But I
EFJ 28	thought of him being ten years old made the children want to	giggle	but they bit the giggles back. Their mother was looking so
G1M 2528	, evolving through a deep guffaw, and ending as a childlike	giggle	, once more behind her. Her lips thinned. Her finger
BMN 2014	dirty children who eyed Corbett boldly, then ran to hide and	giggle	behind their mother's skirts. Corbett bowed. 'Joan Taggart
CAS 588	happens? Right. It's like instructing a schoolchild not to	giggle	. Similarly, your subconscious cannot try not to be a

FIGURE 3.2 Examples of the terms "children", "schoolchild", "childish" and "childlike" collocated with the term "giggle"

(Figure 3.8) appears to connote male laughter. Some may even believe that giggling in grown men may undermine their masculinity just as others may think that guffawing in women may question their femininity. In fact, a search for the word form "giggle" in the British National Corpus returns 254 hits, several of which collocate with terms such as "suppress", "stifle" and "repress", implying that giggling may not be an especially positive thing to do or that it may be perceived as being inappropriate.[1]

Furthermore, the word form also collocates with words like "childlike" and "childish" underscoring the undesirability of this type of laughter in fully grown adults by implying the giggler's immaturity. In addition, in the corpus, "giggle" also collocates with the negative adjective "cheap".

After sifting out expressions such as to "have a giggle" and "for a giggle" from the corpus, the word form "giggle" did indeed emerge more frequently as a collocate of female as opposed to male nouns. For example, out of 47 proper

CMD 1014	names. What is the significance of Marilyn other than a cheap	giggle	? There is a strong danger of a mountain 'twitcher'

FIGURE 3.3 Example of the adjective "cheap" collocated with the term "giggle"

29	APC 223	In Arequipa I had watched women in the church of Santo Domingo	giggle	happily as they dressed the Virgin for a procession;, behaving
41	B38 3370	and they babble Men Talk Men Talk. Women gossip Women	giggle	Women niggle-niggle-niggle Men Talk. Women yatter Women chatter Women chew the
42	B38 3398	philadelphia Cream Cheese. Oh Bossy Women Gossip Girlish Women	Giggle	Women natter, women nag Women niggle niggle niggle Men Talk.
202	HH3 15394	women are overjoyed. Their hard work has paid off. They	giggle	as their men rush forward in front of the TV camera to
178	H94 1488	dark wintry streets with a woman in a tea-cosy. A small	giggle	slipped from her lips. His golden head whipped around and she
	HP0 1019	trees. There was a scuffle, and then a woman's	giggle	, among the undergrowth toward the centre of the small coppice.

FIGURE 3.4 Examples of the terms "woman", "woman's" and "women" as collocates of the term "giggle

The language of jokes and gender   73

36	ATA 417	Kind of image that girls can talk about, laugh at and	giggle	over together. Indeed Katie's group, when I'd pushed
39	ATE 1981	whined, 'pops is tired'. The girls continued to	giggle	and scream and run and hide and generally have fun with their
57	CAD 1643	it !]: We're liking everything today! (they	giggle	, theatrically, like the Philadelphia cheese girls) They're from
187	HD7 269	. Every so often I stood the treat. The girls would	giggle	and tell risqué stories. My ears burned with their crudity at
219	J13 817	'What are you girls snorting?' I ask. They	giggle	into the mirrors. I snap, 'come on !'
42	B38 3398	Philadelphia Cream Cheese. Oh Bossy Women Gossip Girlish Women	Giggle	Women natter, women nag Women niggle niggle niggle Men Talk.
71	CCC 730	want to fuck men.' She forces a false, schoolgirl	giggle	. 'How kooky. That's the real alternative lifestyle!
79	CHA 1018	I've always resented the ideal of the frilly frock and girly	giggle	as the symbols of femininity – dungarees and big boots should not
134	FRS 1989	catch her, and she fell into them with a ridiculous girlish	giggle	. 'If she wants the hotel she can have it,
191	HGF 2302	. I saluted Heil Hitler, you know, with a girlish	giggle	. The Jewish family got back their papers and told me afterwards
195	HGN 2361	bounce off the walls (nothing so trillingly femme as a girlish	giggle	). I don't quite see the joke, but then

FIGURE 3.5 Examples of the terms "girls", "girlish", "schoolgirl" and "girly" as collocates of the term "giggle"

65	CCW 673	the poor man was jealous.' My father had begun to	giggle	. 'Do you know what she told me, Nick?
107	EWH 844	!' he remarked, and the young man gave a high-pitched	giggle	. Sara knew that she had not been intended to understand this
64	CCN 540	boys, they have got it all worked out. They may	giggle	and act as though they have not a serious thought in their

FIGURE 3.6 Examples of "man", "boys" and "father" as collocates of the term "giggle"

nouns either preceding or following the form "giggle" (thus nouns referring to who was actually doing the giggling), 33 are female names and only 14 male. Similarly, against 37 occurrences of the pronoun "she" as a collocate of "giggle", there are only 9 occurrences of "he". Again, 19 other incidences of "giggle" collocate with "her" against 5 for "his". In addition, the corpus contains only one occurrence of the word form "woman"; four occurrences of "women"; one of "women's" and five of "girls" all collocated with "giggle" against a single concordance with the word form "man"; a single concordance with the word form "boy" and a single concordance with "father".

Noteworthy are the collocations "girly giggle", "girlish giggle" and especially "schoolgirl giggle" that occur near the taboo term "fuck!" (Figure 3.5 example 71/CGC730). The corpus displays no similar "male" equivalents – "boyish giggles" and "schoolboy giggles" are not natural expressions and do not occur in the corpus observed. Consequently, the data examined backs up an intuitive hypothesis that giggling is largely perceived as a somewhat unfortunate female characteristic.

In the same corpus, the word form "cackle" returns only 61 hits, implying that it is not especially common usage. Three occurrences of "cackle" collocate with names of fowl, as cackling is the sound birds make, while another six collocate with "Miss" to create "Miss (Amelia) Cackle" a character from the British TV series *The Worst Witch*.[2] In fact, "Miss Cackle" makes up around 10 per cent of all

74 The language of jokes and gender

GVP 2394	?' 'Dressed in mourning?' Iris gave an unsympathetic	cackle	. 'Can't say we didn't warn her.'
GVP 3099	.' 'Oh, yes.' Iris gave a derisive	cackle	. 'The last straw, losing her golfing partner. Enough
GVT 83	'll bring to the pictures next,' she wheezed. Her	cackle	turned into a bronchial cough. Gertrude stopped working, and collapsed
HGV 1572	'Good bye, ma'am. Keep well.' There was a	cackle	from the old lady. 'Ain't me you want to
J54 890	heard you shouting at Mr. Matthew.' 'She gave a little	cackle	and then bent down and began locking the french windows."
KS7 1639	s own excesses — simple, melodic threads he untangles from demonic	cackle	and sheer noise. But some of the astonishment was that we

FIGURE 3.7 Examples of some collocations of the term "cackle"

occurrences. Furthermore, in diverse concordances the form "cackle" is repeated in sequence to create an onomatopoeic effect thereby inflating the number of concordances. Therefore, not only unlike the word form "giggle" does the word form "cackle" appear to be used less frequently as a laughter word, but also, diversely from "giggle", the collocations of "cackle" are less clear in terms of their association with pronouns that mark gender. It is, however, evident in the corpus examined that cackling, like giggling, is another undesirable type of laughter as we find "cackle" collocated with terms like "scornful", "unfeeling", "derisive", etc. Three interesting concordances of "cackle" are "devilish", "demonic" and "lunatic-sounding" that precede the word form, while "old lady" acts as its collocate on two occasions.

However, without resorting to a corpus, Vennochi (2007) notes that "HENS CACKLE. [original upper case] So do witches. And, so does the front-runner in the Democratic presidential contest". In fact, throughout the 2008 US Presidential elections, the media dedicated a large amount of space to deriding Clinton's laughter, so much so that according to Groch-Begley (2015), the "Clinton cackle" and her "record scratch" were constantly adopted as a form of attack. In addition, during the 2016 run-up to the US Presidential elections the media continued to ridicule the candidate's laughter and, above all, her "cackle" while there was no reference to the quality of laughter of her male opposition. Blogger Sonny Bunch (2015) goes as far as dehumanizing Clinton by asking "Hannah Groch-Begley can't *actually* think that Hillary Clinton has a normal, appealing, human laugh, can she? I mean, have you heard it?" while mockery is sustained through the sale of items such as the "Hillary Clinton 2016 Laughing Pen", which, according to the sales' blurb, produces "a crescendo of maniacal and frightening giggles and guffaws".[3] Also known as the "scary as hell" pen, consumers are encouraged on the package to "Laugh with/at Hillary". Video compilations of Clinton's laughter went viral over the internet, together with videos of the Laughing Pen. However, the extent to which dislike of Clinton is justified by the way she laughs is best illustrated through remarks left by YouTube viewers that appear below video clips portraying Clinton's laughter. Many comments reflect sexist attitudes that are apparently vindicated by the quality of her signature laugh. Hillary's laughter is considered "witchlike", "evil", "creepy" with observations such as "who in their right mind would want to listen to that old witch cackling?" Beneath one YouTube video of the Laughing Pen, we find comments such as, "She's not a witch. Witches are technically human"; "LOL comparing Hillary's widemouth laugh next to the Predator was funny! They resemble each other so closely it's scary!!!" (sic.). Again, we also find, "That wicked witch of the west sure can open her mouth wide".[4] Just as everyone has a distinctive tone and timbre of voice, the same applies to laughter. It is odd that in a politically correct world in which we must tread carefully so as not to cause offence through our choice of words and to avoid being indelicate about the physical appearance of others, people can get away with publicly mocking someone because of their way of laughing. Even Dr Annie Evans, a well-known expert on female health, when describing the mood swings which may occur during the menopause in a series of lectures published on YouTube uses Clinton's laugh to exemplify menopausal symptoms. "What women want to know is whether this is normal" asserts Evans, "or am I going stark, staring raving mad", at which point viewers are presented with a close-up of Hillary Clinton with a wide mouthed laugh. The live audience, made up predominantly of women, can be seen and heard reacting with lengthy laughter presumably in agreement with the instance of mockery.

Finally, the word form "guffaw" returned only 28 hits in the BNC corpus, suggesting that, similarly to "cackle", it is not commonly used. However, 16 occurrences of "guffaw" clearly collocate with male names or pronouns compared to 3 that collocate with females, once more backing up the intuition that guffawing is more of a male laughter style. In one occurrence in which a certain Lady Merchiston emits a "cackling guffaw", we find a combination of two types of laughter that endow the character with twofold traits that are undesirable in women in contemporary society, namely ageing and lack of femininity (Figure 3.8 23/HGV1227). As we saw previously, Clinton's antagonists combine their remarks about "guffaws" with "frightening giggles"; thus, while paradoxically linking ageism with immaturity, at the same time they bestow upon her non-human attributes that are intended to evoke fear.

As for styles of humour, according to Tannen (1991), males generally appear to favour a "competitive" style when interacting with each other so it might also follow that a tendency for them to hold centre stage while telling jokes and "topping" those told by other males may be a prominent feature of male comic style. On the other hand, Tannen claims that females display a preference to collaborate with other females and "match" their contributions with those of other participants

23	HGV 1227	when the time comes.' Lady Merchiston let out a cackling	guffaw	, and then noticed her godson's glance going from one to
	ALS 183	Doom the jailer laughed. Jake and his men gave a loud	guffaw	and so did the Town Clerk and the Dragoons. And now
	BMU 8	Wot a night!' wheezed an old farmer, with a	guffaw	that shook the raindrops from his whiskers. 'Granted before asked
	CCD 2270	think . . .' Forest's last words had been accompanied by a	guffaw	, and Edward's half-formed comment was drowned by the slamming of
	HH1 4910	helped out like a dutiful daughter.' He gave another coarse	guffaw	. 'I'll pay in coin like I always does,
	EVC 2533	, but that's all.' Oswin let out a huge	guffaw	.' I admire the man. Two wives and a mistress
	FEE 3228	carry on the Great Name of Graham – She gave a short	guffaw	.' So now you're going to have what might well
	CFY 2339	age to him, he wanted not only to laugh but to	guffaw	, like he used to do when Harry or Martin came out
	CK9 167	yours?' The question was innocent but it brought a great	guffaw	from the youth and he answered, 'Ben Smith, Jones

FIGURE 3.8 Examples of some collocations of the term "guffaw"

within a conversation, thereby creating a sort of alliance (1991: 92). In fact, when it comes to humour, research shows that females tend to use it in a cooperative way and frequently adopt a variety of jocular styles to provide support for others (Coates 2014; Holmes 2006; Holmes and Marra 2006; Holmes and Schnurr 2014; Vine *et al.* 2009).

One difference between the sexes in the performance of humour may lie in the invention and telling of jokes, which appears to be more of an activity engaged in by males (Kuipers 2006: 46). Men create a sort of inclusive atmosphere and cement groups by means of telling jokes. In contrast, women form closer ties through telling each other (funny) stories (Coates 2014). According to Davies (2012), it is males, rather than females, who are responsible for generating joke cycles that reflect their position in the social order.

Based on experimental data, Hall (2015) claims that laughter is a fundamental feature in courtship where the female, through laughter, provides an "audience" for the male who makes jokes. However, in a far-reaching outline of psychology research on gender differences in sense of humour, Martin (2014) highlights how difficult it is to generalize about a multifaceted subject such as humour when there is such wide variability amongst individuals within each gender. Martin, in fact, concludes that there are more similarities between males and females in aspects such as sense of humour and joke appreciation than there are differences. At least, however, the commonplace that women's sense of humour is generally less than that of men's is now considered devoid of foundation.

Targeting gender

Jokes not only have to be about something (see Attardo's "Situation KR" in Chapter 1) but they also require a target, someone or something for the recipient to laugh at. As discussed in Chapter 1, jokes usually target individuals or groups of people who, for the purpose of the joke, are depicted as being intellectually challenged or else duped into acting in a senseless manner through the astuteness of another. Whether the joke is an ethnic joke or one about politics, religion, marriage or any other institution, the target will behave in an injudicious manner or else be the victim of their own stupidity through someone else's canniness. Even so-called "dirty jokes" based on sex, when stripped of their taboo content, are likely to involve a punchline based on one person's inanity or another's astuteness. In other words, titillating content simply tends to serve as a frame in which the joke's target will be either inherently foolish or else tricked into being so by another more artful individual. Either way, the recipient of the joke is intended to laugh at the target.

The target of the ethnic joke, the underdog, typically inhabits a periphery and is joked about and laughed at by those occupying the more illustrious centre. As discussed in Chapter 1, every centre has its own outsider who is in some way depicted as an underdog or as being inferior by the hegemonic majority. As we have seen, Davies (1998) argues that much ethnic humour may arise from feelings of economic or sexual fear in the minds of a consolidated and well-established group directed towards the new "peripheral" group entering their society. This view makes sense and is credible as far as, for example, newly arrived immigrants in a community are concerned. Established inhabitants fear new "others", they fear for their jobs and their spaces. Interestingly, women have traditionally been targeted in sexist jokes, thus rendering them in some way peripheral to the society of which they are an integral part. Could it be that in heteronormative society, women, similarly to migrants, for example, are seen as "other" and thus as an economic or sexual threat?

On the internet, vast numbers of people not only read, but also partake in the circulation of humour that can be, to varying degrees, sexist in nature. If it is given that jokes are founded upon shared ideologies and cultural codes, then, in substance, such jokes may be deemed as being political. In other words, while "only joking", these texts provide significant insight into contemporary perceptions of gender and sexuality (Billig 2005). In their study of gender-related cyber-humour, Shifman and Lemish (2010) classify jokes based on gendered humour on the internet according to whether it is sexist, feminist or postfeminist, three useful labels that will be adopted in the discussion that follows.

Sexist humour

As the term itself implies, sexist humour targets women, "disparaging them as a unified collective" Shifman and Lemish (2010).

> Q. How do you know when a woman is going to say something intelligent?
> A. When her first words are, "A man once told me...".[5]

> I left three notes scattered around the house for my girlfriend. They say "Will", "You" and "Me". That will keep her busy whilst I watch football on TV.[6]

Sexist jokes such as these depict women as unintelligent beings, usually bent on trapping men into marriage. Shifman and Lemish go on to sub-divide sexist jokes into "general" and "specific" jokes". General sexist jokes unite all women under a single classification in which they all behave in the same manner, while specific sexist jokes target only certain women according to a number of stereotypical characteristics, e.g. wives, blondes, nuns, etc.

Significantly, while jokes in general connote men ethnically (Irish, Black, Italian, etc.) or according to a profession (e.g. doctor, lawyer, engineer, politician, cleric, etc.) women in jokes (if and when they happen to have a profession) are typically restricted to the occupation of teachers, nurses and nuns. While nurses and nuns are largely restricted to the category of dirty jokes, wives and mothers-in-law are also popular targets. Walker (1988: 120), in fact, suggested that the ever-present stereotypes of "bimbo and housewife" disguise a society that trivializes women's lives.

Needless to say, the World Wide Web contains countless websites that specialize in collections of jokes – suffice it to google "joke collections" to retrieve 48.1 million hits while other combinations of the term "joke" (e.g. "children's jokes", "clean jokes", etc.) spawn countless other compilations.[7] When googling "joke collections", one of the major websites that emerges is "jokes2go". This website contains a large number of joke categories listed from A to Z ranging from "Animal jokes" to "Yo mama jokes". Most categories appear to be gender neutral apart from the categories of "Men", "Men jokes", "Women", "Women jokes", "Blondes", and, of course, "Yo mama jokes". Another highly visible website is "Jokes4all" that also lists joke categories in alphabetical order.[8] Amongst its numerous categories, the Jokes4all website contains jokes regarding over 50 professions in alphabetical order ranging from "accountants" to "waitresses". Although the vast majority of the listed professions are gender neutral, e.g. doctors, managers, economists, etc., the professionals in the jokes are mainly male:

> A physicist, biologist and a chemist were going to the ocean for the first time.
> The physicist saw the ocean and was fascinated by the waves. He said he wanted to do some research on the fluid dynamics of the waves and walked into the ocean. Obviously, he was drowned and never returned.
> The biologist said he wanted to do research on the flora and fauna inside the ocean and walked into the ocean. He too, never returned.
> The chemist waited for a long time and afterwards, wrote the observation, "The physicist and the biologist are soluble in ocean water".[9]

> "A philosopher", said the theologian "is like a blind man in a darkened room looking for a black cat that isn't there".
> "That's right", the philosopher replied, "and if he were a theologian, he'd find it".[10]

Of course, these two jokes are not about gender at all, they are jokes that target people in high standing occupations and that, according to Davies (2011: 29) undermine stupidity jokes generally aimed at "powerless people at the bottom end of the social order". Nevertheless, the professionals are consistently male and it would be tempting to argue that we are unconsciously primed to consider prestigious professions to be the monopoly of males. On the same website, however, the categories of babysitters, nurses and secretaries, while labelled with gender-neutral terms, include only jokes about female babysitters, nurses and secretaries.[11] Furthermore, with the exception of babysitters and waitresses who are paradoxically targeted both for their stupidity and canniness, jokes about nurses, nuns and secretaries are mainly obscene in nature. Apart from wives and mothers-in law, the only occupations that are strictly female at Jokes4all are restricted to "hookers", prostitutes, princesses and nuns.

A popular brainteaser from the 1990s illustrates how common gender stereotypes are:

> A man and his son are driving in a car one day, when they get into a fatal accident. The man is killed instantly but the boy, although unconscious, is still alive. He is rushed to hospital, and will need immediate surgery. The doctor enters the emergency room, looks at the boy, and says, "I can't operate on this boy, he is my son". How is this possible?

The answer to the conundrum is simple because the doctor is the boy's mother, yet the answer is not always immediate to many recipients because the profession of doctor tacitly implies "male". Surprisingly, in 2016, out of 17 mixed-sex undergraduates majoring in English aged between 21 and 25, only 3 females guessed the correct answer, while the others were mostly unable to solve the enigma with most recipients guessing that the surgeon was the boy's biological father.[12] So again and still, we may be primed to consider some professions more closely associated with one gender than another.

According to Shifman and Lemish (2010: 871), the internet "offers a unique perspective for understanding contemporary perceptions and stereotypes of highly charged issues such as gender and sexuality". They go on to argue that while traditionally jokes in which women were the butts reflected a series of consolidated attitudes and values, the growing visibility of female stand-up comedians together with a platform for humour provided by the web has helped subvert these attitudes with what they define as "feminist humor". In fact, there is a growing trend for jokes made at the expense of men in industrialized countries (Bing 2007; Kotthoff 2006; Shifman and Lemish 2010). Sexist jokes aimed at men include jokes such as when, in answer to the question "Why are women bad at parking?" the female joker replies "Because they are used to men telling them that this much (joker indicates an inch with thumb and finger) is ten inches" (Chiaro 1992). Also:

> The patient's family gathered to hear what the specialists had to say. "Things don't look good. The only chance is a brain transplant. This is an experimental procedure. It might work, but the bad news is that brains are very expensive, and you will have to pay the costs yourselves".
> "Well, how much does a brain cost?" asked the relatives.
> "For a male brain, $500,000. For a female brain, $200,000".
> Some of the younger male relatives tried to look shocked, but all the men nodded because they thought they understood. A few actually smirked. But the patient's daughter was unsatisfied and asked, "Why the difference in price between male brains and female brains?"
> "A standard pricing practice", said the head of the team.
> "Women's brains have to be marked down because they have actually been used".[13]

Specific sexist jokes

Wives

Returning to Walker's suggestion that women in jokes are trapped within the stereotype of "bimbo or housewife", in many jokes women are indeed portrayed as sexual objects or as money-driven beings who use their sexuality to trap men into marriage, yet once they are married, they are no longer keen on sexual relations with their husbands. However, wives in jokes do retain a predilection for sexual activity, but with men other than their husbands. These men can be frequently found in wardrobes by husbands who come home early from work. When not partaking in adulterous activities, women in sexist jokes spend most of their time spending their husband's hard-earned money. In other words, in specific sexist jokes about wives, women emerge as mercenary beings who, to put it mildly, are quite despicable.

As argued by Davies (1998, 2011), jokes poke fun at institutions, so it is of no surprise that there is an abundance of jokes about marriage in general. Yet, traditionally, when wives are targeted it is either because they no longer have sexual feelings for their husbands, or because they spend too much money, or a combination of both:

> A wife arrived home after a long shopping trip, and was horrified to find her husband in bed with a young, lovely thing. Just as she was about to storm out of the house, her husband stopped her with these words: "Before you leave, I want you to hear how this all came about. Driving home, I saw this young girl, looking poor and tired, I offered her a ride. She was hungry, so I brought her home and fed her some of the roast you had forgotten about in the refrigerator. Her shoes were worn out so I gave her a pair of your shoes you didn't wear because they were out of style. She was cold so I gave her that new birthday sweater you never wore even once because the colour didn't suit you. Her slacks were worn out so I gave her a pair of yours that you don't fit into anymore. Then as she was about to leave the house, she paused and asked, 'Is there anything else that your wife doesn't use anymore?' And so, here we are!"[14]

> A husband walks into the bedroom holding two aspirins and a glass of water. His wife asks, "What's that for?" "It's for your headache", he replies. "But I don't have a headache", she says. To which her husband replies, "Gotcha!"

These two jokes both work because of the astuteness of husbands who manage to find shrewd solutions to overcome their deprivation of marital sex. In the first joke, the husband justifies his adulterous behaviour because his wife no longer "uses" his body (for sex), so he therefore chooses charitably to donate it to a needy woman together with other items his wife no longer uses such as her cast-off clothing. Notably, in the joke, the new woman is described as a "young, lovely *thing*" – literally as an object. In the second joke, the husband craftily takes the euphemistic excuse of his wife having a headache for not wanting to have sex literally and provides his wife with painkillers so that he can legitimately have (non-consensual?) sex with her.[15] While on one level this is a stupid/canny joke, i.e. the wife makes up an excuse to avoid sex while her husband cannily finds a solution to her "headache", on another level the joke highlights the power differentials between husband and wife and the "legitimate" entitlement of a husband to sex, regardless of the wishes of his wife. Furthermore, it also reinforces the stereotype that wives have no sexual desire, but that male desire will find a way, despite the lack of receptivity to his desires. Although interpreting this as a rape script may be going too far, as rape is not explicitly foregrounded, a "rape reading" is also possible. The two (distant) poles in the joke are (a) a way to "force" the woman to have sexual intercourse against her will and (b) a (clever) way to prevent the headache excuse (given a subtle interplay of the kind "well I'm not against it, but I do not feel like it right now"). As in most (clever) jokes, a lot is left unsaid. In other words, this interpretation is very much in the mind of the beholder as what is left unsaid is uncontrollable by the teller.

Interestingly, in both jokes, the wife is the guilty party who gets her just rewards, namely betrayal and/or unwanted sex. According to George Orwell (2000), the conventions of what he labels the "sex joke" state that "Marriage only benefits women. Every man is plotting seduction and every woman is plotting marriage. No woman ever remained unmarried voluntarily", and this notion is still constantly reiterated in jokes today:

> A groom waits at the altar with a huge smile on his face. His best man asks, "Why do you look so excited?" The groom replies, "I just had the best blow job I have ever had in my entire life, and I am marrying the wonderful woman who gave it to me". The bride waits at the other end of the aisle with a huge smile on her face. Her maid of honor asks, "Why do you look so excited?" The bride replies, "I just gave the last blow job of my entire life".[16]

Wives in jokes display contemptible personality traits by using sex to trap men into marriage after which they no longer come up with the goods, yet, at the same time, they do engage in extra-marital sex. As we have seen, a popular trope in the "wife/husband" category regards the husband coming home from work and finding his wife *in flagrante* with her lover who will be typically hiding in the wardrobe:

> A man comes home earlier than expected from work and hears his wife yelling. He runs up the stairs and finds her in bed naked and clutching her chest.

"What's the matter?" he asks.
"I think . . . I'm having . . . a heart attack", she gasps.
"I'll call 911!" he cries. As he is reaching for the phone, the couple's two children come running in.
"Daddy, daddy!" they yell. "There's a naked man in the hall closet!"
The man rushes to the closet and throws open the door to reveal his next-door neighbor, buck-naked.
"Fred, I can't believe this!" he yells. "My wife could be having a heart attack, and here you are running around scaring the kids!"[17]

Once more, we have a stupidity joke wrapped up within a joke about marriage. The given within the situation is that the husband is the breadwinner while the (house)wife has the luxury of being able to stay home and engage in an extra-marital affair. In fact, Pressley (n.d.) lists 25 "marriage" jokes of which 5 concern the canniness of wives whose husbands come home from work unexpectedly to find them in bed with another man. This trope endorses the common imaginary of a 1950s household where the woman is the homemaker and the husband is a hardworking dupe. To my knowledge, there are no jokes of women hiding away in wardrobes from homecoming wives. These 1950s style jokes strengthen the stereotype of women being restricted to the domain of the home while men venture beyond – women are stationary and men are in motion. Interestingly, leaving women at home alone is very dangerous for men. Apart from withdrawing sex, wives also typically overspend.

> A man had his credit card stolen. He however decided not to report it because the thief was spending less than his wife did.[18]
>
> Q. What book do wives like the most? A. Their husband's checkbook![19]

Still other jokes about wives focus on unattractive, slovenly women whose husbands rejoice in their demise.

> Q. What worse than finding out your wife's got cancer? A. Finding out it's curable.

In his discussion of seaside postcards, Orwell (2000) notes the ageism upon which their humour pivots:

> Sex-appeal vanishes at about the age of twenty-five. Well-preserved and good-looking people beyond their first youth are never represented. The amorous honeymooning couple reappear as the grim-visaged wife and shapeless, moustachioed, red-nosed husband, no intermediate stage being allowed for.

While it is undeniable that age has always been a target for comedians, it is also true that unattractiveness in wives and, as we shall see below, mothers-in-law, is more acceptable to joke about than unattractiveness in husbands. However, there is also the trope about the rich, old but canny guy who thinks he can have any beautiful young woman, but she is of course (being a woman) taking him for all she can get so it is still the woman who is acting unethically:

> A rich man goes golfing with his friends and he brings along a gorgeous young lady. "Well guys, meet my new fiancée", he says, full of pride. And for the rest of the afternoon the friends can't take their eyes off the beauty. After the round of golf, the rich man goes up to the bar to order drinks for the group. One of his friends accompanies him and quietly asks: "how did you manage to hook up with such a beautiful young lady? You're seventy. She must be at least forty years younger than you!" "I lied about my age". And she believed you!? How old did you say you were?" "I told her I was ninety".[20]

Mothers-in-law

The portrayal of the mother-in-law in jokes is generally that of an intimidating battle-axe clutching a rolling pin. Consistently targeted in jokes in which they traditionally henpeck their long-suffering sons-in-law, these elderly women are hard-line harridans:

> *Wife:* "You hate my relatives!"
> *Husband:* "No, I don't! In fact, I like your mother-in-law more than I like mine".
>
> Two men were in a pub. One says to his mate, "My mother-in law is an angel". His friend replies, "You're lucky. Mine is still alive".[21]
>
> David is finally engaged, and is excited to show off his new bride. "Ma", he said to his mother, "I'm going to bring home three girls and I want you to guess which one is my fiancé". Sure enough twenty minutes later, David walks in the door with three girls following behind him. "It's that one", said his mother, without blinking an eye. "Holy cow", exclaimed David, "how in the world did you know it was her?" "I just don't like her", she replied.

In the spring of 2016, while the Italian parliament discussed the same-sex marriage bill, a common aside by both supporters and non-supporters of the statute regarded the prospect of a man marrying the daughter of two lesbians who would end up with two mothers-in-law, who as is well-known, are nasty, ugly naggers. There is an element of "woe betide" attached to the notion of a mother-in-law so that two female in-laws add up to a sort of double torment. Jokes about the hypothetical mother-in-law allow the male joker to get his feelings about her off his chest. Male audiences and possibly female audiences too associate with these negative feelings.

> "I haven't spoken to my mother-in-law for 18 months. I don't like to interrupt her".
>
> Ken Dodd

> We were having tea with my mother-in-law the other day and out of the blue she said, "I've decided I want to be cremated". "Alright," I said, "get your coat".
>
> Dave Spikey

> "I took my wife to Madame Tussaud's Chamber of Horrors and one attendant said, 'Keep her moving, Sir, we're stocktaking'".
>
> Les Dawson[22]

Davies' (2012) investigation of mother-in-law jokes sets out to demonstrate that such cycles "stem from a male perception of an incongruity in the social order" that is based upon "hidden transgressive thoughts or feelings". According to Davies, the reason these jokes are funny is that they mention the unmentionable and "evade rules about how something may be spoken about". Through a comparative and historical analysis, Davies asserts that the mother-in-law joke derives from the tension between the wife's mother and her son-in-law within the nuclear family. Men tell jokes about their wives' mothers in societies in which extended kin are in an ambiguous situation. While mothers-in-law are kin, at the same time they are also strangers that occupy an equivocal slot in the structure of the family. In fact, in cultures where families include extended kin, such as India and China, there are no mother-in-law jokes. For a series of economic and practical reasons, in the recent past it was common for young married couples in Britain to live with their parents, and the natural choice fell upon living with the wife's parents. The son-in-law would tend to avoid conflict with his wife's mother who was, after all, what could be seen as an interfering outsider. Furthermore, these jokes conceal the stereotypical suggestion that women are closer to their mothers than they are to their husbands and that they are in a collusion with their mothers to infantilize or otherwise persecute the husband. In the USA, there are lots of jokes about Jewish mothers both because of something in the Jewish family set-up and owing to the fact that so many male stand-up comedians of earlier generations were Jewish.

> Two men, old friends, run into each other at the bowls club.
> "I hear that your mother-in law's ill", says the one.
> "Yes, she's in the hospital".

"How long has she been there for?"
"In 3 weeks' time, please God, it'll be a month".

Aarons 2012: 27[23]

In conclusion, Davies sees these jokes as a way to manage hostility between mother-in-law and son-in-law. According to Davies, by joking about them with other men, they avoid direct conflict with their wives' mothers. That of course is not to say that these jokes are to be taken seriously. In the jokes examined so far, sons-in-law do not really want these women dead and neither do mothers-in-law take offence at the jokes.

However, despite scouring the internet for father-in-law jokes, there were very few returns:

> Daughter announcing to her father that she was engaged. The father asked, "What does he do? Does he have any money?" The daughter replies back saying, "You men are all alike. That's the first thing he asked me about you!"

> A young woman brings home her fiancé to meet her parents. After dinner, her mother tells her father to find out more about the young man. The father invites the fiancé to his study for a drink. "So what are your plans?" the father asks. "I am a bible scholar," the young man replies. "A bible scholar, huh", the father says. "Admirable, but what will you do to provide a nice home for my daughter to live in, as she is used to having?" The young man replies, "I will study and God will provide for us". "And how will you buy her a beautiful engagement ring, which she deserves?" asks the father. "I will concentrate on my studies and God will provide for us", replies the young man. The conversation proceeds in this manner, with each question the father asks, the young man replies that God will provide. Later, the mother asks, "How did the conversation go?" The father answers, "He has no job and no plans, but the good news is that he thinks I am God".[24]

Davies also documents a lack of jokes by women about their mothers-in-law, i.e. their husbands' mothers. He explains that this is due to women seeing their mothers-in-law in personal rather than structural terms. In fact, women seriously complain about their mothers-in-law and their aberrant behaviour rather than make jokes about them (e.g. Apte 2009; Hill 2008). The daughter-in-law is an intruder in the mother–son relationship in which the mother's power is illegitimate within a nuclear family structure. It seems that wives have a personal problem with their mothers-in-law rather than a structural one, making the issue a serious subject matter. However, subversive comedian Joan Rivers included mother-in-law jokes in her stand-up routines, such as how she flew halfway round the world to cremate hers and reprimands herself when she says, "I should have waited till she was dead", which is not so different from the typical demise of the mother-in-law joke told by men.[25]

Davies, in fact, puts the preponderance of jokes told by men about wives' mothers down to a gender divide, claiming that joke-telling is a masculine pastime. In contrast, as some have claimed, women's way of joking is in sharp contrast to the aggressive and competitive joke-telling that is typical of men, in that women prefer a more "storytelling" style that forms a sense of comity (Coates 2007; Kothoff 2006).

The dirty joke

Dirty jokes relate sexual matters in an indecent or offensive way and of course, being about sex, in one way or another, they will usually concern gender. As we saw before, there are diverse categories of dirty jokes, yet, apart from their titillating content, like so many other jokes, they tend to be mainly either about someone's stupidity or else about another's astuteness. Sex almost acts as a coat hanger upon which to hang a joke about someone else's stupidity. However, over and above stupidity and canniness, these jokes surely also reflect sexist attitudes in society. For example, one blatantly sexist category of dirty jokes that was especially popular in the late 1990s is about blonde girls and their UK Essex girl equivalents. These jokes play on a combination of the stupid target, i.e. the blonde/Essex girl and a canny male who will take advantage of the stupid target and lewdness.

> Q. What do Essex girls use for protection during sex?
> A. Bus shelters.
>
> Q. Did you hear about the new blonde paint?
> A. It's not real bright, but it's cheap, and spreads easy.

Shifman and Lemish classify blonde jokes as "specific" sexist jokes. Davies has explored these jokes at length (2011: 69–76) without classifying them as sexist in any way, but simply claiming that blonde joke cycles are predated by other jokes about "sexy blonde-haired" women in general. Davies argues that there is a widely held perception that blonde-haired women are remarkably attractive. He then reports Ovid's accounts of the Ancient Romans who would cut off the blond locks of German slave girls captured in war to make false hair for their own womenfolk who had often severely damaged their hair by excessive use of bleach. Davies also relates how, later, Arab and Turkish slave traders acquired blonde female slaves from Poland and the Baltic states, while today pimps from wealthy Arab countries import and exploit blonde prostitutes from the Ukraine. It is no secret that women with other hair colours have traditionally attempted to imitate blondeness with the use of dyes, peroxide, bleach and wigs. Since the time of music hall and vaudeville in Britain, USA and France, blondes have routinely been the subject of jokes in which hair colour was completely irrelevant apart from the fact of its being a cue that the joke would be about sex:

> A stunningly stacked blonde walked into a dress shop and asked the manager.
> "I wonder if I could try on that blue dress in the window".
> "Go right ahead," he said, "It might help business".
>
> *Davies 2011: 71*

According to Davies, the allure of blondeness explains why fair-haired women have become joke targets. In addition, while Davies acknowledges a class-dimension – blondes/Essex girls are associated with material, working class occupations – he attributes the careless use of their bodies for sex to their stupidity. Although Davies does not mention the word "sexism" in his discussions, the language in which blonde jokes are couched does indeed strongly whiff of sexism. The joke about blonde paint in which a substance is compared to a specific group of women cannot be acquitted of chauvinism given the claim that both paint and blonde women are "cheap" and that both "spread[s] easy". Also, the use of the term "stacked" successfully dehumanizes the woman in the joke using a rather vicious way to describe a woman with large breasts and a voluptuous body. That is to say, the words used in these jokes go beyond the beauty and allure of the women and trivialize and humiliate them as merely sexual objects. These words debase women. If these jokes circulate, then there are presumably people who see women in this way and as a matter of fact, the widespread and uncritical circulation of these jokes reflects entrenched gendered power relations. While jokes about blonde-haired men exist, they seem to be based upon pre-existing blonde girl jokes. Furthermore, there is no joke cycle concerning stupid fair-haired men who are also extremely promiscuous.[26] Notably, the fact that jokes about stupid blonde men do not exist as a cycle, means that they are limited to smaller circles of tellers and recipients. An example of gender equality within the context of blonde-haired people concerns a sexually inexperienced couple of blondes:

> Q. Why was the blonde's belly button sore?
> A. Because her boyfriend was blonde too.[27]

However, the absence of promiscuity in the male blond in jokes shows that a double standard regarding sexual mores still exists, as reflected in these jokes. There would be no ambiguity in a fair-haired man seeking (sexual) protection by standing under a bus shelter. A penchant for abundant sexual activity with diverse partners is not perceived in the same way for men as it is for women. As for the joke suggesting the fair-haired woman try on an outfit in the shop window in order to attract customers, if we substitute the "stunningly stacked" blonde for a "well hung" fair-haired man, we might find that while the gentleman would indeed attract a crowd, his nudity would not necessarily help business. There is a trace of ridicule in male striptease well documented in the comic trope represented in films such as *The Full Monty* (directed by Peter Cattaneo, UK, 1997) and, more generally in dance routines that are popular on talent shows in which naked men play a (dangerous) game of peek-a-boo with the help of objects to cover their genitals.[28] Should a dancer accidentally mistake a hand movement, a view of his genitals would cause ridicule and laughter. Compare this to the photograph of Prime Minister Theresa May and First Minister of Scotland Nicola Sturgeon who are ridiculed in the British tabloids for (a perfectly respectable) vision of their legs. "Never mind Brexit, who won Legs-it" reads the headline of the *Daily Mail* encouraging readers to ogle at the two politicians' legs.[29]

The type of ogling that occurs towards the naked male body results in a very different perception of the body with respect to the way the female body is both gazed upon and perceived. If not ridicule, the nudity of a male body in a shop window may project beauty of Greek proportion but not necessarily eroticism. On the other hand, the female body is endowed with erotic capital and hard as we may try, owing to its lack of the same erotic capital, the male body cannot be objectified in the same way. A comic scene from the film *The Dressmaker* (directed by Jocelyn Moorhouse, Australia, 2015) pictures mother and daughter dressmakers (respectively played by Judy Davis and Kate Winslet) ogling at the nakedness of a well-proportioned and muscular male customer (Liam Hemsworth). Interestingly, the humour in the scene is created by making the two women the target of the joke, especially the elderly mother who openly shows pleasure in what she sees and is ridiculed for doing so. The suggestion is that sex is something in which the older woman should no longer be interested. It is an incongruity and therefore material for humour. *Last F**kable Day*, a sketch from the US comedy series *Inside Amy Schumer* backs up the commonplace that older women are not or perhaps should not be interested in sex.[30] In the sketch, Schumer comes across 50+ actors, Tina Fey, Julia Louis-Dreyfus and Patricia Arquette who are having a picnic to celebrate Dreyfus' "last fuckable day". The sketch is a send-up of the way in which Hollywood treats older female actors by putting them out to pasture years before their male contemporaries.

So, blonde/Essex girl jokes reflect and target women behaving "badly" because of their stupidity, and according to Davies these jokes have little or no effect on society, which, of course is probably a truism. In fact, Davies claims that in general "Jokes have no consequences for society as a whole" (2011: 266) and that they are merely a "thermometer" that expresses the status of a society rather than a "thermostat" that can adjust society in any way (2011: 248). However, the consequences of the *Charlie Hebdo* cartoons suggest that some groups see humour as extremely powerful and subversive, and it might be equally sustainable to claim that the thermometer might be recording power relationships. Furthermore, if humour is so inconsequential, the question arises as to why it is so strictly monitored in totalitarian societies. However, we must bear in mind that when jokes travel – and today they travel quickly and ubiquitously – they may easily be received in the "wrong circles" and become a cause for offence. As argued by Kuipers and Van der Ent (2016: 605–33) with regard to ethnic jokes, context is essential. The playful and ambiguous nature of ethnic (and gendered) jokes may reflect entrenched ideologies (Billig 2005; Weaver 2011). After all, who is to deny that when someone targets an old/fat/blonde/promiscuous woman or a gay man or a lesbian in a joke, they are doing so because their audience shares that same mind-set and will align with the joker? A mind-set that will no longer be funny if it accidentally travels into the group being targeted:

> Q. How many feminists does it take to change a lightbulb?
> A. That's not funny.

As long as promiscuous females are targeted rather than licentious men, the thermometer is undoubtedly saying something about society's perception of female sexuality. Whichever way we look at it, the blondes and Essex girls in jokes are taken advantage of by men. It is the blondes who are derided for their stupidity and certainly not the men who benefit from it. However, the cleverness of the men and stupidity of the women may well be only half the story, as so-called "dirty jokes" are not restricted to blondes or Essex girls, yet do frequently target women *tout court*.

> A famous heart specialist doctor died and everyone was gathered at his funeral. A regular coffin was displayed in front of a huge heart. When the minister finished with the sermon and after everyone said their good-byes, the heart was opened, the coffin rolled inside, and the heart closed. Just at that moment one of the mourners started laughing. The guy next to him asked: "Why are you laughing?" "I was thinking about my own funeral," the man replied."What's so funny about that?" "I'm a gynaecologist".[31]

The joke verges on the ridiculous, with an image of a coffin sliding into a vagina like a probe. It is an analogy of the equally ridiculous image of the coffin going into the heart. No human organ inserts itself into a heart, so the image of the coffin going into the heart is a giveaway as to how one is primed to interpret the punchline. What is going into the heart is a foreign object, but the scene as described demonstrates the heart specialist's love for his work (the image of the heart functioning both as a sign of the specialization in cardiology, but also as an expression of his love for his work). The gynaecologist thinks of the vagina in the same way, as a way of penetrating the physical object of his work, while expressing his gleeful desire to do so (clearly a huge professional taboo).

The gynaecological part of the joke picks up only on the penetration reading, not on the love for his work reading. This joke could indeed fall into Davies' category of canny jokes as the triumphant gynaecologist imagines himself in his coffin penetrating a huge vagina, i.e. priming with the "huge" heart at the start of the joke. In terms of "priming prosody" (Hoey 2005), the word "gynaecologist" immediately primes with the word "vagina" even though the latter term itself is missing from the joke. In the joke image, the coffin would still be tiny when compared to the huge vagina, yet the triumphal sense of accomplishment conveyed by the gynaecologist's unstated implication suggests that there is something else going on here beyond canniness. Could this joke appeal to someone who does not spend their (his?) time with his hand in women's vaginas? Is the coffin a symbol of a hand, or a phallus, or indeed a whole body? The idea of a man being swallowed by a vagina might be both exciting and terrifying at the same time for an imagined male audience and certainly, if what we fear most is what we most desire, and jokes are a way of escaping the internal censor, then a Freudian interpretation of this joke would carry some weight. One reading of the joke reflects a social association between humour and power that is entrenched in the notion of domination present in the act of penetration itself, as argued by radical feminists like Dworkin (2006 [1987]). The gynaecologist is so powerful, he (in the form of his coffin) can dominate and enter the huge vagina; another reading, however, might suggest the humiliation of the coffin/corpse being sucked into the all-powerful vagina. The second reading reveals a deep fear that a vagina has the power to swallow up and consume. That reading implicates a different kind of joke: one in which desire and fear are linked. Is it possible that a male audience would laugh out of fear? What would this interpretation mean for a female audience, for whom the first interpretation may be a very offensive form of objectification in which the vagina is seen as only the sexual province of a man, and further, does not acknowledge women's desire or their autonomy.

As Billingsley points out (2016: 24) while excluding power relations in his discussion of blonde jokes, Davies does, however, begin to theorize about the relationship between humour and supremacy in his discussion of jokes by heterosexuals that target gay men. Here Davies links these jokes to an obsession with penetration, dominance and *becoming like women* (Davies 2011: 155; my italics). Davies also stresses that the relationship between penetrator and penetrated reflects "patterns of social domination" (2011: 166). If this argument counts for the heterosexual obsessions about gay men, then might it not also count (*a fortiori*) for heterosexual men's relationship with women? The gynaecologist joke is certainly about some kind of power play. In fact, let us see what happens if we alter the joke slightly:

> A famous heart specialist doctor died and everyone was gathered at his funeral. A regular coffin was displayed in front of a huge heart. When the minister finished with the sermon and after everyone said their good-byes, the heart was opened, the coffin rolled inside, and the heart closed. Just at

that moment one of the mourners started laughing. The guy next to him asked: "Why are you laughing?" "I was thinking about my own funeral" the man replied. "What's so funny about that?" "I'm a proctologist".

By replacing the gynaecologist with a proctologist in the joke, an anus would then have to replace the vagina in the image, thus changing the joke quite radically. The punchline no longer says, "I'm about to penetrate my way into a vagina and enjoy this feeling for eternity", but "I'd hate this to happen to me (i.e. get swallowed up by an anus) when I die". This is quite a different kind of laughter compared to the man who is happy to penetrate a vagina. The assumption is that heterosexual men do not like being penetrated. In this case, it is the proctologist doing the penetrating. We are left to wonder whether or not he would enjoy it, as it is the act of penetration that is key to the joke. In fact, while it is common to hear remarks made by men regarding the good luck of gynaecologists who spend their time inserting their hands and enjoying the company of female genitalia, it is extremely rare to hear envious remarks about proctologists who examine anuses for a living. With the idea of a proctologist penetrating an anus, arguably the power balance shifts because of either the suggestion of anal sex and/or the implied homosexuality. In this joke, being penetrated is scoffed and feared rather than being the (fortunate? delighted?) penetrator which is always seen as an act of power. Another reading entirely could imply that the coffin is like a medical probe being inserted into an orifice, thus making it funnier than the original, but in a different way, as it picks up on the reading that medical professionals probe different bodies, and the anus is the bottom of the barrel – no pun intended. A similar kind of sexual domination and power play can be seen in the following joke:

> A man gets the words "I love you" tattooed on his penis. His wife says, "Stop putting words in my mouth!"
>
> *Tucker 2012*

As before, on one level, we can explain the joke in terms of the man's canniness in getting such a tattoo, as a "romantic" reading overlaps and clashes with an "oral sex" reading. Stereotypically women want men to say, "I love you", and men want women to show them how much they love them by giving them oral sex. The man in the joke is literally putting words into the woman's mouth so that she can stereotypically demonstrate how much she loves him by saying so, but also by performing oral sex on him, without her permission. She tells him to stop, so there is no consent in this act. On another interpretation, the act of fellatio itself, particularly without mutual consent, could be considered an act of power and dominance on the part of the man receiving it. Rather like the use of the term "my bitch" in rap culture to refer to a person someone "owns" – and note, "bitch" can only be feminine even if "someone's bitch" can be of either sex – jokes like this one highlight (and some would say, reinforce) the idea of male superiority in the social hierarchy.

Rape jokes

No discussion of gender and humour would be complete without a discussion of rape jokes. Rape jokes fall into the category of specific sexist jokes that straddle two categories: that of the dirty joke, owing to their coarse content, and that of the sexist joke. Rape jokes are very different from what I shall label more mainstream dirty jokes as they take unwholesomeness up a notch by joking about a heinous crime – something that has rendered these jokes, those who tell them and recipients' reactions to them, the subject of much public debate. These jokes have become significant on the humour scene in the digital age because of the numerous discussions that appear on the web regarding the phenomenon. In a study analysing disputes on the internet regarding the funniness of rape jokes, Kramer discusses the difficulty in defining what we actually mean by "rape jokes" (2011: 139). Is a rape joke one in which the main plot element is rape? A joke that describes rape? Kramer wonders if it is sufficient simply to "implicitly gesture towards it" for a joke to qualify as a rape joke. As we saw previously, in a joke in which a husband resolves his wife's headache with an aspirin to be able to have sex with her, a rape reading may be possible in a joke where significant sense depends on variables like the recipient's perspective and the joker's intentions. Owing to their violent content, jokes that are widely considered to be highly controversial are those in which the main plot element is rape and those that describe rape. Disputes on the internet principally concern whether such jokes can be funny in the first place. As Kramer argues, if rape jokes exist then some people obviously find them funny. The point is that the "rape joke" debate is about whether people *should* find rape jokes funny, hence endowing humour, and especially humour about rape, with what Kramer labels "moral weight" (2011: 138). To some, telling a rape joke is seen as breaking social norms because rape is a crime about which it is inappropriate to adopt a non-serious stance. Furthermore, for others, telling a rape joke or laughing at one may indicate alignment with rapists, almost as though the verbalization and report of the act becomes the act itself. There are others for whom not being able to tell jokes about rape impinges upon their freedom of speech. Problematically, laughing at a rape joke may render whoever laughs morally reprehensible; not laughing may see him accused of lacking a sense of humour. It is worth considering this question: if the process of laughter is involuntary, are some people saying that in the face of rape jokes laughter should be supressed? And if this is indeed the case, how could this suppression be achieved?

As Davies has argued, whole categories of disaster jokes and sick jokes have always existed, and people are always going to joke about any subject, no matter how unpalatable. An example of the fine line between serious and non-serious discourse can be exemplified by an incident that occurred in 2012 during a performance in which stand-up comedian Daniel Tosh told a rape joke.[32] Whether or not the joke was in good or bad taste is not at issue, but what is at issue is the comedian's response to a woman in the audience who heckled him and shouted out that rape is never funny. To this, Tosh replied, "Wouldn't it be funny if that girl got raped by, like, five guys right now? Like right now?" Clearly, Tosh tried to humiliate the woman by asserting his power, as stand-up comedians will do when heckled. However, his comment caused much controversy on social media and soon led to his having to apologize. Tosh's initial joke may have been in bad taste, yet we do joke about everything and anything. The problem with Tosh's response to his heckler was that it sounded like an invitation to rape and a celebration of a violent crime. In addition, and this is likely to have been the issue, he stepped outside the play frame for his riposte. Although he was standing on stage, and in a comedy club, and the rape joke which the heckler disputed took place within a play frame, context matters. Tosh was knowingly or unknowingly approving and giving authenticity to a crime.

Additionally, over and above the viciousness of the act of rape itself that is described in such jokes, these jokes also tend to include and describe other diverse forms of violent acts. Only very rarely can rape jokes be quite innocuous, such as the one-liner, "Rape: small word, long sentence", that puns on the terms "rape" and "sentence" and is in any event a warning about rape, not an encouragement to engage in it.[33] Naturally, this joke is not part of the norm of rape jokes. The typical rape joke can be quite graphic and hence disturbing. These jokes remind us that although we are human beings that distinguish ourselves from other non-human animals, behaviour such as rape is non-human, animal-like conduct. Critchley provides us with many examples of satire from the literary works of authors such as Aesop, Kafka, Swift and Orwell to Gary Larson's *Far Side* cartoons in which animals take on human features (2002: 31). Critchley argues that while the animal who becomes human is endearing and amusing, when the reverse happens and the human becomes a beast, the effect is disgusting. The rape joke evokes the epitome of animal behaviour in the human.

> I was walking down a street when the woman in front of me dropped her bags. She asked me for help. "Of course I'll help", I said to her, "With how beautiful you are, I bet you can get a man to do anything". She giggled and flirted back by touching my arm and saying, "With how strong you are, I bet you can get a woman to do anything". I laughed and said, "Yes, I can actually". Then I raped her.

On one interpretation, the joke is a typical example of two scripts that overlap and oppose each other to create a single script. The joke contains an apparent "two people flirting" reading/script in which the couple flatter each other reciprocally for their physical attributes of beauty and strength through which they can get the opposite sex to do "anything". A second "sexual" reading/script is concealed and hinges on the term "anything" thereby setting up the rape in the punchline. A person who is being raped is passive and does nothing but gets something done to her. This is reflected syntactically through use of the passive voice. It is more common to read, "X was raped by Y" rather than "Y raped X". Yet "Y raped X" is more forceful than the more common alternative. Perhaps if the active form was used more frequently more people would become aware of the gravity of the offence. In fact, one feature that makes rape jokes especially horrifying is the fact that these jokes are typically couched in the first person. In other words, the joke-teller is the rapist himself. The use of the first person combined with the backdrop of an ordinary situation provides further incongruity and at the same time brutality to the narrative. The punch is quite unambiguous, there is no pun or duplicity in "then I raped her". Of course, there are other joke cycles that are couched in the first person like the "I walked into a bar/pub the other day" that prime the recipient for what is to come, but the use of "I" in rape jokes does not occur within a fixed joke cycle signalled, for example, by the "bar/pub" frame. Also, very seldom are those "walked into a bar" jokes dependent on the person (first or third) in which the joke is told. They usually simply depend on context and personal style. Additionally, the heterogeneity of the manner in which rape jokes are framed does not immediately signal a Knowledge Resource (cf. Attardo). These jokes are delivered in a nonchalant tone – even though they are to be read on websites rather than recited – that continues right to the punchline where the use of the throw away "then" highlights an ordinariness contained in the action of rape. Whoever posted this joke is, in fact, being openly tendentious while at the same time covertly reinforcing the "woman asking for it" discourse because of the way in which the victim giggles and flirts with her aggressor/rapist.

In a collection of "sick" jokes, Jardon (2014) provides 44 jokes under the heading of "Sex Crimes", 17 of which are specifically about raping women – the remaining jokes being more specifically about necrophilia and paedophilia. Nine of these jokes are told in the first person, in other words by the rapist himself:

> I was raping a woman the other night and she said "Please, think of my children!" Kinky bitch.

> I hate having to walk through parks alone at night. Makes me wonder why I became a rapist in the first place.

> For me having sex is a lot like spreading butter on toast. It's easier with a credit card but much easier with a knife.
>
> *Jardon 2014*

These three jokes are all set against a background of normality. If the oppositeness and overlap of Attardo and Raskin's GTVH is created simultaneously by both the duplicity and the incongruity of the situation, undeniably, inherent illogicality manifests itself in the casualness of the language. Consider the insouciance of "I was raping a woman the other night" in which the heinousness of the felony is cushioned by the normalcy of actions conveyed through the past continuous tense as the rapist's misdeed casually occurred "the other night". In the second joke a person claims that he is frightened of walking "through parks alone at night" while in fact, it is he, the narrator himself, who is the perpetrator of violence and not an unknown other. The utterance "Makes me wonder why I became a rapist in the first place" weakens the crime of rape when it is set against other possible forms of criminality that he might encounter in the park at night (and also, it makes being a particular type of criminal a career choice). The third example begins by comparing sex with spreading butter on toast, a contrast that evokes the congeniality and warmth of a kitchen but which ends in vulgarity and violence. All three jokes insult women further by suggesting that sex is only obtainable via payment or violence. However, the most striking rape jokes juxtapose what at first sight appears to be consensual sex, with pure brutality:

> It's a fact that 9 out of 10 people enjoy gang rape.
>
> Hello, my name is Rape. Remember it; you'll be screaming it later.
>
> I like my wine how I like my women. 15 years old and locked in a basement.
>
> My favourite sexual position is the JFK. I splatter all over her while she screams and tries to get out of the car.[34]

Finally, a sub-category of rape jokes ends with the violent death of the victim. These jokes too are contained within a linguistic framework of ordinariness as discussed previously.

> I never do well with women, they always want to hug, cuddle and pillow talk after sex. I just like to slam the boot shut and push the car into the river.[35]

A further adverse aspect of rape jokes is that they play on the assumption that the victim may actually enjoy being raped. Many rape jokes concern the sexual desire of nuns. Presumably, nuns are targeted because of the unnaturalness of choosing a life of celibacy that some may consider bizarre. Yet the fact that nuns are continually stereotyped in jokes suggests that these particular sexist jokes transfer perfectly normal physiological sexual desire into a craving to be raped. In a sense, these jokes implicitly justify a felony on the part of the rapist as a case of satisfying the sexual need of the victim.

> A nun is walking down a deserted road when a man grabs her and starts raping her. After the rapist is done, he says, "Hey Sister, what are you going to tell the other Sisters now?"
> "I'll tell them the truth, that you grabbed me, threw me to the ground, and raped me twice . . . unless you're tired", she responded.[36]
>
> Two nuns, Sister Mary and Sister Elizabeth are walking through the park when they are jumped by two thugs. Their habits are ripped from them and the men begin to sexually assault them. Sister Elizabeth casts her eyes heavenward and cries, "Forgive him Lord, for he knows not what he is doing!" Sister Mary turns and moans, "Oh God, mine does!!!"[37]

Presumably, the world has its share of sexually frustrated beings, but such jokes imply that these women actually want to be raped. Whether a person is not getting their share of sex by choice or because they are old or irretrievably unattractive, does not necessarily mean they cannot wait to be raped. Rape is a heinous crime, the crime is not at all funny and, as we have seen, many rape jokes are extremely unpleasant. However, to quote outspoken comedian George Carlin, we should be able to joke about anything; it clearly depends on how the joke is constructed.[38] This is demonstrated in Carlin's own words: "Feminists do not think all men are rapists. Rapists do".

> A 14-year-old boy was arrested for raping an 8-year-old girl in Cardiff. He was later released without charge, after a judge ruled the girl was dressed provocatively in her woolly fleece.

The joke that plays on the commonplace that Welshmen (like Sardinians and other sheep farmers around the world) partake in sexual activities with sheep. However, on another level the joke mocks the discourse of rape in which the victim, the girl, actually provokes rape and becomes the accused because she is dressed provocatively. Of a similar ilk is the remark made by British female stand-up comedian Bridget Christie at the Edinburgh Fringe festival in 2015:

> I know you didn't come here today to hear a rape joke but you've all come here dressed like you want to hear one so it's not my fault.[39]

The final example is similar. It too is a meta-joke that subverts the genre even further by couching the joke within the typical structure of the rape joke, i.e. use of the first person and casualness of both situation and language. The joke is set in an ordinary pub where an ordinary young girl is sitting having a drink. Equally "normal" is the supposition that the speaker is about to take advantage of her:

> I was in the pub last night and I took advantage of a young girl. When she went to the toilet, I nicked her chair.

In 2015 the Thames Valley Police promoted a short video cartoon, *Tea Consent*, which compares initiating sex to making a cup of tea.[40] The voiceover describes a number of ambiguous situations in which sex is implied, yet never mentioned as the text always keeps within the tea analogy.

> Maybe they were conscious when you asked them if they wanted tea, and they said "yes". But in the time it took you to boil the kettle, brew the tea and add the milk they are now unconscious . . . Don't make them drink the tea. They said "yes" then, sure, but unconscious people don't want tea.

For the sake of completeness, I would like to add a short video that, after being broadcast as a preview of BBC television's *Tracey Ullman's Show* (Season 2, Episode 6) in mid-March 2017, immediately went viral online.[41] In the clip, a well-dressed young man is in a police station being interviewed after he has reported that he has been mugged at knifepoint. The man is noticeably in a state of shock when Ullman, in the persona of a rather unsympathetic detective, interrogates him. The young man is wearing a suit and tie and Ullman asks, "Is this what you were wearing when it happened? You look quite provocatively wealthy". When the young man says that he fails to see what he is wearing has anything to do with the incident, the detective Ullman insists, "Just a bit of an invitation, isn't it? Like you're advertising it". Of course, the parallel with a post-rape interrogation is quite evident. Police detectives in films and TV series typically accuse rape victims of wearing inappropriate clothes such as short skirts and therefore the victims are implicitly "asking for it". Furthermore, the cold manner in which police officials grill victims is replicated in the parody. The young man's visible distress is clearly heightened by the callous manner of the detective; when Ullman brings in a counsellor to assist the victim she tells her, "This gentleman's a bit upset; he was mugged earlier", to which the counsellor replies "Oh dear!" According to a seminal work on women's language by Robin Lakoff, expressions such as "Oh dear!" that are typically connected to the speech of women, diminish the force of what has caused their use. Lakoff (1975: 10) famously argued that expressions such as "Oh fudge my hair is on fire" and "Dear me, did he kidnap the baby" underscore how inappropriately soft expressions often adopted by females in place of a stronger four-lettered taboo word favoured by males, will weaken the importance of the matter at hand. In this clip, the use of such traditionally female language actually becomes a strong weapon so that "Oh dear!" sounds like a mockingly feeble reaction to mugging, yet simultaneously highlights how rape is all too often belittled. Donning a smug expression, the counsellor then asks the man whether he had been drinking after which, accusingly and without a shred of sympathy the detective adds, "Yes, because if you'd had a drink it could send out confusing signals . . . Lead somebody on with the nice suit and the phone, and then at the last minute, say, 'I don't want to be mugged!'" As in the "tea" parody discussed earlier, simply replacing the word "rape" with "tea", blaming the victim of mugging for the crime derides the widespread narrative that puts rape victims at fault. When the man repeats that the mugger pointed a knife at his throat, the detective coldly wonders, "How is somebody to know that you don't enjoy handing over your possessions unless you make your intentions clear?" The man repeats that he did not scream because the mugger had a knife and he was "really scared", but the detective tells him that he will have to accept some of the responsibility for what has happened to him. The parody closes with a policeman who interrupts the interview because of someone who is complaining about receiving abusive emails. The detective asks about the font adopted in the mails, "If it's something coquettish like Helvetica, he has probably brought it on himself!" The parody, of course, highlights how in cases of rape, a double standard is often applied.

Feminist jokes

Alongside sexist female jokes, the internet is full of plenty of what Shifman and Lemish label "feminist" jokes that parallel conventional male sexist jokes such as the one below.

> Q. How do you know when a woman's about to say something smart?
> A. When she starts her sentence with "A man once told me".[42]

Traditional sexist jokes reflect gender inequalities and hegemonic stereotyping. Feminist jokes, on the other hand, subvert heteronormative expectations and according to Franzini (1996) are "ground in criticism of the patriarchal structure of society and aspire[s] to reform it".

> Q. Why did God create men first?
> A. Because we learn from our mistakes.[43]
>
> Q. What did God say after creating Adam?
> A. I can do better.
>
> Q. Why don't women blink during foreplay?
> A. They don't have time.

According to Shifman and Lemish, feminist humour opposes the present state of affairs and at the same time empowers women by giving them a sort of freedom of (humorous) speech for which the internet provides a convenient and ideal platform. However, the internet is not the only platform for feminist humour as female stand-up comics in theatres and television are also significant drivers of feminist humour. However, the internet plays a part in the consumption of these routines as recordings of these comedians' live performances are available on platforms such as YouTube and therefore spread to millions of users.

> "The best way to a man's heart is through his hanky pocket with a bread knife".
> *Jo Brand*

> "I blame my mother for my poor sex life. All she told me was, 'The man goes on top and the woman underneath'. For three years my husband and I slept in bunk beds".
> *Joan Rivers*[44]

> "In advertisements, there are just two types of women: wanton, gagging for it; or vacuous. We're either coming on a window-pane, or laughing at salads".
> *Bridget Christie*

These examples provide a mix of feminist attitudes. While Brand and Rivers provide traditional script oppositions: a nurturing/murder script by Brand and a sexual/furniture script by Rivers, Bridget Christie's asides are especially interesting because there are no oppositions as she is actually telling it like it is. In other words, the incongruity of the remarks lies in the absurdity of reality itself where in advertising, women are indeed often portrayed as hypersexualized and/or vacuous. Indeed, the script contains hyperbole and a mixture of registers, but it is also the case that advertisements do make use of women displaying happy and/or erotic expressions while handling foodstuff and cleaning products. Christie's gag is an example of "charged" humour that according to Krefting, is humour that challenges "social inequality and cultural exclusion" (2014: 2).

Postfeminist humour

The so-called postfeminist movement is multifaceted and diverse. What is certain is that postfeminism has turned away from traditional issues concerning women's oppression to embrace women's abilities and accomplishments by positively focusing on many and different areas of lifestyle. The movement, however, is heavily influenced by and involved in mass media and consequently spills over into questions about consumerism, i.e. beauty products, fashion, etc. The individual female body and sexual empowerment are brought to the forefront of audience consciousness as opposed to an older fashion of public debate regarding equality and the breaking of the socio-political glass ceilings. Thus, whereas in traditional sexist humour there is a hierarchy of males and females – as we have seen so far, domination plays a central role in sexist male/female jokes – postfeminist humour pivots on the differences between the two sexes. It especially hones in on differences in communicative styles and emotional needs and, by focusing on these differences, a concept that owes much to the writings of Tannen (1991) who initially made these differences respectable long before postfeminist arguments. Rather this humour seemed to reinforce the idea of "equal but different". Postfeminist humour obliterates some elements of the hierarchy woven into traditional sexist humour.

Typically, these jokes will highlight, for example, women's need to discuss feelings and males' apparent lack of a similar need and the diverse sexual necessities of the two sexes.

> One evening last week, my girlfriend and I were getting into bed. Well, the passion starts to heat up, and she eventually says, "I don't feel like it, I just want you to hold me". I said, "WHAT??!! What was that?!" So she says the words that every boyfriend on the planet dreads to hear. . . "You're just not in touch with my emotional needs as a woman enough for me to satisfy your physical needs as a man". She responded to my puzzled look by saying, "'Can't you just love me for who I am and not what I do for you in the bedroom?" Realizing that nothing was going to happen that night, I went to sleep. The very next day I opted to take the day off work to spend

time with her. We went out to a nice lunch and then went shopping at a big, big unnamed department store. I walked around with her while she tried on several different very expensive outfits. She couldn't decide which one to take, so I told her we'd just buy them all. She wanted new shoes to compliment her new clothes, so I said, "Let's get a pair for each outfit". We went on to the jewellery department where she picked out a pair of diamond earrings. Let me tell you . . . she was so excited. She must have thought I was one wave short of a shipwreck. I started to think she was testing me because she asked for a tennis bracelet when she doesn't even know how to play tennis. I think I threw her for a loop when I said, "That's fine, honey". She was almost nearing sexual satisfaction from all of the excitement. Smiling with excited anticipation, she finally said, "I think this is all, dear, let's go to the cashier". I could hardly contain myself when I blurted out, "No honey, I don't feel like it". Her face just went completely blank as her jaw dropped with a baffled, "WHAT?" I then said, "Honey! I just want you to HOLD this stuff for a while. You're just not in touch with my financial needs as a man enough for me to satisfy your shopping needs as a woman". And just when she had this look like she was going to kill me, I added, "Why can't you just love me for who I am and not for the things I buy you?" Apparently, I'm not having sex tonight either.[45]

This narrative neatly fits into the category of canny jokes in the sense that the husband reciprocates his wife's behaviour in which she does not consent to sex following ample foreplay, so he retaliates by not buying her the clothes she desires after a long day's shopping. The joke, however, mostly highlights what are traditionally considered to be the different emotional and physical needs of males and females. Stereotypical or not, it would appear that women pass in the public imaginary as needing embraces and heart-to-heart dialogue while men's foremost desire is to engage in sexual activity. Women's stereotypical love for shopping stands for sexual foreplay in this joke, so the butt of its particular narrative is the woman, because the husband gets his revenge for not being able to fully have his arousal satisfied by penetration and ejaculation. But, of course, the story also plays on clichés and stereotypes. A user called Iamrb posted the "story" in 2015 on the Reddit entertainment website under the heading *Venus vs Mars* and is pre-empted as follows:

[n]ever quite figured out why the sexual urge of men and women differ so much. And never have figured out the whole Venus and Mars thing. Never figured out why men think with their head and women with their heart.

Although Iamrb tries to make the story pass as something that really happened to him, a commenter in the thread following the story points out that the same story had been published two years earlier on Facebook. In fact, the joke scores 8,410

When Women Pack When Men Pack

FIGURE 3.9   Source: http://9gag.com/gag/6854629/-when-women-pack-vs-when-men-pack-true-or-not

hits on Google showing that it is by no means either true or original.[46] However, even though this humorous story is supposedly generated from a male perspective (and contains a certain degree of spite), it is structurally typical of a category of jokes that mirror the positive and negative traits of the two sexes. Generally, these "Venus versus Mars" jokes are better balanced than the story in question in which the man comes out trumps. Figure 3.9 illustrates a classic cartoon of a highly organized woman versus a highly disorganized man packing their respective suitcases. Clearly, each sees the other as being either too excessive or too cavalier, and the joke shows how they are both equally right but also equally wrong. The joke underscores the stereotypical weaknesses of each gender.

Similarly, the illustration in Figure 3.10 displays the meticulous analysis carried out "when a girl receives a text message from a guy". Starting from "How long did it take him to respond?" the complex flow chart worthy of the best scientific analysis purportedly follows the female brain as she thinks about why the man texted and how she should respond. The male response to the same text message is reduced to two options, both involving the prospect of sex.

Likewise, The Female and Male Dictionary (Figure 3.11) also plays upon the divergent communicative styles of males and females. According to this dictionary, men are imagined, rightly or wrongly, to say exactly what they mean and to always get straight to the point. For example, when a man says, "leave me alone" he means just that, whereas the same remark uttered by a woman appears to

102 The language of jokes and gender

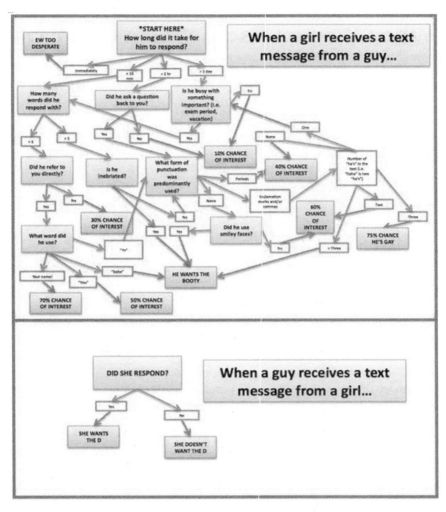

FIGURE 3.10   Source: https://plus.google.com/108531052526575991056/posts/
WnjH2b4xXjc

actually mean the opposite as she typically expects the male to read her mind, or rather, that he should automatically understand that she wants him to engage in dialogue with her. Women in these jokes come across as emotionally overflowing and men as unruffled beings who are unable to infiltrate women's minds and true needs.

Extremely pervasive on the internet are the Human Brain Analysis jokes. These visual/verbal jokes have many variants but are similar in that they feature a sketch of a female brain and one of a male brain in which different areas varying in size are supposedly dedicated to gender-specific interests. Stereotypically, sex

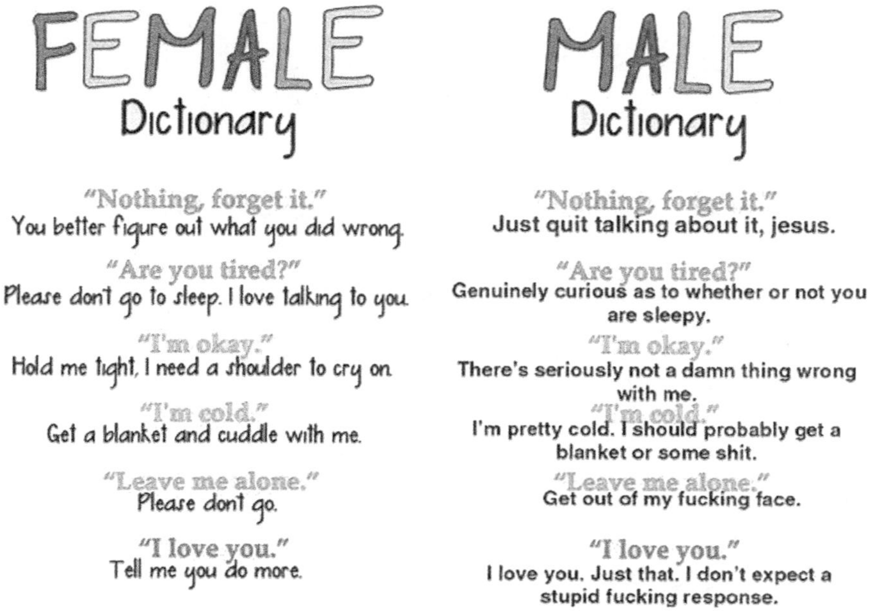

FEMALE Dictionary

"Nothing, forget it."
You better figure out what you did wrong.

"Are you tired?"
Please don't go to sleep. I love talking to you.

"I'm okay."
Hold me tight, I need a shoulder to cry on.

"I'm cold."
Get a blanket and cuddle with me.

"Leave me alone."
Please don't go.

"I love you."
Tell me you do more.

MALE Dictionary

"Nothing, forget it."
Just quit talking about it, jesus.

"Are you tired?"
Genuinely curious as to whether or not you are sleepy.

"I'm okay."
There's seriously not a damn thing wrong with me.

"I'm cold."
I'm pretty cold. I should probably get a blanket or some shit.

"Leave me alone."
Get out of my fucking face.

"I love you."
I love you. Just that. I don't expect a stupid fucking response.

FIGURE 3.11   Source: http://cavemancircus.com/2012/02/09/the-female-vs-male-dictionary/

and/or women take up large areas of the male brain, while shopping, talking and shoes occupy large areas of the female brain. However, over and above large areas of the brain dedicated to chocolate, sport, cars and shoes depending on the sex, what is most interesting is brain space dedicated to the communicative style of each sex. "Mysterious moods and behaviours" occupies a large part of the female brain, while in the corresponding male brain we find "getting lost and not admitting it" (Figure 3.12). These features display two forms of silence triggered by different reasoning. Presumably, the female wants the male to understand why she is moody, she wants him to engage in talk and explore her emotions. On the other hand, not admitting to being lost may be seen to be an affront to a man's masculinity that would explain why he is unlikely to admit that he is at fault. Other features that challenge a man's masculinity may be asking for directions and avoiding personal questions paralleled by women's huge need for commitment (Figure 3.13). A minuscule area of the male brain is dedicated to listening compared to the large area occupied by talking in the female brain. Good or bad driving skills, a predilection for chocolate or beer and even being unable to aim correctly while using the toilet may refer to superficial aspects of gendered behaviour that the opposite other may or may not approve of, but these features are hardly of great pith and moment (Figure 3.14). On the other hand, the male inability to listen and the female expectation of the other to interpret what she means through her silence or for him to deduce that what she actually means is the opposite of what she is

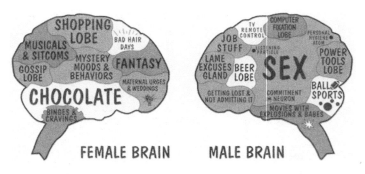

FIGURE 3.12 Source: https://ellebeaver.com/2014/05/13/human-brain-analysis-men-vs-women-with-jack-uppal-a-breakdown/.

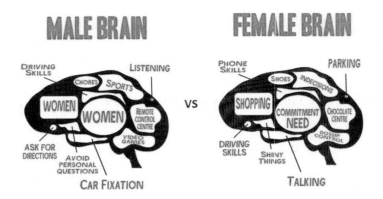

FIGURE 3.13 Source: http://community.dipolog.com/media/male-vs-female-brain.226/

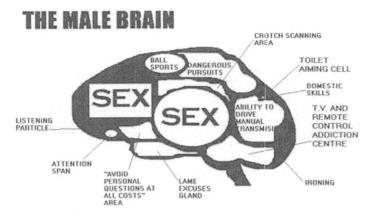

FIGURE 3.14 Source: http://mylipsissealed.blogspot.it/2010_06_25_archive.html

saying are significant aspects of communicative styles. This kind of humour is indeed a thermometer that reflects people's perceptions of aspects of communicative behaviour that can make or break relationships.

Women and self-deprecatory humour

The internet has given the general public access to a huge amount of comedic materials especially thanks to users who upload audio-visual clips onto platforms such as YouTube so that they can share them with other people. This allows researchers like myself to access vast amounts of materials from the past and from the present, with the ease of a click. The discussion that follows is the result of numerous YouTube searches, especially for performed humour on stage and in clubs. Obviously, I would not have been able to access such materials with such ease in the past. Now from the comfort of my desk I have a world of performers readily available at the click of a mouse.

Stand-up female comedians appear to be especially fond of particular topics upon which they build a humorous discourse that is often self-deprecatory in nature and that makes up a large part of their repertoire. While these comedians parallel male sexist humour by aiming disparaging remarks at themselves especially with regard to their appearance, they also produce humour that is specifically about their relationships with their male partners, female friends, mothers and offspring as well as humour about the strong effect of hormones on their wellbeing at different stages of their lives.

In an age where appearance is paramount and various media promote the body beautiful and eternal youth especially for women, it is not surprising that many (most?) women are insecure about their body image. A fat body is certainly not seen favourably and the fact that many women struggle with keeping their weight down through dieting in a perennial quest to obtain an ideal body shape may well underlie the rising number of girls and women with eating disorders in the western world. Although people come in all shapes and sizes, consumer culture undoubtedly promotes a single female body type that is preferably tall, slim and at the same time curvaceous in the right places. As most women probably do not correspond to this ideal body type, joking about inadequacies is an obvious choice of comic material together with the subject of the decline of the female body due to ageing. As Joan Rivers ironically puts it,

> It is all about looks, this is my message ... looks count, education? (She pauses and spits at the floor). Looks count. I have no sex appeal and it screwed me up for life. Peeping Toms looked at my window and pulled down the shade ... my gynaecologist examines me by telephone.[47]

The GTVH may not be adequate to deal with this type of self-detrimental humour. Rather than opposing or hidden scripts pertaining to the joke form, the humour in female stand-up routines seems, first, to occur outside the joke frame proper and, second, appears to involve saying the unsayable in a pseudo-naïve manner. Rivers uses exaggeration and absurdity to create incongruity in answer to the bitter truth that according to herself, and much of the media, looks do indeed count more than education, and, as Rivers frequently asserted: "no man ever put his hand up my skirt looking for a library card". Rivers yells as she utters her lines as though needing to convince the audience of something that should be a truth universally acknowledged. In other words, while the incongruity of disgusted Peeping Toms and distant gynaecologist present linguistic and cognitive duplicity, "looks count" is unequivocally a single script. It is an example of charged humour that is highlighting the double standards of the world in which we live.

UK comedian Bridget Christie takes the issue of the importance of women's looks further by being ironic about the way advertisements use women. In many TV ads, women are seen spinning around in a circle for no particular reason. This in itself should be funny, although of course it is designed presumably to show the woman twirling so that audiences can admire her body, and especially her legs, if she is wearing a flared skirt:

> A woman's looks are very important, in fact the way a woman looks is more important than anything she can ever think do say or achieve er women's looks are so important in fact that women are often asked in fact to give people a twirl so she can be approved in 3D.[48]

Christie is telling it like it is but in a pseudo-naïve fashion so that what she says could be perceived as irony, but in effect, what she is saying is anything but. As discussed previously, as well as twirls women in ads are "wanton, gagging for it; or vacuous. We're either coming on a window-pane, or laughing at salads" (see page 98). If these lines contain any opposition or incongruity it is surely with the real world that depicts women twirling and looking vacuous rather than in a script that is hidden within Christie's overt discourse. Of course, in terms of script oppositions we can see a "sexist fantasy" reading and a "reality" reading, and regarding the twirls, Christie continues,

> [e]r but us women don't just turn around in circles all day long looking hopeful and getting dizzy er we do lots of other things as well. For example, when Christine Lagarde isn't twirling around in a circle she's the head of the International Monetary Fund, Angela Merkel fills her time between turns by being the German chancellor. Jayne Torvill is not a good example to use here.

The absurdity of these twirling women in advertisements lies in the fact that women do not spend their time turning and actually have other more significant roles and things to do in life. Thus, we find a second opposition between "getting dizzy" and the downplayed "[doing] lots of other things as well". Christie chooses two high profile women to make her point, but even women in less prestigious occupations do not spend their time twirling around. The incongruity lies in the equivalence of the sexist image of women as objects to be looked at and the reality of accomplished women world leaders going about their work. Now, if irony is meaning more than what you are actually saying or something different from what you are actually saying, what exactly is going on here? Christie is certainly *not* saying the opposite of what she means. Lagarde and Merkel do many things other than twirling. It is the idea of twirling gormlessly itself that is absurd. The GTVH remains silent on such matters although we possibly have two overt oppositions, or rather incongruities, in twirl + Head of IMF; twirl + Chancellor of Germany. We have here a conflict between the trivial and the serious, and Christie underscores the absurdity by giving twirling status that is as serious as being a political figure. However, I would argue that the only true opposition comes in the final line where Christie implicates Jayne Torvill, an ice skating champion, as a poor example of the point she is making because Torvill really does literally twirl for a living by virtue of the sport in which she participates. She therefore does not fit into the previous discourse ridiculing the idea that women spend their lives twirling.

British comedian Jo Brand is a well-built and robust woman who uses her weight as the subject of many of her gags. In a performance in which she recounts how people often ask her whether she would take a pill to make her thin, she responds:

> [c]ourse I bleedin' well would. I would like to take a pill that made me six stone then I could eat my way back up to ten! What a bloody brilliant weekend that'd be wouldn't it![49]

While she adopts exaggeration and intensification to get her audience laughing, her spiel also strikes a chord with all those familiar with comfort eating. While it is highly unlikely that a person could feasibly put on so much weight in such a short period of time, it is certainly possible both to binge and put on some weight. And the success of Brand's punch consists in the surprise contained in the amplification of how much weight she could gain in such a short amount of time. Brand goes on to compare the way she binge eats biscuits to people who have exceptional control over what they eat and thus continues to strike a sympathetic chord with her audience.

> You see I think there's two types of people in the world, right, and it's all to do with how they eat biscuits right. 'Cos the first type of person makes a cup of tea, gets a plate out, [PAUSE] opens the packet of biscuits and takes one biscuit out, puts it on the plate, eats it very daintily off the plate, folds the packet back up, bit of sellotape over the top to keep it fresh for next month, now those sort of people should be executed shouldn't they because the rest of us get a packet out eat the whole fucking lot without taking the cover off do we and consequently end up looking like me.

She portrays herself as someone with an eating disorder (although she questions who or what is disordered) but at the same time highlights the normality of a love for food and the temptation to overeat. She accomplishes this by placing herself in the position of being laughed at while at the same time not sparing any irony or sympathy towards slim people who watch what they eat. Brand delivers her monologue with a deadpan expression and her signature matter of fact, even tone of voice. Her timing is perfect especially when she pauses and emphasizes the word "plate" when describing the type of person who "makes a cup of tea, gets a plate out" showing her indignation about anyone who would dream of placing a single biscuit on a plate before eating it. Here we can find a hidden and opposing script when she describes the saintly eaters who carefully store their remaining biscuits. Normality, according to Brand, is to quickly devour the lot straight from the packet. Through a combination of stance, gesticulation and facial expressions and above all timing and clever use of pauses, she waits for the audience's positive reaction through laughter. Following the "biscuit" episode, she then goes on to tell the audience how she has always had a weight problem and how a teacher at school had asked her what she wanted to be when she grew up. When Brand replied that she wanted either to be a nurse or get married, the teacher suggests "You'd better be a nurse then". As well as underscoring her perceived unattractiveness, Brand is also pointing out the social credit attached to married women, getting a laugh when she claims, "You'll be surprised I managed to get a husband, but I did".

Another British comedian, Sarah Millican also makes ample use of the issue of fat and body image in her stand-up routine.[50] She tells the audience that she is on a diet and recounts her disappointment at not being able to fit into clothes when she goes shopping. She goes on to discuss the irony of the song she typically listens to after an unsuccessful shopping trip in which she is unable to find clothes in her size, namely, "Big Girls Don't Cry" but, according to Millican, they do cry. The comedian then tells the audience that she cries because she is fat, because she cannot get a boyfriend and because "there's no trifle left". Millican cannot get a boyfriend because she is greedy, the underlying message being that fat girls are ugly because they are greedy. Her love and craving for fattening foods overrides her desire to diet and become slim – she must forgo the idea of obtaining a man. Like Brand, who pokes fun at the control of slim people eating a single biscuit, Millican pokes fun at slim women by describing her unease at swimming pools. Here other women are wafer thin and Millican avoids these women for fear that others might think she has eaten one – although she says she could not eat one as there is "no meat on them". She also tells her audience that she has developed "something of a cake shelf . . . it's bigger than a muffin top so I call it a cake shelf. I call it a cake shelf 'cos that's where I keep me cake". Again, Millican pokes fun at her consumption of cake. And of course the large quantities of cake she eats adds inches to her midriff, cause it to bulge and turn an endearing muffin top into a shelf. Beautiful women do not eat cake.

The style of all the comedians quoted so far could be described as coming from the "alt com" (alternative comedy) tradition. Apart from performing, at least initially in venues such as clubs, these women break from mainstream comedy tradition by telling stories rather than reciting a string of jokes. They use a story telling technique to subvert mores and create incongruity through surreal situations that surprise the audience – of course men do this too, but differently. We suspend our disbelief when Brand tells us she intends to put on four stone over a single weekend and when Millican recounts an episode in which she accidentally placed her belly on the scales at an automatic checkout till. The result was that she "just put it down as satsumas and legged it", because she did not want to pay for her own fat. While we are dealing with simple narrations, the contrasting scripts rely heavily on our suspension of disbelief rather than linguistic duplicity. Millican provides a rare example of a female comedian adopting a pun when referring to her "cake shelf". When someone asked her if she was pregnant she replied, "Only if I've been shagged by Mr Kipling" and after the audience's laughter subsides she adds, "It was exceedingly good". Here Millican provides us with an example of two overlapping and contrasting scripts by referring to both the Mr Kipling brand of pastries and a hypothetical person of the same name followed by a reference to the advertising slogan of the same cakes ("exceedingly good") and her opinion of a sexual encounter she had with Mr Kipling.

US comedian Margaret Cho also requires audiences to suspend disbelief when she recounts the unfortunate effect on her bowels after going on a diet that consisted of eating only persimmons for six months.[51] After surviving on this fruit alone, as might be expected, she develops the need to defecate copiously and the performance pivots on her attempts at retaining oncoming diarrhoea while driving on a motorway. The basic scatological humour is multiplied because she is a young, attractive female. Young attractive females do not need to diet. Focusing on women's obsession for slim bodies, Cho asserts:

> I think everyone should go on my diet. It's called the Fuck It Diet. Basically what it is, is if I want to eat something but it has a lot of fat or carbs, I just take a moment, and I go within, and I say "Fuck it" and I eat it. You have to do it 6 times a day. It works really well with the Fuck That Shit Exercise Program.

Cho's anti-diet rant exemplifies Krefting's notion of "charged humor". Like Brand, Christie and Millican, through her irony Cho is ridiculing the ordeal of the lives of many women that are dominated by an obsessive control over what they eat coupled with strenuous exercise regimes. Much of the incongruity between what she says and what she means can be found in the tone of what Cho says rather than the content itself which sounds perfectly sensible. Her tirade includes many taboo terms and she certainly tells it like it is, as she verbalizes what many people think. Rivers, Brand, Millican and Cho all give strength to the argument that men, rather than women, tell jokes consisting of a framed narrative containing a narrative build-up and a punchline while women opt for a more "narrated" style of humour embedded in a less-regimented frame (Coates 2007). If we attempt to apply the GTVH to the *Fuck It Diet* text, while we could agree that the hidden text might refer to any well-known diet such as Weight Watchers' or the Atkins Diet, Cho is surely expressing not only what many women really think of dieting, but also how they truly eat, namely ignoring "fat and carbs".

Ageing is another subject favoured by female comics, especially older ones. Joan Rivers, famous for having gone under the plastic surgeon's knife numerous times, made the effects of ageing a central part of her routines. Apart from her hyperbolic descriptions of sagging bodies ("My boobs have dropped so much I use the left one now as a stopper in the tub"; "It all drops, I can have a mammogram and a pedicure at the same time")[52] she also uses very dark humour to joke about the effects of osteoporosis. She considers the effect of Viagra on elderly men who then attempt sex with their wives whose bones are audibly cracking and whose vaginas are so dry that sexual activity could create a fire. She describes the "good" positions for what she labels "old sex". She lists nonsensical positions such as "reaching for the phone to call the doctor" advising the elderly to "make sure you groan into the good ear" when faking orgasm and noting that the fact that "the nurse changes the sheets" is one of the great advantages of "old sex". Jo Brand on the subject of elderly sex gives us "Laughter is the best medicine but does not tend to work in the case of impotence" (uttered during a performance at the Edinburgh Fringe 2015).

Of course, the subject of strictly female conditions that range from motherhood through pregnancy childbirth, menstruation to menopause are all favourite topics of female stand-ups. A classic remark regarding childbirth regards comparing the size of a baby's head to the part of female anatomy involved in the birthing process: "I remember looking down and thinking, there's a design fault here" says comedian Victoria Wood.[53] As before, there is no incongruity in the reality of the female body and the size of a baby's head. Bridget Christie takes a different view of motherhood when she says of new-borns:

> Obviously, they're very cute, if they weren't cute obviously the human race would have died out a long time ago because early humans would have gone "OK I've done three days now I'm out, that's enough". I just think they're overrated. I think they contribute the least to society but they are the most worshipped and revered people on earth . . . they create chaos, if you replaced any of us with a baby there would be chaos.[54]

This discourse goes against the grain, but similarly to other incongruities thrown up by reality, tackled by female comedians, here too Christie tells it like it is from the point of view of her persona, presumably shocking audiences as she dares to criticize babies in a culture that holds motherhood and new-borns in high regard. In fact, women with no maternal instincts or a desire for motherhood are often regarded as less than women in mainstream discourse.

Not only do professional comedians joke about these subjects, Dr Annie Evans, a physician specializing in women's health who has a channel on YouTube where she posts lectures in which she talks about symptoms and remedies of/for a variety of female ailments, adopts humour in her talks.⁵⁵ Her videos are full of scientific data yet at the same time are extremely user-friendly, as Dr Evans makes the scholarship accessible via humour. Talking of the menopause and changes that may occur in the vulva during this period, Evans says "we vary rarely talk about changes in the appearance of the vulva . . . it isn't a family car". Now, unlike the type of language used by the female comedians we have seen so far, Evans uses the technique of straight overlap and opposition where the term "vulva" is placed in opposition to, for example, Vauxhall Viva, Vectra and Nova or Renault Thalia. These short feminine sounding names ending in an "a" to most people supposedly prime with the name of a car. Interestingly, towards the end of one of her talks on menopause, Evans uses the kind of postfeminist humour we saw earlier in which males and females are seen as similarly complex. "We have all kinds of little tweaky buttons which get affected by time and age and our hormonal changes" says Evans, as her PowerPoint slide displays a remote control with dozens of buttons labelled "Women's Remote", "but never let it be said" she continues "that men are not just as complex as we are". At this point, a second remote control labelled "Men's Remote" appears on the PowerPoint slide with simply two large red buttons, namely "Food" and "Sex" (Figure 3.15).

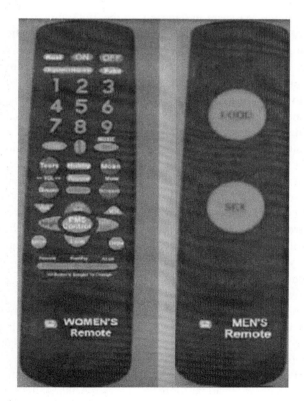

FIGURE 3.15 Women and men's remote controls

Significantly, Evans resorts to several techniques adopted by professional comedians. She uses self-deprecatory humour at the start of her talk when she shows her audience the painting of the *Seven Ages of Woman* by Hans Baldung Grien. "I wish that I was still down at the other side" says Evans, pointing towards the younger stages of a woman's life and then adds, "I know of course I am up at this side with the Grim Reaper looking over my shoulder". Evans gets a laugh from the audience; she is not being ironic but simply telling it like it is.[56]

Gender bending

Comic representations of male cross-dressing

Hollywood has a long tradition of portraying men who see dressing up in women's clothing as the only solution to get themselves out of some kind of sticky situation. In mainstream filmic comedy, men who cross-dress mainly do so in order to solve a problem. In Billy Wilder's 1959 comedy *Some Like It Hot*, saxophonist Joe becomes Josephine (Tony Curtis) and viola player Jerry becomes Daphne (Jack Lemon) when the couple opt to masquerade as unlikely looking women as a solution to escape from Spats and his mafia hitmen after accidentally witnessing the St Valentine Massacre in Chicago. In the 1983 movie *Tootsie* (directed by Sydney Pollack) cross-dressing as Dorothy is the only way Michael (Dustin Hoffman) can get work and similarly, Daniel (Robin Williams) cross-dresses as Mrs Doubtfire in the eponymous 1992 film (directed by Chris Columbus) in order to be able to see his children following his divorce. These comedies, as well as many others in which men dress up as women, have a number of features in common. Cross-dressing does not come naturally to the main characters in these films; instead, having to do so is the only solution to solve some kind of impossible problem. Audiences suspend their disbelief, as these men, who belong to artistic professions in the first place, think nothing of donning a disguise and performing the part of another gender. In addition, much screen time is dedicated to the protagonist's transitioning, in other words, scenes in which these men get dressed up as women, apply make-up and so on. Naturally these scenes are those which add to the farcical elements in the films and create tension as the protagonist runs the risk of being caught out in the wrong persona, i.e. as a man, by the very person he is trying to trick into believing he is really a woman. Throughout these films, the protagonist's heterosexuality is continually reiterated, especially when he receives sexual attentions from another man.

In dramatic films and in those in which the protagonist regularly wears women's clothes and adopts a series of female characteristics as his consistent lifestyle, cross-dressing is not part of a lifesaving scheme. In fact, if we look at the *The Crying Game* (directed by Neil Jordan, 1993) and *Kinky Boots* (directed by Julian Jarrold, 2006) for example, the two cross-dressers do not don women's clothing as a ploy but because it is natural for them to do so. Although both films contain comic scenes, their respective protagonists Dil and Lola are not comic characters but regular men to whom wearing female outfits is a necessary lifestyle choice. However, whether in comedy or in drama, male characters who perform the feminine on screen are usually already some kind of performer. Joe/Josephine and Jerry/Daphne are out of work musicians, Michael/Dorothy is an out of work actor, and Daniel is a dubbing actor before he turns into Mrs Euphegenia Doubtfire. Presumably, the fact that they had all already set out as entertainers becomes an asset as they set out to play the part of females in their everyday lives. In the dramatic *The Crying Game* and the mixed genre comedy/drama *Kinky Boots*, the cross-dressing protagonists are also performers, yet in both films they play drag artists. In other words, in mainstream comedies, the men dressed up as females look ridiculous, especially because of their old-fashioned, matronly style of attire, whereas the drag queens of the more serious movies choose sexy attire, look more credible as women and make fun of themselves during their stage performances.

Comedies based on cross-dressing include at least one scene that highlights the sheer effort involved by the male hero to transition into his female other. The scenes in which the actor is seen shaving, plucking, curling, painting, dyeing, donning prosthetic boobs, women's clothing and, last of all, high heels, are usually the lengthiest and amongst the funniest in each movie. While audiences are supposed to laugh at or be intrigued by the absurdity of the sheer effort involved by these men donning the female mask, it is what many women do on a regular basis in real life. Interestingly, some of these movies pre-date Judith Butler's (1990) concept of gendered performativity by decades. The idea here is that male is the baseline and that maleness requires no further embellishment. The cross-dressing men in these movies enact the "stylization of the body"; indeed, in our films, we see the same individual who, despite having one unequivocal biological sex, actually presents two body variants thanks to the artifice of disguise. The outward body essentially presents us with a display of signifiers denoting gender. In terms of comedy, these signifiers require hard work. We laugh at these actors as they wobble in their high heels and adjust their bosoms in a performance of the female – something that is void of incongruity when enacted by females simply performing the female in everyday life.

Comedies based on cross-dressing will typically include at least one comic scene that focuses on the main character transitioning into the female character. As the plots are farcical, much time involves ensuring that the protagonist's true gender does not emerge to those he wants to convince that he is female. This, of course, implies a lot of rushing around and changing appearance as quickly as possible so as not to be unmasked and caught out. A lot of the action therefore takes place "backstage" in bathrooms and bedrooms as much shaving of legs and making up and removing make-up occurs in these rooms, and so they are handy places to switch disguises. However, rather unsurprisingly, another topos in these films is the male character forgetting to remove a piece of female attire when he is in his male persona. Most famously, Joe/Josephine forgets to remove her earrings when he is pretending to be heir to the Shell Oil Corporation and Jerry is still wearing Daphne's shoes in one of the final scenes in *Some Like It Hot*. Bedrooms and bathrooms are the spaces in which much of the physical transitioning typically occurs as actors dress in and out of their two personae. A bubble bath can hide a multitude of sins and above all, a penis, as in the scene in *Some Like It Hot* where Lorelei (Marilyn Monroe) sits on the edge of a bathtub in which Josephine aka Joe is submerged. The unmasking of Mrs Doubtfire occurs in a restaurant bathroom. However, bedrooms and bathrooms are also the spaces where the heterosexuality of the cross-dresser may be restored. In *Some Like It Hot*, it is in a sleeping car of a train where Jerry, disguised as Daphne, almost seduces Lorelei and in *Tootsie*, Michael is looking for outfits for Dorothy and is trying on dresses in his girlfriend's bedroom when she walks in. Not wanting to admit that he is trying on women's clothes, Michael pretends that he wants to have sex with her. If there was any doubt regarding Michael's sexuality, it is now restored through a sexual encounter with his girlfriend. Connected to the possibility that they might be unmasked is their insecurity regarding their looks, so we find these men asking others whether their female outfits look good on them or not, which is stereotypically female behaviour. Heterosexuality is also restored on occasions in which female personae take on a masculine stance out of necessity. Mrs Doubtfire attacks a young man who tries to snatch her handbag and Dorothy, tired of waiting patiently for a cab and being physically usurped by men finally adopts the same tactics and uses strength (kicking and elbowing) in order to catch a cab. Thus, they resort to male privilege when they have to because they can. Quite the opposite occurs in *Kinky Boots* when Lola, a trained boxer, deliberately loses a wrist fight so as not to challenge her opponent's masculinity. Unlike in drag, where the two bodies and the two identities coexist in a juxtaposition, comedic cross-dressing aims at obliterating the original body/identity, in place of a brand new performed gender.

But what is interesting in the comedies is how asexual these men dressed up as women are! For some reason all them opt for frumpy clothes buttoned right up to the collar, liberty florals, long hemlines, old-fashioned permed hair, and unlikely glasses combined with ridiculous accents and tones of voice – also interesting is that they all transition into women who are older than their true selves are. This is quite the opposite of the dress code of the main actor in a drama whose character is a genuine transgender male who prefers tight slinky sparkly dresses. The beautifully dressed Lola in *Kinky Boots* has a predilection for sexy red thigh boots. While Lola certainly has the gift of the gab, she is in no way a comic character. For example, she never disguises the husky tone of her voice. Paradoxically, it is in the comedies that cross-dressed protagonists are courted by other men. Despite their matronly aspect, at some point an unsuspecting male will make a pass at them – a bus driver makes allusive remarks to Mrs Doubtfire; a man proposes to Dorothy in *Tootsie* as does a billionaire, Osgood Fielding III, to Daphne in *Some Like It Hot*. Yet, in the more dramatic films, where the female personae are far more credible, their effect on people is quite different. When Lola's landlady asks him if he is a man, she does so only so that she knows in what position she should put the toilet seat.

The process of unmasking in comedy aims at provoking laughter. When the characters are finally unmasked, chaos sets in. In the dramas, however, a slightly misplaced wig in *Kinky Boots* is sad as is the scene in which Dill cuts her hair short in *The Crying Game*. While the topos of the heterosexual man who falls for the cross-dressed man is considered humorous, the discovery that the object of desire is really a man tends to cause shock and anger in the thwarted lover. The unmasking of Dil as a male provokes vomit and disgust in the man who had previously thought Dil was female.

In the media we are made accustomed to stereotypes of sexuality that create two polarized sexualities, hetero and homo, and people who belong to these poles are easily identifiable – especially in the recurring presence across media texts of the screaming queen. Comedian Eddie Izzard, on the other hand, dressed in female clothing, and donning full make-up, has nothing of the drag queen. He may be dressed like a woman, but he embraces very masculine gender in his movements and in his speech, with nothing remotely camp in his self-performance. The overlap and oppositeness that make up Izzard's humour consists of a performance of his own masculinity superimposed upon a female frame so that self and other blend and merge. In fact, with his tongue firmly in his cheek, he considers himself to be a "a straight transvestite or a male lesbian" and has also described himself as "a lesbian trapped in a man's body" (Sommers 2016). And as he stomps heavily across the stage in high heeled boots and kimono, swearing like a trooper, he resembles more a prize boxer than a fairy. In the case of Izzard, gender and sexuality clearly refuse to remain invisible and their visibility does not lend itself to the creation or repetition of familiar clichés and polarized identities. In his show, *Dressed to Kill*, Izzard appears on stage wearing a kimono and full make-up and, as he declares, "In heels, as well. Yeah" and then goes on to explain:

> Yes, I'm a professional transvestite so I can run about in heels and not fall over. If women fall over in heels, that's embarrassing but if a bloke falls over in heels, you have to kill yourself. End of your life. It's quite difficult.

Izzard begins to laugh at himself and at his feminine side yet immediately enlightens the audience regarding the erroneous notion that transvestites are homosexuals. Izzard is a heterosexual who enjoys wearing women's clothes and explains this in a tirade about his wanting to join the army:

> I was going to be in the army when I was a kid. Yes. I say that and people go, "Oh, yeah, yeah". No I was going to be in the army when I was a kid. Cos if you're transvestite, you're actually a male tomboy. That's where the sexuality is. Yeah. It's not drag queen. No. Gay men have got that covered. And this is male tomboy. And people do get them mixed up. They put transvestite there.

> No no no no! Little bit of a crowbar separation, thank you. Gay men I think would agree. It's male lesbian. That's really where it is. Because . . . It's true, cos most transvestites fancy girls, so fancy women, so that's where it is. So running, jumping, climbing trees, putting on make-up when you're up there, that's where it is. I used to keep all my make-up in a squirrel hole up the tree and the squirrel would keep make-up on one side, and they keep nuts on the other. Sometimes I'd get up that tree and that squirrel would be covered in make-up.

In an attempt to have audiences understand the liquidity of gendered identities and sexuality, Izzard describes his transvestitism as "male tomboy" and "male lesbian". As he describes his running, climbing, masculine side combined with his make-up wearing feminine side, he mimics a squirrel alternating putting on make-up and eating nuts in a style of humour reminiscent of the Pythons.

Izzard counterpoints the "cave man" transvestite, the man who feels something is amiss and therefore cross-dresses with his own brand of transvestitism, namely the "executive" transvestite and the "action" transvestite, two labels to which he constantly refers throughout his shows. Ironically and comically, Izzard claims that he did not sign up because of the haphazard way soldiers camouflage their faces that would be in contrast to his flawless make-up:

> They [soldiers] only have that nighttime look and that's a bit slapdash. And they look a mess. You can't join. Even though the US armed forces have a distinct policy of "don't ask, don't tell" if you're a bloke wearing a lot of make-up, they don't need to ask. So you can't join. They go, "No, it's the wrong shade of lipstick for the army". They're missing a huge opportunity because one of the main elements of attack is the element of surprise. So what could be more surprising than the First Battalion Transvestite Brigade? Airborne wing. The airborne wing parachuting into dangerous areas with fantastic make-up and a fantastic gun.

The young men who form Out of the Blue, an all-male capella choir consisting of Oxford University alumni, also play with gender, but they do not cross-dress.[57] Out of the Blue adopt the notion of camp to create a witty effect. In their version of Shakira's *Hips Don't Lie*, the choir members sing in falsetto and prance around wiggling their derrières and other body parts in exactly the same way as the Columbian star Shakira does in her original video. The amusing incongruity occurs because a bunch of gawky male undergraduates in dark suits, shirts and ties act like the scantily dressed and sensual Shakira. The contrast between Shakira and the boys displaces the expectations of audiences and thus amuses. What was an erotic text originally, namely a video clip in which a half-naked Shakira gyrates and pouts into the camera as she is seen and projected through the male gaze, is transformed playfully as that same male gaze gives us fully dressed men gyrating and pouting into the camera in place of Shakira. Thus, the choir members subvert female objectification through a conceptual blend thanks to which they make a political point as here, gender is bending, rather than snapping.

Yanis Marshall, Arnaud and Mehdi are a dancing trio who perform dance routines wearing high heels and, similarly to Out of the Blue, emulate feminine movements in an exaggerated fashion, thus creating an incongruity between their masculine selves and their feminized movements. In their first appearance on the talent show *Britain's Got Talent*, they danced to a medley of songs by the Spice Girls and immediately after their performance one of the (female) judges commented, "That was ten times better than any female dancers we've seen on that stage today". This remark highlights the fact that the desired effect was achieved, in other words, the three dancers are clearly men, and they perform femininity better than the women do. Yet the incongruity of their act provokes a mirthful response in the audience. After their performance in the semi-final, judge David Walliams, who had openly flirted with the trio after their previous performances cried out "Sisters that was fierce!" Walliams, on several occasions on the show, plays on his ambiguous sexuality by flirting with attractive male competitors (see pages 45 and 46).

The presenters ask the trio "The big question is of course what do your wives and girlfriends make of this routine?" to which the three dancers pretend to look embarrassed and do not answer. "That was just a joke", responds the presenter, but of course it wasn't. Or rather, the question was deliberately asked to make the audience laugh as they are supposed to presume that the dancers are homosexual – something still considered incongruous and worthy of laughter by many. So a certain element of ambiguity lies in the fact that men dressed up as women are seen to be funny and that men who like other men are funny, too. Funny odd and/or funny haha?

Walliams is also famous for his persona from the *Little Britain* TV series in which he plays the part of the "Rubbish Transvestite" Emily Howard, a "lady" who dresses in long floral dresses, uses a parasol, has a high-pitched voice and participates in what she refers to as "lady-like" activities. Emily spends much time trying to convince people that she is "a lady" as she attempts to use female only facilities and generally pass as a woman. Walliams dressed up as an unlikely looking woman creates dissonance between himself as a man and as a cross-dresser, especially when he doth protest too much about his sexuality.

In an episode of *Little Britain in the USA*, two US police officers arrest Emily for having stolen a frock from a store. As she is handcuffed and led away, the British accented voiceover tells us "One of the most popular pastimes in Great Britain . . . is transvestitism". At the police station, Emily poses sexily for mug shots and does her best to answer the police officer's questions posing as a female. However, try as she might to insist that she is "a lady" in answer to her name, sex and general information, a severe glance from the police officer forces her to admit she is a man and answering in her male persona and in a male tone of voice.[58] This stark contrast of two genders that Walliams creates is quite original. Walliams insists to all and sundry that she is a she and then, when we least expect it, suddenly reverts to her "he" persona. In a sketch for the 2009 *Comic Relief* Emily and another "lady" Florence, own a dress shop. In her signature high-pitched voice, Emily tells Florence that it is important for women to have somewhere they can buy "ladies' things . . . our little lace handkerchiefs, our parasols, our general ladies' . . ."; at this point Emily hesitates and changes facial expression and tone. Lowering her voice and reverting to the masculine, she adds the word "shit". When pop star Robbie Williams enters the dress shop by accident, Emily and Florence convince him to dress up as a lady. As Williams walks away from the clothes shop dressed in a long flowery gown and holding a parasol, Walliams, dressed as Emily looks on and in a masculine voice utters "Bloody poof!"[59]

Emily behaves in a similar way in 2010 when she joins singer Sting on stage as he is performing *Fields of Gold*.[60] Emily openly flirts with Sting, inviting him back to her hotel after the show and insisting she is a lady who spends her time doing "lady's things". In answer to Sting's question as to what "lady's things" actually are, Emily responds "I bathe in rose petals, skip through meadows, I play the harp" then reverting to her male persona lowers her voice and adds, "that sort of bollocks". As in the sketch with Robbie Williams, Emily at times seems to be a half-hearted transvestite who considers – what Emily considers to be – "ladies' things", "bollocks" and "shit". Again, when Emily sings with Sting she does so in a flat, harsh, male tone of voice, after which she kisses Sting at length on the lips. Walliams jumps backwards and forwards from he to she and back again when the audience least expects it.

Notes

1 The concordances were generated in KWIC format from the BNC, extracting the corpus from two diverse platforms: the University of Lancaster BNC-baby and the BNC online version by Mark Davies at Brigham Young University.
2 *The Worst Witch* is a TV series about a group of witches attending a school for magic that ran on ITV between 1998 and 2001. Miss Cackle, played by Clare Coulter, is the school's headmistress.
3 On sale at Amazon www.amazon.com/Hillary-Clinton-2016-Laughing-Pen/dp/B0125 51IEE. Retrieved 15 February 2016.
4 Comments randomly retrieved from threads below the following videos: "Hillary Clinton Evil Laugh Compilation" available at: www.youtube.com/watch?v=btgLIgPK YsE and "Hillary Clinton's Laugh" available at: www.youtube.com/watch?v=a2VMB HCzfr8. Retrieved 15 February 2016. Crackerwv, The Viper of Death and Andrej Pejcic are the names of the three people who left the comments.
5 Available at: www.jokes4us.com/dirtyjokes/womenjokes.html. Retrieved 1 December 2016.
6 Available at: www.funny-jokes-quotes.com/jokes-about-women-wife.html. Retrieved 2 December 2016.
7 This figure refers to a search conducted on 26 October 2015.
8 See www.Jokes4all.net. Retrieved 21 October 2015.
9 Joke available at: http://jokes4all.net/physicist-jokes. Retrieved 22 October 2015.
10 Joke available at: http://jokes4all.net/philosopher-jokes. Retrieved 22 October 2015.

11 See http://jokes4all.net/nurse-jokes; http://jokes4all.net/babysitter-jokes; http://jokes4all.net/secretary-jokes. Retrieved 22 October 2015.
12 I would like to thank the second year students of my 2016 English Linguistics class for their help and enthusiasm. The imaginative answers to the conundrum included those of the two 21-year-old males, one of whom answered, "Maybe the doctor had an affair with the mother of the young man" and the other who thought that "Doctor is bored and tells a lie to avoid operating on the boy".
13 Joke available at: www.singlix.com/417/jokes/braintr.html. Retrieved 4 September 2016.
14 Available at: http://unijokes.com/joke-8572/. Retrieved 25 February 2016.
15 Thank you to Debra Aarons, Giuseppe Balirano, Janet Bing, Alison Bron and Giselinde Kuipers for their helpful insights on this joke.
16 Available at: http://unijokes.com/marriage-jokes/. Retrieved 25 February 2016.
17 Available at: http://www.jmpressley.net/humor/marriage.html. Retrieved 23 November 2015.
18 Available at: http://jokes4all.net/wife-jokes. Retrieved 22 October 2015.
19 Available at: www.jokes4us.com/dirtyjokes/husbandwifejokes.html. Retrieved 25 February 2016.
20 Available at: www.reddit.com/r/Jokes/comments/3we3z3/a_rich_old_man_goes_golfing_with_his_friends/. Retrieved 4 September 2016.
21 Available at: http://betterafter50.com/2013/06/these-in-law-jokes-will-make-you-smile/. Retrieved 25 February 2016.
22 Joke available at: www.dailymail.co.uk/news/article-1263846/Mother-law-jokes-new-lease-life-online.html. Retrieved 10 March 2016.
23 Interestingly there is no mention of Jewishness in the joke yet we "know" it is a Jewish joke. Thanks to Debra Aarons for pointing this out (personal communication).
24 Joke available at: www.quora.com/How-come-you-never-hear-father-in-law-jokes. Retrieved 9 March 2016.
25 See www.youtube.com/watch?v=knxuG_hYe-8. Retrieved 12 July 2016.
26 Although, see for example: www.realjock.com/gayforums/4203439/ and www.realjock.com/gayforums/4203439/. Retrieved 17 July 2016. According to Christie Davies, "They are fakes" (personal communication).
27 Available at: www.jokes4us.com/blondejokes/blondejokes.html. Retrieved 26 January 2017.
28 See "The Naked Chef" (les hommes à poêles), Available at: www.youtube.com/watch?v=tuTVGjZea3o, and a similar dance carried out with towels available at: www.youtube.com/watch?v=ae69-9lIIhQ *France Got Talent* (towels). Retrieved 2 May 2017.
29 For more on this issue see: www.theguardian.com/media/2017/mar/28/daily-mail-legs-it-front-page-sexist and www.theguardian.com/media/2017/mar/28/theresa-may-refuses-to-comment-on-daily-mail-legs-it-front-page. Retrieved 2 May 2017.
30 *Inside Amy Schumer – Last F**kable Day* – Uncensored. Available at: www.youtube.com/watch?v=XPpsI8mWKmg. Retrieved 7 September 2016.
31 Available at: http://jokes4all.net/funeral-jokes. Retrieved 17 February 2016.
32 The rape joke told by Tosh is available at: www.youtube.com/watch?v=isSJjwdXgho. Retrieved 6 June 2016.
33 Slogan adopted by the South Wales Police Rape Awareness Campaign on TV and radio. Available at: www.youtube.com/watch?v=COujGHikiqM. Retrieved 22 February 2016.
34 Available at: www.reddit.com/r/Jokes/comments/26gfos/rape_jokes_general/. Retrieved 29 February 2016.
35 Available at: http://thedingers.eu/viewtopic.php?f=42&t=25&start=540. Retrieved 29 February 2016.
36 Available at: http://www.jokes2go.com/jokes/19762.html. Retrieved 22 February 2016.
37 Available at: www.reddit.com/r/Jokes/comments/3ipnl9/two_nuns_sister_mary_and_sister_elizabeth_are/. Retrieved 22 February 2016.

38 "George Carlin about Rape". Available at: www.youtube.com/watch?v=fwMukKqx-Os. Retrieved 29 February 2016.
39 Edinburgh Fringe 2015: The 50 Best Jokes, *Independent online* 28 August 2015. Available at: www.independent.co.uk/arts-entertainment/edinburgh-festival/edinburgh-fringe-2015-the-50-best-jokes-10476941.html. Retrieved 24 July 2016.
40 *Tea Consent.* Available at: www.youtube.com/watch?v=oQbei5JGiT8. Retrieved 7 September 2016. It was part of the Thames Valley Police #ConsentisEverything campaign against rape.
41 "What were you wearing?" Available at: www.youtube.com/watch?v=51-hepLP8J4. Retrieved 13 March 2017 shortly after being broadcast by the BBC on *Tracey Ullman's Show* see: http://bbc.in/2mWxDTW.
42 Available at: www.jokes2go.net/joke/3192/how-do-you-know-when-a-woman-s-about-to-say-something-smart. Retrieved 26 October 2015.
43 Available at: www.jokes2go.net/women-jokes/3. Retrieved 26 October 2015.
44 Jokes reported by Katy Brand, "Feminists have never been funnier – and here's the proof" *The Telegraph.* 9 January 2015. Available at: www.telegraph.co.uk/women/womens-life/11334783/Feminists-have-never-been-funnier-and-heres-the-proof.html. Retrieved 3 March 2016.
45 Joke available at: www.reddit.com/r/Jokes/comments/355cz2/venus_vs_mars/. Retrieved 9 July 2016.
46 Joke googled 9 July 2016.
47 Examples taken from *Joan Rivers Live at the Apollo*, available at: www.youtube.com/watch?v=knxuG_hYe-8. Retrieved 12 July 2016.
48 Bridget Christie: *A Woman's Look*. Available at: www.youtube.com/watch?v=5aUHZhKbf6o&spfreload=10. Retrieved 25 July 2016.
49 Examples taken from *Jo Brand Live at the Apollo*, available at: www.youtube.com/watch?v=d9vjyAizwQU. Retrieved 10 July 2016.
50 Examples taken from *Sarah Millican Live at the Apollo*, available at: www.youtube.com/watch?v=Gyuo9ZH3frE. Retrieved 11 July 2016.
51 Margaret Cho, *Persimmon Diet*, available at: www.youtube.com/watch?v=hF1pIMgE8FA&spfreload=10. Retrieved 20 July 2016.
52 Joan Rivers performing, available at: www.youtube.com/watch?v=YNUkLzi46OI&spfreload=10. Retrieved 12 July 2016.
53 Victoria Wood – *Talking About Having a Baby LIVE*, available at: www.youtube.com/watch?v=Qwkpba2zOV4&spfreload=10. Retrieved 25 July 2016.
54 "Bridget Christie does not like babies" – *BBC Room 101*: Series 5, Episode 7, available at www.youtube.com/watch?v=2DP_fai-FpM. Retrieved 25 July 2016.
55 Dr Annie Evans, *Menopause Facts, Signs & Menopause Symptoms* Part 4, available at: www.youtube.com/watch?v=2CY4D9qfCiU. Retrieved 26 July 2016.
56 Dr Annie Evans, *Menopause Facts, Signs & Menopause Symptoms* Part 1, available at: www.youtube.com/watch?v=I1RtnxKy8TI. Retrieved 26 July 2016.
57 Videos available at the choir's official website: www.ootboxford.com/. Retrieved 2 August 2016.
58 Video clip available at: www.youtube.com/watch?v=vvH1LLZeef4&index=4&list=RD4THO9-N--k4. Retrieved 27 January 2017.
59 "Little Britain meets Robbie Williams" *Comic Relief* 2009. Available at: www.youtube.com/watch?v=AJ8e6UVpLNg. Retrieved 27 January 2017.
60 *Emily Howard from Little Britain with Sting*, available at: www.youtube.com/watch?v=gM7O8PMNdtA&index=5&list=RD4THO9-N—k4&spfreload=10. Retrieved 27 January 2017.

4
THE LANGUAGE OF JOKES ONLINE

In the early days of the internet, users had a somewhat passive relationship with its content. Although initially they could access and view the content of web pages, they were unable to interact effectively with what appeared on their screens. Thanks to the innovations of Web 2.0, today users can interact more actively in a virtual environment and with a certain amount of ease. No longer do they passively access websites and simply look and/or read, as they are now able to engage dynamically with content and interact with other users in real time.[1] More importantly, users can now generate, upload and display their own content, manipulate the content of others' as well as react, and build upon the interaction of others. At the time of writing, many people spend a large part of their daily lives online and engage in a wide range of activities that are digitally driven. Such online activities can be carried out anywhere there is a wireless connection to link an electronic device such as a smartphone or a tablet to the gigantic network such is the World Wide Web. Furthermore, Web 2.0 has enabled, amongst other things, social networking, media sharing, bookmarking and tagging. In fact, the focus of Web 2.0 is very much on users' collaboration and sharing. And what can be more collaborative and worthy of sharing than humour?

It is at present possible to carry out numerous activities within at least two parallel worlds. While we can take part in various actions online such as browsing, chatting and finding directions, we can also engage in commercial activities like banking, calling a cab and shopping as well as playing games and participating in leisurely activities, at the same time we can (still?) carry out exactly the same undertakings in the real world too. According to Weitz (2017), the "fullness" of online life is still in its "teenage years" as many people straddle reality and a virtual environment. Moreover, and importantly, just as humour is an integral part of real life, it plays a significant role in the digital environment of the internet too. To demonstrate this, Weitz examines an episode of the ABC sitcom *Modern*

Family that is entirely filmed through the lenses/screens of numerous devices and asserts that the misunderstandings that create the humour in this particular episode serve as a "state-of-the-artform cultural snapshot and comic critique of a rabidly networked lifestyle that many of us know so well".[2] A much darker, satirical view of this lifestyle is also portrayed in the aptly named series *Black Mirror*.[3]

Verbal language is of utmost importance in users' relationship with the internet; after all, it is principally words that drive the internet. When we look for something via a search engine, we do so by typing words onto a screen by means of a keyboard. The alphanumeric keyboard governs and mediates users' relationship with the massive network of the World Wide Web. As for conversational interaction, although chatting, as the word itself implies, can be carried out vocally, with participants speaking synchronously, so-called chatting online actually involves reading and writing. Indeed the foundations of social networking are written messages and their responses. Although many social networks also provide a "talking" option so that users can record a message (e.g. WhatsApp), the written mode of texting is more prevalent. However, although these texts are technically written, the language resembles that of speech rather than writing. Someone posts a thought in writing and others read and then perhaps evaluate it with a thumbs up signal indicating a "like"; they might share it with others thus making the original message "go viral". Even though important networking sites such as Instagram and Pinterest are primarily based on pictographic rather than verbal content, written captions attached to visual materials as well as verbal responses in writing to each pictorial post are inescapably present and constitute a significant part of these texts in their entirety.

When we think of online humour, so-called internet memes spring to mind. These often take the form of a text applied to an image to create a humorous effect, but memes may also occur in the form of video clips, gifs or hashtags.

Starting with examples of purely verbal online humour, the following is an overview of some of the different types of computer-mediated humour available on a variety of virtual platforms and easily accessible on our diverse screens.

Conversational humour online

Given that we know humour is a social activity, is humorous activity mediated by a smartphone, say, any different to face-to-face joking, and if it is, in what way? Have users needed to adapt the conversational rules of joking outlined by Norrick (1993, 2000) to the virtual environment? And what about timing? In a space where it is beyond the poster's control exactly *when* other users pick up another person's remark, will this time lapse affect responses? Furthermore, when someone posts a witty comment, he or she will presumably expect friends and followers to appreciate the quip. But what if someone with whom we are not familiar reads our witty post – or rather what *we* consider to be a witty post? If we are unsure about the person with whom we are communicating – after all, the internet is a place where we may not have met our interactants in real life – a wisecrack can be a way of testing the waters to see if a person will align with us. If they share our values and if they find the same things funny as we do, we have every reason to believe that there is room for comity. On the other hand, as we do not really know our audience, the Wild Wild West of the internet can also be a place where there is a high risk of causing offence. A joke about a socially delicate subject that touches politics or religion, for example, is launched into unchartered waters and our unfamiliar audience may be sensitive to these topics and take offence. Humour may indeed hurt the feelings of others when it wrongly estimates their comfort zone. With humour, we need to tread carefully. With internet humour, more so.

Signalling laughter online

As pointed out by Glenn (2003: 42), while it is common for people to report the speech of others word for word, it is unlikely that we would report someone else's laughter by uttering the expression "ha ha ha". Over and above the fact that the expression has something of a sarcastic overtone, we do not actually laugh in such a well-ordered and regular manner. Yet it is unexceptional to "write down" laughter using items like "haha", "ha ha ha" or "hee hee hee" even though these canonical transcriptions are nothing like the sound of real laughter. In fact, these multiples of "ha" (or indeed "he/e") are quite common in online interaction. A Facebook study on "e-laughter" carried out in 2015 observed how over the course of a week, users transcribed laughter. First, the study revealed that during the week under observation, 15 per cent of users who posted comments had used at least one "e-laugh". For the purpose of the survey, an e-laugh included any way of conveying laughter in online communication by typing variants of "haha" (e.g. "hahaha", "haahhhaa" etc.), "hehe", "lol" or else the use of emoji (Adamic *et al.* 2015; Lobrutto 2015). As in real-life writing, "haha" (as well as variants thereof) appears to be the preferred way to express laughter and is used by 51.4 per cent of Facebook users. The acronym "lol" ("laughing out loud") was popular with mainly older users, suggesting that it is possibly going out of fashion in this context.

Second to the use of "haha" came the use of emoji, smiley-type faces, with 33.7 per cent of subjects. The report claims that in this study, when laughter was expressed using an emoji, a single emoji is used 50 per cent of the time and people rarely posted a string of more than five identical consecutive emoji. This suggests that emoji may offer a concise way to convey various forms of laughter online. As Weitz quite rightly highlights, "Despite the inability of our bodies to accompany us into the virtual sphere, we seem unable to ignore their insistence on playing parts in the online humour transaction" (2016). The large set of disembodied smiley faces or the need to type colon+dash+left-facing brackets into our emails and into our online conversation in general, reflects the need to include physical behaviour within the virtual sphere. Skype, a programme that allows users to make telephone calls from computers, goes a step further by including a set of animated emojis portraying entire bodies engaged in a wide range of actions.

Earlier we discussed how laughter is a characteristic feature in that by sharing virtual content we find funny with others, we are encouraging them to laugh with us. Web 2.0 allows users, amongst other things, to allow others to hear our laughter. Vlogger Alonzo Lerone posts videos of things he finds funny on YouTube and on his Facebook page together with his own running commentaries. So, for example, he will typically film himself together with a screenshot of an amusing tweet someone has posted that he reads aloud while laughing. In particular, he retweets Gordon Ramsay's "roasts" from the celebrity chef's Twitter account (see below). Ramsay's "roasts" are not his recipes for joints of meat, but good-natured jokes that he makes at the expense of his followers for the amusement of others. Ramsay, in this "angry chef" persona, encourages his followers to post photographs of their disastrous dishes, after which he will post derogatory comments that are intended to be funny. Lerone will read out the tweets and often burst out laughing because of the obnoxious looking dishes and Ramsay's clever/rude/hilarious responses. Users see and hear Lerone laughing alongside the tweet and post appreciative comments and emojis and, in the space for users' comments known as "BTL" – below the line – they will typically post appreciative comments like "I like watching you laugh" as Lerone's contagious laughter encourages us to laugh with him.[4] A sort of echo of laughter happens as we laugh at the awful looking dish someone has subjected to Ramsay's scrutiny; we laugh with Ramsay at his clever response, but above all, we laugh with Lerone. This is a sort of game of Chinese boxes where users laugh at someone laughing at something/one else who was encouraged by a third person to provoke laughter in the first place. This interconnectivity is further highlighted in emulations of this game. Like most successful people, Lerone has his imitators. In particular, there is a vlogger who also comments on Ramsay's tweets but without showing his face and using a very high pitched voice reminiscent of Alvin and the Chipmunks and, above all, a Chipmunk style laugh.[5] Significantly, users are irritated by this laugh, and BTL, we find much criticism of his laughter. Comments include: "Are those that funny you have to laugh out loud after reading each of them?"; "The laugh is so over the top fuck, Gordon what do you rate this laugh, fucking dreadful?" and "Ok fk these, I just can not stand that FKN voice, Ugh AND annoying FAKE ASS LAUGH". It could well be that readers have simply distinguished Lerone's true laughter from the other poster's affected laugh, something that the human brain is primed to differentiate (Hurley *et al.* 2013; Provine 2000).

Ping-pong-punning

One of the features of wordplay that has remained constant over time must surely be the occurrence of a phenomenon that I have labelled "ping-pong-punning" (PPP) (see Chapter 1). In a real-life joke-capping session people will typically take turns at telling a succession of jokes, with each joke being different from the next and separated by laughter or at the very least by the verbal evaluation of the joke by other listeners. The phenomenon of PPP is quite different from joke-telling proper as it consists of a series of puns that while being uttered by different speakers, do not stand out from surrounding discourse within separate joke frames or formats. PPP sessions consist of diverse speakers who intertwine instances of wordplay within the principal surrounding discourse. These witty remarks are not framed and rarely take on the semblance of a formulaic joke. However, similarly to what occurs in a session of joke-capping, a string of puns arising in "ping-pong" style will tend to be non-intermittent. PPP is further similar to joke-capping in that something in the ongoing regular, albeit informal, discourse prompts someone else to tell a joke or to emit a pun that will trigger more of the same. As with joke-capping, that first witticism will stimulate others, in turn, to do the same resulting in a lengthy succession of jokes and/or puns on related subject matter or belonging to a similar cycle. Unlike joke-capping however, PPP involves someone who deliberately picks up and puns and/or plays upon an ambiguous word or phrase contained within an ongoing conversation. Conversation participants follow with banter containing other puns that are in some way semantically connected to the initial pun or wordplay. In contrast to joke-capping, in PPP there are no actual jokes involved. In fact, when the phenomenon of PPP occurs, the tendency is for the whole discourse to border on the nonsensical, although it will contain a clear leitmotiv. The following exchange evolved as part of an informal conversation involving Peter, a person with a broken arm:

> *Initiator:* "No 'arm in it, eh Peter?"
> *Participant 1:* "Yeah got to hand it to you".
> *Peter:* "That's not funny".
> *Initiator:* "Put my finger on it have I?"
> *Participant 2:* "'Armless enough".
>
> *Chiaro 1992: 115*

Peter's arm in plaster prompts four independent yet simultaneously concatenated puns roughly based on the semantic field of limbs. The punsters play on the acoustic similarity of the terms "arm/(h)arm", "armless/(h)armless" as well as on idioms containing the terms "hand" and "finger". PPP resembles a battle of wits in which each participant tries to top, or at least match, the attempt at punning produced by the previous punster. It is likely that PPP occurs more frequently in social interaction than joke-capping sessions, as the latter are feats of memory and jokesters position themselves front-stage as they recite their joke, whereas the former consists of on-the-spot and off-the-cuff inventive in which single participants are only foregrounded for the space of a short quip (Chiaro 1992: 113–17). PPP originated as a strictly conversational phenomenon that could only occur in oral communication. Today, as diverse types of writing on the internet resemble speech more and more and as social interaction seems to take place as much as, if not more, online than in real life, predictably this type of wordplay frequently occurs online too, albeit in written form: it reflects spoken language.

So, while the actual way of playing PPP has remained constant, what has changed is its occurrence on a variety of virtual platforms. This makes sense if we consider that much social networking does occur in real time just like conventional conversation does. PPP would be impossible or would at least lose its verve, if it occurred in the mode of traditional written communications that require time to be read and for a riposte to be written, parties being both temporally and spatially distant. Social networking occurs in real time and thus provides an ideal platform for PPP to flourish. Nonetheless, it is true that others will not necessarily immediately pick up a post on a virtual platform. Furthermore, what we post is likely to remain there forever. This would suggest that the practice of PPP online is radically different from its live counterpart. If we look at the examples of PPP in Chapter 1, though, it emerges that chains of puns are not always created in real time and ripostes to puns are not always posted immediately. The timeline in Figure 1.1 illustrates that while a punning response can indeed be posted within minutes, i.e. closely enough to real time, reactions can also occur after several hours. The first pun on the word "correctness" in Figure 1.2 "correct-egg-ness" appears on 12 January at 20.32. However, someone picks it up and revises it with the term "corr-egg-ness" only the following day at 14.02. Interestingly, the initial punster may not necessarily even see the rejoinder. Thus, in a sense, this changes the essence of PPP that should be all about quick thinking and immediate rejoinders. Furthermore, the rectification/modification of the first pun "correct-egg-ness" to "corr-egg-ness" appears to remain hanging, unobserved and unchallenged by the initial punster, who only responds and challenges someone who criticizes him with "Did you read about puns in a textbook and not really understand" so that another separate exchange becomes embedded within the initial ping-ponging discourse. This embedded discourse also contains an example of PPP with two adjacent puns created by two speakers ("Dairy me" followed four hours later by "Eggsactly"); there is no response to "corr-egg-ness". In other words, paradoxically, PPP online appears at times to lose its real-world time rules. It ceases to be an event in which speed is an essential element; pun – immediate evaluation – simultaneous and swift rebuttal.

Therefore, in virtual life, we can never be sure when an instance of wordplay we post on Facebook for example, will actually be seen. If I want to post a clever riposte, I have all the time in the world to do so thus losing the spontaneity of live PPP and transforming my extemporaneous rejoinder into something closer to a well thought out enactment. So, this type of verbal play online resembles (comic) literature that is written to be read at a distance from the author both in terms of time and place. In fact, the concept of conversational adjacency pairs becomes difficult to apply to online PPP because of the possibility of a time lapse between the time of posting the initial quip and its pick-up time by others. Not only that, but a member of a chat or a thread can leave the conversation at any time, just as they may return at any time at a different point within the whole thread. Absurdly, PPP online both is, and at the same time is not, about comity.

PPP BTL

Many national newspapers now appear in online formats and contain a function that enables readers to post comments directly below articles. The online version of UK daily newspaper *The Guardian* has a thriving community of readers who regularly post in the "comment is free" sections of the paper. The number of people who participate in these BTL comment sections can sometimes be so high as to create lengthy threads of observations and remarks. These threads seem to follow many rules of real-life conversation, as they are extremely interactive with participants making remarks on each other's comments, agreeing, disagreeing, getting angry or even participating in trolling. Consequently, as these rolling threads resemble traditional oral interaction and conversation, they often display instances of PPP. Whether the subject of the preceding article is serious or lighthearted, it is common practice for someone to start punning in the comments section and for other posters to notice the pun and follow suit.

An article in *The Guardian* online regarding the excessive amount of sugar contained in breakfast cereals (Usborne 2016), triggered numerous comments from readers that included many witticisms. In truth, the journalist himself was quite liberal with puns in his article although the content itself was serious. Regarding the amount of sugar contained in one cereal, Usborne claims that "It is not the first time Special K has been 'oat of order'" after which he apologizes for the pun with a "(sorry)" – journalist's brackets. Usborne also plays on brand names in his article with "Dreaded Wheat", "Confessquick" and "Cheatabix". A lengthy thread of comments from readers follows the article and at one point (at 14.47) a reader, unexpectedly, inserts a complete joke about muesli, picked up by a would-be ping-pong-punster almost three hours later (at 17.26) with "Is there a raisin you posted this sad tale here?" (Figure 4.1)

DoTheBartman   21 Jul 2016 14:47

Did you hear about the man who drowned in his muesli?

He was pulled under by a strong currant.

WandaDelamere ↪ DoTheBartman   21 Jul 2016 15:00

Nice one.

Doofer1903 ↪ DoTheBartman   21 Jul 2016 17:26

Is there a raisin you posted this sad tale here?

FIGURE 4.1   Ping-pong-punning below the line ("muesli")

As I pointed out in 1992, recipients do not necessarily evaluate jokes by laughing, but also verbally. BTL laughter is only possible with the use of smileys, emojis and verbal conventions. However, someone evaluates the "muesli" joke within three minutes of its being posted with the comment "Nice one". Interestingly the muesli joke is a real joke in terms of form and structure; it is a one-liner and the "reason/raisin" evaluation seems ironic; it highlights the story-like structure of the muesli joke by referring to it as a "tale" thus exemplifying a different type of play from that normally expected in an online feed.

An article about a policy in the Italian city of Turin to promote vegetarianism not only triggers fiery comments from *Guardian* readers, but also some punning (Kirchgaessner 2016). The mayor of Turin who had had the idea of promoting vegetarianism is a member of Italy's Five Star Movement, so, in answer to a post claiming that "Her policy is nuts" – punning on the term "nuts" both as a vegetarian food and as a slightly batty person – someone replies "Five star nut roast". The comment is followed by a string of puns related to food from others (Figure 4.2) such as "Let's hope she's not telling porkies" in which the punster cleverly combines the concept of pork – meat – with that of lying ("pork pies" are "lies" in Cockney rhyming slang, hence "porkies" in mainstream English). The string of puns ends with "doughnut take her policy lightly" as it is a "big dill". Puns may be the lowest form of wit, but they are possibly one of the highest forms of mental dexterity.

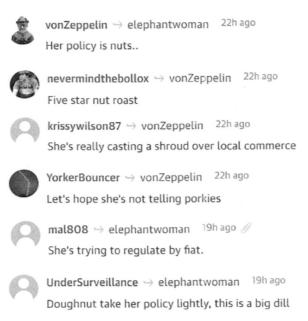

FIGURE 4.2 Ping-pong-punning below the line ("nuts")

In July 2016, Brexit and its surrounding narrative provided a good excuse for ping-pong-punsters on *Guardian* BTL threads to engage in witty inventiveness, as the portmanteau "Brexit" itself paved the way for dozens of others based on the names of other EU member states.[6] Encouraged by the neologisms "Brexit" and "Bremain", posters participated in a lengthy battle of wits in which they alternated serious discussion around the crisis affecting the EU and novel portmanteaux such as "Czechout", "Italeave" and "Fruckoff", etc. (Figures 4.3 and 4.4). Especially interesting in these threads is the meta-discourse regarding the puns themselves, "Quitaly?" says one poster. "Man that's a low humor pun" retorts another (Figure 4.3). Furthermore, the (un)seriousness of some participants is unclear. "All words are made up!" says one contributor, while another wonders "whether these things are genuine, or just made up in order to invent new words" (Figure 4.4.) Again, punsters argue about the exactness of each portmanteau. Should it be "Portugoer", "Portugout", "Portugaleave" or "Portugone"? "Spanish Armadoor" or "Spaxit"? "Quitaly", "Ex.it", "Filtaly" or "Italeave"? The inventiveness is endless and every so often, someone tries to enter the thread with

ReinerNiemand 1h ago

"Quitaly", really?
Man, that's a low humour pun. As american stand-up you'd now get peanuts thrown at you.
What will be next, The Spanish Armadoor, or maybe Portugoer?

GBscript → ReinerNiemand 52m ago

It's Spaxit and Portugout.

Simon_1956_Vintage → ReinerNiemand 49m ago   0

I call it Italexit and it is a movement that is gaining pace rapidly throughout the country.

saintabroad → ReinerNiemand 48m ago

Byelgum.
Departugal.
Italeave.
Fruckoff.
Czechout.
Outstria.
Finnish.
Slovlong.
Latervia.

Until what is left is Germlonely.

DesertTortoise → GBscript 40m ago

Surely it's Portugaleave, as in Portugaleave it, they voted out!

FIGURE 4.3 Ping-pong-punning below the line: Brexit portmanteaux 1

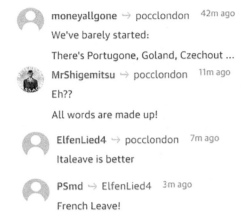

FIGURE 4.4 Ping-pong-punning below the line: Brexit portmanteaux 2

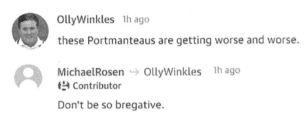

FIGURE 4.5 Ping-pong-punning below the line: Brexit portmanteaux 2

a serious comment that posters completely ignore. In fact, it appears that any suggestion for a portmanteau goes unless a contributor tries to put a stop to the play: "These portmanteaus are getting worse and worse", says one contributor who is promptly met with the punning rejoinder: "Don't be so bregative" (Figure 4.5).

Trolling, the practice of disrupting online discourse by posting inflammatory messages with the intent of provoking an emotional response in readers seems to be impossible when surrounded by people with a good sense of humour.

Of course, it is not always the case that a pun or a joke made by a commentator turns into PPP. Participants in online humour do not notice all instances of wordplay; neither will a single wisecrack necessarily trigger PPP. In fact, participants may completely ignore a pun, as in the case of a person who interrupted a long thread in which readers reacted BTL to a satirical cartoon by Steve Bell that featured an image of the corpse of the late conservative anti-migration parliamentarian Enoch Powell. A heated debate followed this cartoon consisting of 516 comments. In the midst of a serious argument by readers on the issue of Brexit, migration and politics, there is a sudden interruption as one reader posts, "Rule Theresa, Theresa rules the graves" in reference to the image of the (Tory) corpse in the cartoon and (Tory) Prime Minister Theresa May. Other pundits completely ignore the joke that remains hanging there all alone amidst serious political debate.[7]

BTL communities

There is a marked tendency for groups of *Guardian* newspaper readers to meet up online, seemingly deliberately, to comment BTL on a newspaper feature. This occurs with many regular features from political and economic issues to articles on beauty and fashion and is the case for followers of Rhik Samadder, a journalist who writes a weekly column in *The Guardian* in which he regularly describes a quirky kitchen aid he has put to the test. Samadder writes in a tongue-in-cheek manner using saucy double-entendres as he describes gadgets such as sausage stuffers, milk makers, pizza scissors and the like. After trying out the device, in his "Inspect a gadget" article (Inspector Gadget?) Samadder explains what the object is, how it works, its "redeeming features" and whether it should go to the "counter, drawer, back of the cupboard?" The comments in the thread that follows each weekly article contain lengthy concatenations of puns by readers. Mostly verging on the double-entendre, provoked by the journalist himself, these threads mainly occur in real time and, as in real life, contributors (seem to) actually know each other personally. Samadder's first review appeared in May 2015 when his assessment of a cake server received 62 comments from readers while, two years later in March 2017, his review of "Silicone bagel moulds – holy snack heaven!" was followed by 756 comments, and his review of "onion goggles" in April 2017 by 806. Many of the commentators – especially the punsters – are regulars, as each week they emerge online as soon as the article appears, greet each other, wait for one another, note when a regular is missing, apologize for being late and generally adopt the rules of real-life conversational etiquette. Samadder's review of a coconut grater opens with the headline, "Coconut grater – an ugly pleasure of the flesh", clearly provoking his regulars to contribute with double-entendres, was followed by 493 comments.[8] A handful of contributors who emerge as leaders each week, dominate in the creation of puns as can be seen in Figure 4.6. In fact, two punsters practically take over the feed as they produce 10 out of 11 puns in a stretch of PPP, all of which are based on the names of chocolate confectionary available in the UK and use a wide variety of punning techniques. A third contributor evaluates this string of PPP after the ninth pun, "Thank you for being the inspiration that spawned so many replies, haven't giggled so much for ages". However, the contributor who is being thanked and who actually triggered the puns does not actually take part in the long succession of chocolate-based banter. It is also clear from the last two posts of the PPP session, that the person who posted the tenth quip, was actually responding to the eighth pun, "don't milka it too much" telling that particular punster not to be a "smartie".

Figure 4.6 is an illustration of the timeline of digital PPP. Unlike in real life, people can come and go from a virtual conversation, add comments to a comment posted at any time and generally can be unaware of surrounding discourse. Whereas in real life when someone enters an ongoing conversation they will eventually be filled in, or else they themselves will contextualize and understand the discussion, in online discourse, someone who enters this virtual fray *in media res* will not necessarily have caught up with all that was said previously.

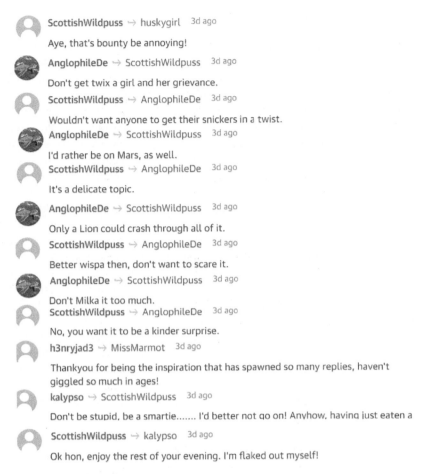

FIGURE 4.6 Ping-pong-punning below the line ("confectionary")

Thus, online discourse runs the risk of becoming non-linear. Occasionally the same pun is repeated in different places within the same thread. This seems to be especially evident in longer stretches of PPP. A reader needs to reconstruct both the timeline and adjacency pairs that are no longer physically online. It can become confusing to outsiders who attempt to read these threads post hoc, as it is not always clear who is responding to whom. Of course, a newcomer (newbie) could catch up by reading the entire thread from the beginning – as well as other threads below similar articles – but as that might involve reading several pages of comments, it would not always be feasible. Furthermore, a reader needs to reconstruct both the timeline and adjacency pairs created by posters who are no longer physically online. Another problem is inclusion. Threads contain numerous "in-jokes" that contributors make to one another that are quite incomprehensible to a newbie. This incomprehensibility exemplifies the necessity for shared knowledge resources in the uptake of humorous discourse. Significantly, in-jokes create

susyrosy ↪ susyrosy
Best laugh I've had for ages! Ride and funny - just how I like it

susyrosy ↪ susyrosy
Rude of course

kumano ↪ susyrosy
The rudeness is all in your head, I detected none here but got what I expected, a professional objective review of the utility of a kitchen implement, you remind me of the story about Samuel Johnson who upon being congratulated by two ladies for not including any 'rude' words in his dictionary allegedly replied "What, my dears! Then you have been looking for them?"

How low the readership of this great paper must have sunk to find smut in a harmless gadget review!

AnglophileDe ↪ kumano
I blame the TV and this newfangled interwebsy thing.

FIGURE 4.7 Ping-pong-punning below the line

comity amongst those who are included and understand the jokes, but exclude those on the outside looking in. Comments amongst contributors following Samadder's articles exemplify a similar kind of exclusion that may occur in real-life joking when for lack of knowledge we may find that we are unable to be amused by the banter of others. This is especially common in inter-cultural exchanges in which there may be a lack of common ground in terms of both language and shared cultural knowledge.

There appears to be a lot of self-awareness in these comic communities as people partake in a sort of performance of the self they wish to portray online. Not only do regular contributors to Samadder's reviews consistently congratulate the journalist for his comic abilities, but they also pat each other's backs for each other's skills in creating lengthy stretches of puns connected to the gadget under scrutiny; they also post parodic poems, songs and funny stories. Much as we evaluate verbal humour in real-life discourse, we also do so online. Following one of Samadder's most popular articles, a review of the "Ham Dogger" – a device to stuff bread rolls with a sausage (I know, the mind boggles), amongst the 667 mostly witty comments that follow the article (and 438 "shares"), evaluation is rife.[9] Someone who suggests the article was "rude" – albeit in a positive sense of appreciation of its raciness – is followed by a contributor who attempts his or her hand at irony (Figure 4.7) and gains 39 "likes" followed by 21 ripostes. However, it is evident from some of the replies that not everyone picks up the irony in "How low the readership of this great paper must have sunk to find smut in a harmless gadget review!" Online, in fact, it is hard to distinguish irony from trolling. After 15 posts, the friendly banter gets very out of hand, with the ironist having to post:

> FFS! It was a fucking trolly wee joke; do you honestly have any doubt in your mind? In which case, if you do, I suggest we part paths now and we have nothing more to say to each other (that sounds harsh, but what the fuck else am I meant to do?).

Another regular to the community ends up having to act as moderator "xxx is just joining in with the joke, not taking you for serious! After all we have all read your comments over the years". This is a clear example of how it is easy to misunderstand the intent of others within an online environment where, unlike in a real-life situation, it is not easy to contextualize the surrounding milieu and thus the appropriateness of what we are about to post. Devoid of so much "real-life" information, it is challenging to understand the context sufficiently to grasp the intention of the poster.

Threads containing long stretches of PPP also appear in online newspapers during live coverage of televised events. It is, of course, fairly common for viewers to post comments on social networking platforms such as Facebook and Twitter during live television programmes so that their posts and/or tweets will appear in real time on the lower part of the TV screen as they watch. However, if we wish to examine the interaction and flow of banter between more than a couple of viewers, newspaper threads occurring in real time and at the same time as a TV programme provide a goldmine of material for humour scholars.

The examples that follow have been extracted from live feeds in *The Guardian* newspaper online in which a group of fans of *The Great British Bake Off* (GBBO) comment and generally chat about what they are watching on screen, as they watch it. As have devotees of Rhik Samadder's articles discussed previously, these *GBBO* fans have created a small online community that interacts each week during the programme in real time. Until 2016, journalist Heidi Stephens was responsible for the weekly live coverage of the programme, while for the 2016 series, Stephens was replaced by Samadder in *"The Great British Bake Off 2016 Episode x as it happened"*. At the same time as the journalist provides a commentary, in the BTL comments section readers/viewers provide their comments too.

Here too, it is clear from how contributors interact with one another in the thread that they know each other, at least virtually. In fact, they make use of communicative and politeness strategies that would be adopted in real-life conversation such as greetings, apologies and so on, just like contributors to the comment section following Samadder's articles on kitchen gadgets. The difference here is the presence of another screen, i.e. a television screen. This is because as well as a smartphone or tablet, contributors are also watching a TV screen. Of course, this is not to say that they might be watching *GBBO* from the same device from which they are typing, but even so, they are privy to a more complex text than that of a traditional newspaper article and its accompanying photographs. *GBBO* itself sports dialogues coupled with moving images as well as written text, illustrations, music, special effects, graphics, etc.

Figure 4.8 illustrates an example of PPP captured from a special episode of *GBBO* that involves competitors making a flan.[10] We have a rather different style of wordplay from those examined so far as one participant opens up play by simply playing with the word "flan" – "Isn't flan a lovely word flanflanflanflanflan" to which another responds "Not as good as tart tarttarttarttarttart" while a third joins in with an attempt to joke on the term "pie". While we are not strictly in the realm of puns, we are still dealing with humorous discourse and wordplay.

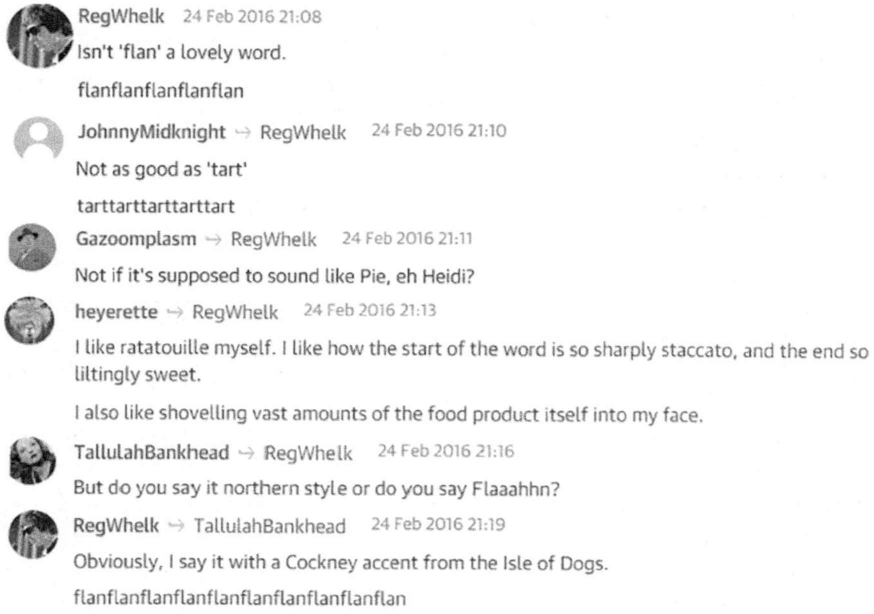

The language of jokes online   135

RegWhelk   24 Feb 2016 21:08
Isn't 'flan' a lovely word.

flanflanflanflanflan

JohnnyMidknight ↪ RegWhelk   24 Feb 2016 21:10
Not as good as 'tart'

tarttarttarttarttart

Gazoomplasm ↪ RegWhelk   24 Feb 2016 21:11
Not if it's supposed to sound like Pie, eh Heidi?

heyerette ↪ RegWhelk   24 Feb 2016 21:13
I like ratatouille myself. I like how the start of the word is so sharply staccato, and the end so liltingly sweet.

I also like shovelling vast amounts of the food product itself into my face.

TallulahBankhead ↪ RegWhelk   24 Feb 2016 21:16
But do you say it northern style or do you say Flaaahhn?

RegWhelk ↪ TallulahBankhead   24 Feb 2016 21:19
Obviously, I say it with a Cockney accent from the Isle of Dogs.

flanflanflanflanflanflanflanflanflan

FIGURE 4.8   Ping-pong-punning below the line ("Bake off")

A fourth participant joins the fray by analysing her love of the term "ratatouille". The entire exchange consists of 6 moves made by 5 players in the space of 11 minutes. The players are there online throughout the exchange as each move follows another in rapid succession. Journalist Heidi is slightly confused as to what to call the dish the contestants are baking, "I would argue strongly that a pie without a top is a tart, or maybe a flan, but definitely not a pie", she writes. In fact, the third contributor does not engage in wordplay but directs his riposte to "Not as good as 'tart'" to Heidi, "Not if it's supposed to sound like pie, eh Heidi?" However, a more traditional "punning" exchange occurs towards the close of the thread when one participant hopes that life is "flan-tastic" for the others, which is followed by the response "flan-queue very much".

Contributors to all the threads described are very much aware of their linguistic flair for punning and wordplay. They encourage one another to play with words and they constantly evaluate each other on their display of clever banter. This type of linguistic activity highlights the extent to which the internet is language driven.

Hashtaggery

Twitter is a social network that allows users to post short messages known as "tweets" that are restricted to 140 characters. In a sense, this limit in the number of characters is a challenge in itself, a sort of a game. In addition, Twitter users signal messages according to subject matter with an appropriate hashtag – # – followed by a word or phrase. Many hashtags promote largely humorous tweets:

#crazy #epic #friend #friends #fun #funny #funnypictures #haha #hilarious #humor #instafun #instagood #instahappy #joke #jokes #joking #laugh #laughing #lmao #lmfao #lol #photooftheday #silly #TagsForLikes #tweegram #wacky #witty

However, if as Highfield (2015) asserts, "play and silliness are popular strategies for the coverage and presentation of the topical and mundane online" and Twitter is a suitable vehicle for presenting "the topical", it follows that all that is newsworthy (and boringly un-newsworthy) will incite joking. Unsurprisingly, the subject of politics and those engaged in politics takes up a large amount of space on this platform and Twitter hashtags can be inventive, funny and politically charged in order to target those in power. Numerous hashtags in 2017, for example, target President Donald Trump, such as #AnnoyTrumpIn3Words. As the hashtag suggests, contributors have to think up ways to restrict their badinage to a mere three words in a manner that should supposedly annoy the President.[11] The tweets for this hashtag include references to the notorious wall the President wishes to build between the USA and Mexico, his dislike of minority groups as well as his infamous hairstyle (Figure 4.9).

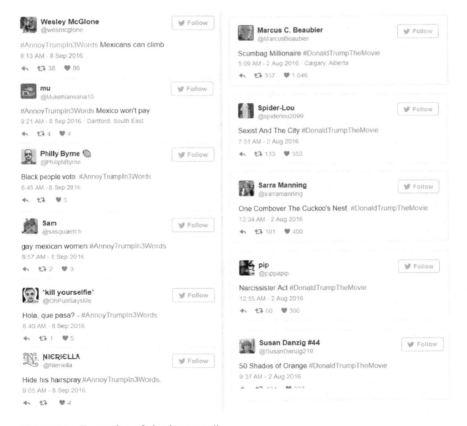

FIGURE 4.9 Examples of "hashtaggery"

Another of the abundant humorous hashtags regarding Donald Trump is #DonaldTrumpTheMovie.[12] Here users go to town with parodic tweets that include "Sexist And The City #DonaldTrumpTheMovie" that obtained 353 likes; "Scumbag Millionaire #DonaldTrumpTheMovie" that gained 1,046 likes and "One Combover The Cuckoo's Nest #DonaldTrumpTheMovie" with 400 likes (Figure 4.9). What is significant is the number of times users "re-tweet" these messages to other users. The "Scumbag Millionaire" tweet was shared 357 times. If each person who receives the tweet shares it with at least one person who in turn will re-tweet to others, it is easy to see how virulent these verbal gags can become. If it is true that humans are physiologically wired both to connect with others and to laugh with others (Hurley *et al.* 2013; Provine 2000), it should come as no surprise that someone who thinks up or reads something funny should want to connect with others through the wireless medium so they will laugh at this too. Even though another person may be on the other side of the planet, they will laugh at something that we have generated, and above all, that we both support – especially in the case of political banter. If once we would have casually slipped, "Have you heard the one about the POTUS?" into our conversation and thereby gained consensus through the affiliative laugh of our interlocutor, today we have the means to greatly multiply the number of people who will be amused by what amuses us within a few seconds. Of course, we need to be careful in the face of an unknown audience. The following exchange was recorded from naturally occurring conversation:

Initiator: "What's rich and thick and full of clots?"
Participant 1: "I've no idea".
Participant 2: "I don't think I'm going to like this".

Chiaro 1992:104

The second participant anticipates that the joke she is about to hear will criticize the Tory party with which she sympathizes. In real life, we can put a stop to such awkwardness quite quickly, but online, where users are often invisible and protected by pseudonyms, a gaffe may easily offend and in a worse scenario possibly lead to verbal aggression, hate speech and even much worse scenarios. In fact, there are numerous closed groups on Facebook where people with similar extremist political ideas post humorous materials knowing that others will appreciate them because they are politically like-minded. In the privacy of a closed group, these people who are on the same wavelength may joke to their hearts' content knowing they will not irritate or shock those of differing political tendencies, neither will they themselves be attacked by those who do not share their points of view or sense of humour.

However, seeing our posts shared and liked makes us feel good about ourselves. Studies suggest that Facebook activity stimulates the release of dopamine, a "feel good" chemical in our brains. Making others laugh, seeing that others "like" what we post, appears to give us a chemical high.[13] Unknowingly, the internet has provided us with the tools for positive face strategy.

Finally, it is traditional to poke fun at the establishment, institutions and especially at leaders (see Chapter 1), but what such hashtags allow us to do is, first, to rise to an intellectual challenge (e.g. to mock a President in three words or manipulate a film title). Second, hashtags render our output visible to thousands of other users in real time. As we can see, then, the language of jokes is no different from what it has always been. However, the many ways and modes we convey jokes has changed, and perhaps it has never been so true that the medium is the message.

The hashtag, however, is not simply restricted to categorizing or tagging tweets on the Twitter platform, after migrating to Facebook and Instagram it has now made its way into everyday speech. Rather like the term "lol" that is no longer limited to online communication but is also used in speech, it is quite common amongst younger people to punctuate their speech with the term "hashtag". This migration from internet to real life exemplifies how writing and speech influence each other. If tweets (and short message texts in general) exemplify speech in writing – in the sense that although technically they are written they actually mirror speech rather than writing – it should come as no surprise that people utter the word "hashtag" too. As, in the past, a more formal style of writing favoured a more formal manner of speech; today the opposite occurs with the informality of much written online language seeping into speech.

When the verbal meets the visual: in and around internet memes

The computer-mediated humour we have looked at so far has been purely verbal in form. Online communities argue and chat with words, and the basics of Twitter are set within a character count limitation. Let us now move on to consider what may well be the most popular form of online humour, namely the so-called "internet meme".

Richard Dawkins (1976) first introduced the concept of the cultural meme as "a unit of cultural transmission, or a unit of imitation", more specifically a sort of behavioural equivalent of a biological gene. Dawkins' examples of cultural memes include, amongst other things, tunes, styles of dress, styles of architecture and catch phrases. For instance, in the 1960s, Mary Quant invented the mini-skirt and very soon women and girls the world over were wearing similar skirts. These millions of copied skirts were not identical to Quant's original prototype, but in essence, they were simply different versions of the same short skirt. If we compare the memetic component of the mini-skirt to the biological theory of natural selection, we see that mini-skirts vary in shape, colour and even length; people replicate them easily worldwide and they respond positively to the concept of "fitness". Mini-skirts are "fit" because they successfully "competed" with other objects of fashion to survive and endure through the 1960s, 1970s and beyond. Mini-skirts survive within a cultural meme pool, as opposed to a biological genepool. Eventually, the midi and the maxi-skirt replaced the mini, but Quant's short skirt continued to evolve and exists to the present day, thereby underscoring its cultural fitness. Jokes, especially those belonging to a cycle (e.g. lightbulb jokes, blonde jokes etc.) are instances of culturally transmitted memes.

The world online is rife with memetic activity. When we think of memes today, we might visualize stock images of personalities in particular poses, funny videos and different versions of the same humorous picture with a clever, but always divergent, caption materializing on our smartphones via Facebook, Twitter or WhatsApp. These memes become viral as they quickly spread through the internet. In the same way as Dawkins' social memes (such as the mini-skirt) caught on and spread very quickly, humorous internet memes act in a similar way. Bjarneskans *et al.* (n.d.) compare contemporary memes online to more traditional examples of memetic texts such as the "Kilroy was here" graffiti of the 1970s and 1980s in which the fact that the Kilroy phrase was actually scrawled on walls was part of the message itself (see Chiaro 1992). Seeing "Kilroy was here" in different unrelated places around the world was likely to raise a smile of recognition. Why write on a wall? "Because it's there", declares a famous graffito.[14] The same is true of internet memes. The fact that memes travel and are spread online is actually part of the message. lolcats and gifs, stock character memes and photoshopped politicians can only exist through the medium of the internet. The effect of the image alone would not be the same in a newspaper or on a TV programme – also because of the fact that "old" media do not allow us to share images in the same way, with so many people and with such immediacy. If in the past, we would need to travel widely to experience the wealth of the world's graffiti, nowadays the digital equivalent of graffiti comes to us. Furthermore, this content no longer comes to us on a distant screen, but on our smartphones – in our pockets, in our handbags and in our hands, thus almost becoming part of the private space of our bodies. We live in a face down society, connected to each other and constantly checking our electronic gadgets in fear of missing out – FOMO. This is in contrast to what was once a face up society before we engaged with each other electronically. Although this memetic behaviour occurs privately, in reality it is inextricably linked to an extremely public space that is the online environment, so that public and private spheres mingle and merge. We laugh alone and we laugh together – albeit at a distance in space, and probably in a time lapse of anything from a split second onwards. Last, but certainly not least, it is important to note that users can create their own memes and, above all, adapt pre-existing memes with the aid of many available tools that generate them.

We choose the people with whom we decide to share a humorous meme and we do so because we believe that they will share our sense of humour. We feel we are socially gelling with the recipient by saying, "Hey, you will find X, Y and Z funny/silly/hilarious too. You and I are alike", thereby creating more positive face politeness. If we were to print out a few images of a popular stock character meme, say that of Gene Wilder in the persona of Willy Wonka, leaning on his hand with

FIGURE 4.10   Manipulation of an image macro

a clever catchphrase framing his face and then hand out the copies to members of our family, it would not be the same as posting the meme on Facebook. Similarly, posting on Facebook would not be the same as forwarding the image to members of our family via their smartphones. To understand this, we return to the ideas of Marshall McLuhan. These memes are inseparable from their online abode. Consider the meta-joke within a meme of Willy Wonka with the caption reading, "So, I'm a gif now? I guess pictures aren't enough" (Figure 4.10).

In the same way, millennials tease their elders in scores of posts such as the one entitled, "Oh dear, Dad tried to print a video" that features the image macro of a scrunched up sheet of paper with a blank square with a play button in the middle framing Deep Purple's *Smoke on the Water*. The post simultaneously mocks Baby Boomers' IT inadequacy and their taste in music that has not changed since the 1970s (Figure 4.11).[15]

Still, one significant difference between the example of the mini-skirt as a meme and many internet memes is their restricted fitness. It is unlikely that we will still be laughing at Theresa May and Jeremy Corbyn in the parody of the viral *Thor* trailer in 2027.[16] Just as the seemingly endless memes regarding Silvio Berlusconi's hair transplant have lost their edge, so will those regarding Donald Trump's quiff and orange tinted skin. This is because an important feature of internet memes is their here and nowness. Unlike the possibilities for updating the traditional targets of oral jokes occurring in old media, it would be difficult to find a way to update these memes. We might easily substitute the names of the President, politician and the Pope in the parachute joke in Chapter 1 with the names of those holding the same positions of authority today. The same cannot be done with these somewhat fleeting images referring to a particular moment

FIGURE 4.11 Sharing "deep purple"

in political time. Crucially, internet memes are part of our consumer throwaway society and cannot be refreshed or updated precisely because of their specific link to the present moment. Moreover, a meme that is frozen in the moment clashes with the concept of "fitness" as, on the one hand, a meme such as the *Thor* trailer has 2.5 million views; on the other, it is likely to be outdated long before 2027. When we look back at the early internet parodies of the post-9/11 warmongering in the form of movie posters featuring then President George Bush and his entourage, we find they have lost their relevance and hence their humorous impact.

Shifman, the scholar who has devoted much research to computer-mediated humour, defines the internet meme as: "(a) a group of digital items sharing common characteristics of content, form, and/or stance, which (b) were created with awareness of each other, and (c) were circulated, imitated, and/or transformed via the internet by many users" (2014: 41). She then divides them into nine meme genres that she places under three different headings: "documentation of real life moments", "explicit manipulation of mass-mediated content" and "a new universe of digital and meme-oriented content" (2014: 18). Shifman does not claim these categories to be either comprehensive or watertight as there are many fuzzy edges between one category and the next. We also need to consider cross-pollination where user generated content might appear alongside commercial production of memes (Weitz 2017). However, Shifman's categories are a good starting point to attempt to unravel some of the humorous content roaming around the internet. There is an immeasurable amount of humorous material online and much of it is memetic in nature. In order to obtain a representative sample of all possible instances it would require extensive data mining that is beyond the scope of this chapter. Thus, what follows is an overview of a self-selected assortment of internet memes that were popular around the time of writing.

Real-life moments

Of course, social network sites are places where users may present to others whatever they please about themselves whether in writing or in the form of a snapshot or a video, or indeed a mixture of all three. Cameras on smartphones not only allow users to take photos and make videos but they also allow them to manipulate and enhance results. Users can upload their photos and videos onto platforms such as YouTube and Facebook or simply send them to family and friends. However, apart from cute images and videos of babies, toddlers and pets, there are several other categories of funny "real-life moments" that users can generate, share and with which they allow others to align with them.

Countless compilations of video clips posted on YouTube are of the "funny moment" variety, namely home videos of people having accidents while carrying out everyday tasks. People fall off trees, bump into walls and belly flop into swimming pools. These slipping-on-a-banana-skin moments are funny because the victim is not seriously hurt and usually participates in the laughter thereby signalling that it is OK for others to laugh too. We, the audience know that all is well and good with the victims and that we are free to laugh with them.

Shifman includes photofads within her "real-life moments" category (2013). Photofads refer to a sort of online game in which people take a photo of themselves posing in a certain way before sharing the picture online. There have been a number of fads in which people take photos of themselves "planking" (balancing face-down in a plank position); "owling" (crouching like an owl in odd places); posing as mannequins or even pretending they are dead. These poses are doubly memetic, both in the act of people copying each other's poses and in the continuous repetition of the appearance of the pose itself online, as users attempt to trump each other as they appear in different environments or else think up the most extreme variation of the pose. In terms of meme, the fitness of each photofad is short-lived.

I would like to include photobombing in this category too. Photobombing involves accidentally or purposely putting oneself into the view of someone taking a photo, usually by jumping up behind those posing. In this sense, photobombing is a sort of virtual practical joke. Whether purposeful or accidental, the photo will go online and the effect is comic. Well-known personalities tend to engage in photobombing (e.g. Benedict Cumberbatch and Donald Trump) as they know that their popularity will gain them numerous "likes". Whether this was the intention of Queen Elizabeth II when she photobombed a couple of Australian athletes taking a selfie is dubious; however, the snapshot did go viral (Figure 4.12). The smile on Her Majesty's face reflects her awareness of what she is doing thereby increasing the comic intent of the photobomb.

Related to photobombing are occurrences of people posing for a group photograph and deliberately disrupting it by surreptitiously making a "V sign" or, as Silvio Berlusconi was prone to do, the cuckold sign behind the head of a personality, without them being aware that this is happening. Again, these photos go viral very quickly but just as quickly lose their impact.

The language of jokes online **143**

FIUGRE 4.12   Queen Elizabeth II photobombing Australian hockey players' selfie

Challenges

Diverse online challenges fall into the category of "real-life documentation". The "ice-bucket challenge" of the summer of 2014 involved people throwing a bucket of ice and water over their own or another person's head in order to raise money worldwide for research into motor neurone disease. Numerous heads of state and media personalities took part in the challenge together with members of the public. The point of the challenge was to film and then post the event online for others to view and enjoy. Obviously, personalities like Bill Clinton and Italy's Matteo Renzi received more views than my (not so famous) brother Joe Chiaro did.

Manipulated content

This type of content may well make up the bulk of memes on the internet. Taking an image, or making a video clip and transforming it, even minimally to humorous ends, we create what appears to be the type of humour that many of us are engaging with right now. These visual/verbal memes are easily accessible, they simply arrive on our gadgets, we swipe right in order to access them, we consume them, share them and move on to the next memes that have landed in our pockets. Being mainly visual, unlike verbally dense written texts, memes do not require much cognitive effort in order to be understood and appreciated. Memes are a reflection of a consumer society that is visually oriented and fast moving. I would go as far as defining traditional jokes in terms of slow humour, while memes exemplify fast humour – or better still, McHumor. We see them; we laugh and move on to a newer more topical meme. However, it is nonetheless essentially verbal language that surrounds, sustains, supports and contextualizes these memes.

Churchill's notorious "V sign", Fonzie's (Henry Winkler's) "thumbs up" and Einstein sticking out his tongue are frozen photographic moments that are continually replicated online.[17] These images are reminiscent of the works of art by Andy Warhol in which he would create a pattern by repeating the same picture over and over. Likewise, the same, or almost the same, image of an iconic personality will endlessly be repeated across the web. However, once verbal content is added to the visuals, they cross over into Shifman's second category of "explicit manipulation of mass-mediated content".

An "image macro" is a broad term to describe a picture superimposed with text for humorous effect. These macros can range from the famous image of Einstein writing on a blackboard or sticking his tongue out to scores of stock characters from stage and screen, the world's political arena and beyond. The Willy Wonka/Gene Wilder meme (487,000 Google hits) is a classic meme featuring "condescending/creepy" Wonka making a sarcastic remark.[18] The four images presented in Figure 4.10 show a few possibilities of the way a stock meme may be varied and manipulated. The image macro with the reference to Harry Potter represents the meme's baseline. Wonka is simply making a sarcastic remark as is expected of the meme. Countless images of Wonka in the same stance exist online. Only the verbal text differs from image to image as he makes a different sarcastic remark. A child dressed up and, in a sense, photofadding Wonka and Johnny Depp, the actor who played the role of Willy Wonka in the film's remake, is not only a physical manipulation of the original meme but a memetic imitation that straddles both Shifman's previous category of "explicit manipulation of mass-mediated content" with her category of memes that refer to real-life moments. Lastly, the meme featuring Johnny Depp as Willy Wonka literally mirrors the original meme – the actor is actually positioned in reverse as though looking at Wilder – making a sarcastic and, at the same time, intertextual, remark. These are just four varieties of a single image macro. Multiplying this by the number of innumerable users and we begin to have an idea of the breadth and scope of the phenomenon.

Memes as ethnic jokes

Shifman highlights the low percentage of ethnic jokes in a web-based sample she examines (2007: 202) explaining how this may be due to changes in society that now views such jokes as being politically incorrect. There are internet image macros that target just about every ethnic group on the planet. However, those targeting Jews and the Italians are, generally speaking, probably those in the worst possible taste imaginable. Those targeting the Jewish people are usually Holocaust jokes, those about Italians range from mocking their obsession with food to their participating in organized crime. While in the main Jews as a people have overall trumped Holocaust humour by creating their own jokes and laughing at themselves, Italians are yet to do so. Mintz (1998) has outlined four developmental phases in ethnic humour. In the first stage, the central group is critical of the peripheral group via jokes. During the second stage, the peripheral group becomes critical of itself by telling self-deprecating jokes that target aspects of its own culture. By the third stage, the peripheral group can realistically laugh at itself. It is not until stage four that those on the periphery can joke about the centre. Jewish humour is definitely at stage three by now – and possibly beyond. Italian humour is stuck at stage one.

Here I examine three sets of memes that target Italians; those regarding what is commonly considered to be Italians' excessive use of gesticulation, those regarding their obsession with food, and jokes about their military cowardice.

These three subsets of memes in fact are no more than an online equivalent of traditional ethnic jokes that target Italians, as they play on exactly the same stereotypes exploited in film, television and comedy in general, things like a love for food, the importance of family, military inefficacy, organized crime and so on. An especially virulent internet meme that produces 1.35 million hits on Google is "How Italians do things" and features people (Italians) carrying out a range of everyday actions while holding their hand in a finger purse stance (Figure 4.13). This is a typical Italian gesture in which the fingertips of either hand are brought together upright and pursed to form a cup, while the hand is waved up and down. The gesture can mean a variety of things, but Italians tend to use it especially to implore, "What on earth are you talking about?" or "What the hell do you want from me?" The image macro simply consists of a close up of the gesture and the most basic meme features this image and a caption declaring that "Italian speaking mode" is "on" thereby informing recipients that knowing the gesture is all that is required in order to communicate in Italian. However, users replicate the basic meme and apply it to various contexts so that the gesture appears in a variety of more complex environments. In the simplest emulations of the hand gesture, the memes consist of selfies of hands cupped in the "Italian gesture" posing while playing the guitar or the piano, reading a book, holding a mug of coffee or a smartphone. The suggestion is, of course, ridiculous as none of these actions would actually succeed with hands held in that position, but the meme feeds into a typical stereotype regarding Italians who are allegedly unable to speak without moving their hands. Furthermore, users create other memes within this sub-genre by manipulating images of objects into the shape of the hand gesture to create a set of Italian objects.

However, users create other memes within this sub-genre by manipulating images of objects into the shape of the hand gesture to create a set of Italian objects. There is an "Italian fork" in the form of a pursed hand and an "Italian plug" in which its three prongs meet, while a cat (overlapping with the LOLCat category?) illustrates how Italian felines argue by moving their paws backwards and forwards.[19]

So far so good; however, many memes feature the hand gesture positioned over and covering another body part (Figure 4.13). By superimposing a photo of the gesture onto a pair of feet we see "how Italians walk"; a de-humanized mother and baby whose heads are replaced with hands represents an "Italian mother [who] holds her newborn child for the first time". To underscore the

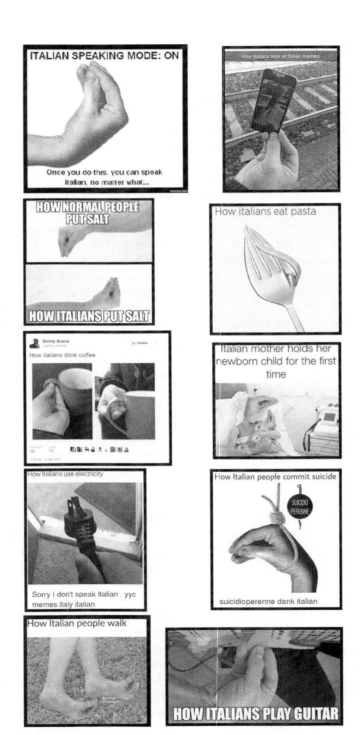

FIGURE 4.13 A selection of internet memes that parody Italian hand gestures

lifetime brevity of these memes, this Italian gesture meme peaked in popularity online on 15 March 2017 and only two days later began to be considered as being overused.[20] On the other hand, these memes remain online long after they go out of fashion amongst younger internet geeks who presumably created the memes in the first place.

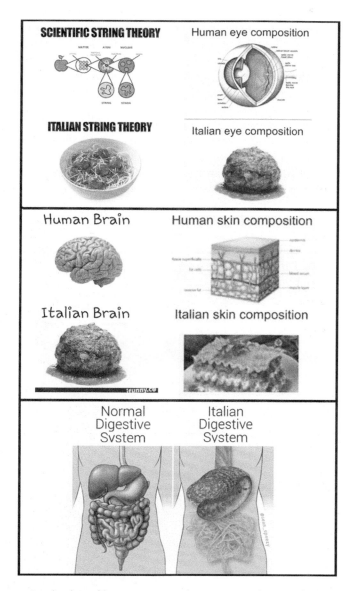

FIGURE 4.14 A selection of internet memes that compare "human" body parts to "Italian" body parts

148 The language of jokes online

A different set of memes pokes fun at Italians' relationship with food. One image macro consists of the image of a plate of pasta with a superimposed punning caption that is heavily dependent on the stereotypical Italian-American accent that reads, "Did you hear about the Italian chef that died" – "He pasta away". Again, the term "impasta" ("imposter") is superimposed over an image macro of a box of vegan pasta while another meme features a T-shirt with a print of tomatoes on the front with the slogan that reads "Legalize marinara". Another common "Italians be like" image macro displays enormous spreads of food captioned with phrases like "We are just having a small meal" or "I don't think I made enough food" to hone in on Italians' obsession with abundant food. Again, an image of hordes of people is captioned with "the family are coming over". Essentially, these memes can be pun-based as in the "pasta/marinara" examples, or they can play on very specific clichés about Italians by juxtaposing images of amplification (of food, people, etc.) with something an Italian might actually say.

In a sub-category of food related memes we find text book illustrations of different parts of the human body, e.g. the eye, the skin, blood cells, etc. The illustrations are accordingly labelled "the human eye", "human skin", "human blood cells", etc. and are set against corresponding images of an Italian food item so that the dermis is compared to lasagne, the eye to a meatball, blood cells to slices of salami, etc. (Figure 4.14). Notably the Italian body part/foods are not compared to say, US

FIGURE 4.15 A selection of internet memes regarding Italian military

body parts, but to "human" parts. Thus, as in some Italian hand gesture memes, Italians are dehumanized in these last memes, which are neither innocent nor jovial.

Finally, a set of very nonsensical memes in which slices of pizza topped with tomato and cheese replace warships and tanks seem to have supplanted the classic joke regarding Italian military inadequacy (Figure 4.15). These memes first appeared in January 2017. The simplest meme replaces the wings of a fighter plane with slices of pizza and a donkey's saddle is replaced with a pizza to represent the Italian cavalry. However, in more surreal memes, triangular pizza slices represent soldiers or warships. As with other memes discussed earlier, they pivot on the dehumanization of Italians, especially when a scantily dressed woman is transformed into a slice of pizza representing the disguise of an Italian soldier. Over and above the ethnic slant of the memes, it is interesting how traditionally women are seen as food, animals or body parts. Here too we have instances of good humour, but bad taste.

Exclusive to the internet

Some internet humour has no real-world equivalent. Shifman includes Rage Comics in her category of a "new universe of meme-oriented content" referring to forms of humour that were born online, thrive online but have no correspondence with reality. Rage comics consist of comic strips containing "rage faces" that are crudely drawn, scribbled sketches of faces or stick people created with

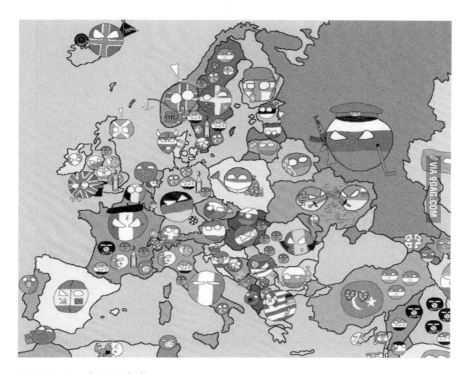

FIGURE 4.16 Countryballs

software like MS Paint. Each face represents a different emotion. These comic strips depict a real-life experience that ends in a punchline. While at the time of writing these rage faces appear to have passed their peak in popularity, some of the faces like the "Troll face" and the "LOL face" are still prevalent, both online and, as we shall see, in real life.

"Countryballs" are a similar phenomenon. The first countryball to appear was Polandball, a cartoon character drawn in the shape of a ball with the white and red colour schemes of the Polish flag. Polandball wants to go into space but feels threatened by Germany and Russia. Soon other countryballs appeared all in the guise of different national flags. The countryball for the USA, which wears the stars and stripes and cool sunglasses, is egocentric, with no idea of anything that happens outside the USA but always ready to rush in to bring "freedoms" whenever required. The UK ball is a man donning a top hat and a monocle, nostalgic for his lost empire. France always surrenders immediately; the Netherlands is usually tripping on drugs and loves tulips and windmills; and so on. Therefore, in a sense we have (yet another) online equivalent of Davies' ethnic jokes. Figure 4.16 illustrates a Countryball map of Europe in which several

FIGURE 4.17 A selection of lolcat memes

subjects are actually similar to rage balls, as opposed to the more usual well-drawn and precise countryballs.

Finally, this category includes the phenomenon of lolcats and "animal humour" in general. As we saw earlier, according to Critchley, when animals act in a way that mirrors human behaviour they are seen as endearing. We therefore smile at photos of cats that according to the person who posted the snapshot, look like famous personalities or the "bread catting" meme in which kittens are photographed with their heads poking through a slice of bread.

As cat owners know, cats may often take on a stance of quasi-superiority as in the image of the "uninterested cat" or they may position themselves in odd places (Figure 4.17), which is amusing enough to trigger a meme. Of course, the addition of a cat-based pun enhances the fun, especially when we consider cats' affected, grammatically incorrect speech present in many memes.

Criss-cross humour

Communication online is not restricted to bimodal means alone. We have seen the emulation of real-life conversation in threads and feeds; we have seen purely visual clips, gifs and images, as well as visual content coupled with verbal elements typical of memes. However, what is particular about Web 2.0 is that users themselves can participate and become part of the content they are posting. The baseline for this could be the vlog (a video blog) in which users can see the speaker instruct viewers on how to do something – this can be anything from playing the guitar to making a cake – and as s/he speaks viewers can actually see what s/he is doing. Therefore, here we have different, distinct narratives all rolled into one. The viewer can see the vlogger, listen to the instructions and, simultaneously, see what s/he is actually doing.

A phenomenon that takes multimodality one step further in terms of humour consists of people who report something funny that they have seen elsewhere online but instead of simply sharing what they have found, they elaborate and comment on it. As we have seen, we tend to laugh at the mistakes made by others (Chapter 1) and that, furthermore, accidental slips of the tongue are very similar to deliberately invented wordplay – otherwise so-called "Freudian slips" would cease to amuse. Hockett provides an interesting example of the comic self-awareness of a slip of the tongue made by two colleagues as they are driving to work in Berkeley:

> "This is how we go to Berkland and Oakley? – Erkland and Boakley? – no, Berkland and Erkley? – Darn it Oakland and Berkeley!"

The first slip is an example of metathesis in which the speaker accidentally inverts the first syllable of the name of each suburb, while in the second accidental slip he shifts the first sound of the name of the first town onto the second (wrong) town name. Hockett (1977) suggests that once the speaker is aware of his mistake, recognizes its comic potential, and deliberately plays on it by twisting the initial syllables in different ways. Hockett classifies the example as a "half witticism". Accidental jokes such as this are formally similar to deliberate jokes. However, in the same way we can make people laugh by reporting an amusing incident, we can also provoke laughter by reporting a linguistic faux pas made by someone else, as Hockett himself does with the example he provides. In fairness, Hockett is making a serious point, but he is also amusing his readers.

In old media, people would send examples of amusing utterances made by small children or ambiguous writings that they had seen to special columns in the press where they would be published (see Chiaro 1992: 21–4). These examples allowed readers to laugh *with* the person who discovered the linguistic mistake and *at* the "culprit" of the mistake. In new media, we find dozens of updated examples of this.

As we saw previously, Alonzo Lerone posts a wide variety of humorous materials on various online platforms. What is of particular interest here is his reporting and comments of a (memetic) online phenomenon known as "food fails" from celebrity chef Gordon Ramsay's Twitter account. Ramsay who has 4.93 million followers appears to have quite a sense of humour. Ramsay's followers will typically tweet a photograph of a dish they, or someone they know, have just prepared together with queries such as "@gordonramsey what do you think of my uncle's chicken?" or @gordonramsey Rate my cream cheese pasta", etc. The images of the dishes that posters query are anything but mouth-watering and Ramsay will typically reply in a very sarcastic or ironic manner expressing his disgust directly.[21] Obviously, Ramsay does not encourage people to post photos of successful dishes because that would not allow him to respond in a humorous manner. Now what Lerone does is to make a compilation of both users' queries and Ramsay's responses and comment upon them.[22] Followers see the meme, the photo of the dish and accompanying tweet that Lerone reads aloud. He reads both question and response in exaggerated tones thereby adding to the amusement of his followers who see both tweets and Lerone. He also uses a laugh voice as he tries hard not to laugh, and will often cover his face. When someone asks Ramsay what he thinks of flight food and the chef answers "I'd rather walk!", we can see and hear Lerone in fits of laughter – and that is contagious. Ramsay is funny per se, he will pun or will just be downright rude, but it is Lerone's laughter and comments that more than double the fun.

Lerone is criss-crossing categories. He is using tweets (someone else's) that in turn rely on user generated content from elsewhere that he points out to his remote audience. He films himself reading out the tweets and reacts. His followers then react to his reaction. This chain reaction continues in the copied version posted online by his imitator.

Meme transference

Finally, Figure 4.18 is the ultimate example of criss-crossing. It illustrates the way in which internet memes transfer, almost by osmosis, into real life. The sweatshirt

The language of jokes online 153

FIGURE 4.18 An example of osmotic meme transference

of the girl in the photograph (taken in Berlin) has the image of a rage face printed on the back.

While we are used to merchandise that cashes in on box office successes, such as products on sale at Disney stores that sell goods that reference the latest Disney film, at one point someone came up with the idea of making money by creating goods that mirror the kind of things that thrive on the web. A commercial website like "Red Bubble" sells everything from clothes and stationery to home furnishings that cash in on of the popularity of the internet meme. These items sport either a meme proper, or else a reference to a meme. The site sells T-shirts with the phrase "Meme Queen" or "Meme Lord" printed on them; duvet covers repeat the word "meme" dozens of times, mugs that display puns like "You meme a lot to me", etc. In addition, merchandise with popular rage faces, especially the troll and LOL faces, are also available.

This merchandise exemplifies how what originated as an internet phenomenon cross-pollinates into the real world. Take for example T-shirts that sport the phrase "All your base are belong to us". This has crossed over into the real world from a video game called *Zero Wing*. The translational error found in the European version of the original Japanese version became an internet meme that was especially popular in the early to mid 2000s. In 2006, when YouTube had taken down the site for maintenance, the phrase "ALL YOUR VIDEOS ARE BELONG TO US" was placed below the logo leading users to believe that the site had been hacked. YouTube responded to these rumours in "Engrish" with the phrase: "No, we haven't be hacked. Get a sense of humor".

Notes

1 At the time of writing, technology is moving towards (what might be called) Web 3.0 that "will be more connected, open, and intelligent, with semantic web technologies, distributed databases, natural language processing, machine learning, machine reasoning, and autonomous agents" (Spivak 2017).
2 *Modern Family*, "Connection Lost" Season 6, Episode 16. First aired 15 February 2015.
3 *Black Mirror*, created by Charlie Brooker. Series 1 and 2 broadcast by Channel 4 (2011–15) and Series 3 and 4 (2016) by *Netflix*.
4 See Alonzo Lerone's Facebook page at www.facebook.com/ItsAlonzo/?hc_location=ufi.
5 See: www.facebook.com/OfficialMonstah/videos/vb.192772410856761/1047516225 382371/?type=2&theater&notif_t=comment_mention&notif_id=1493550164206653.
6 Thread no longer available but consulted at www.theguardian.com/business/econo mics-blog/2016/jul/26/Italy-economics-banks-loans-crisis-europe on 26 July 2016.
7 Thread including comment available at: www.theguardian.com/commentisfree/picture/ 2017/jan/31/steve-bell-on-enoch-powell-and-brexit-cartoon. Retrieved 1 February 2017.
8 Article and thread available at: www.theguardian.com/lifeandstyle/2017/feb/22/kitchen-gadgets-review-coconut-grater-ugly-pleasure-flesh. Retrieved 14 March 2017.
9 Rhik Samadder, "Kitchen gadgets review: The Ham Dogger – possibilities as endless as a nightmare". *The Guardian* 15 March 2017. Available at: www.theguardian.com/ lifeandstyle/2017/mar/15/kitchen-gadgets-review-the-ham-dogger-possibilities-as-endless-as-a-nightmare#comments. Retrieved 23 April 2017.
10 *The Great Sport Relief Bake Off*, Episode four – as it happened. Available at: www. theguardian.com/tv-and-radio/live/2016/feb/24/the-great-sport-relief-bake-off-episode-four-follow-it-live#comments. Retrieved 16 August 2016.
11 Ryan Barrell 2016, "Tweeters share hilarious ways they would annoy Donald Trump with just three words". *Huffpost Comedy UK* 8 September. Available at: www.huffing tonpost.co.uk/entry/annoy-donald-trump-funny-tweets_uk_57d13953e4b0ac5a02 dd6306. Retrieved 23 April 2017.
12 Ryan Barrell 2016. "Twitter is suggesting hilarious titles for 'Donald Trump the Movie'". *Huffpost Comedy UK*. 2 August. Available at: www.huffingtonpost.co.uk/entry/ donald-trump-the-movie-hashtag_uk_57a0492ee4b0459aae5e1b24. Retrieved 23 April 2017.
13 Libby-Jane Charleston 2016. "How Facebook is making us fearful". *Huffington Post* (Australia). Available at: www.huffingtonpost.com.au/2016/07/03/how-facebook-is-making-us-fearful/. Retrieved 25 April 2017.
14 Roger Kilroy. 1984. *Graffiti. The Scrawl of the Wild*. London: Corgi, p. 9.

15 See "Oh dear, dad tried to print a video". Available at: http://imgur.com/gallery/NDX nJqe. Retrieved 26 April 2017.
16 "Snap Election – coming soon". Available at: www.facebook.com/www.JOE.co.uk/videos/878259955671405/?pnref=story. Retrieved 25 April 2017.
17 *Happy Days* was a popular US sitcom that was broadcast from 1974 to 1984.
18 For the technicalities and further details see "Condescending Wonka/Creepy Wonka" at *Know Your Meme*. Available at: http://knowyourmeme.com/memes/condescending-wonka-creepy-wonka. Retrieved 26 April 2017.
19 See https://media.gihpy.com/media/DoJreqKz4McZG/giphy.gif. Retrieved 24 August 2017.
20 See http://knowyourmeme.com/memes/how-italians-do-things. Retrieved 27 April 2017.
21 Gordon Ramsay at Twitter available at: https://twitter.com/gordonramsay?lang=it.
22 Alonzo Lerone available at: www.facebook.com/ItsAlonzo/. Retrieved 30 April 2017.

CLOSING REMARKS

Ever since humans began to write, they wrote on walls and much of what they scribbled was supposed to be funny. According to a wall in Pompeii, we discover that in AD 79, *Festus hic futuit cum sodalibus* – "Here is where Festus did it with friends". Again, in Chancery Lane, London in 1719 someone wrote, "Here did I lay my Celia down; / I got the pox and she got half a crown". More recent lavatory graffiti in the UK includes "Beware of limbo dancers" written at the bottom of cubicle doors and the punning OOAQICI82QB4IP, a traditional graffito to be found in women's public conveniences. However, not all the so-called "scrawl of the wild" are about sexual encounters. Graffiti that are more sophisticated include the classic "Queen Elizabeth rules UK?" a spin-off of the "Arsenal rules OK" meme, literary oriented quips like "Oedipus phone your mother!" and homemade philosophy such as "Life is a hereditary disease!" (Kilroy 1984). Graffiti exemplify humour created by the people for the people. Today, Banksy, the well-known graffiti artist sends out serious messages through drawings that are both ironic and funny. Originally, Facebook adopted the wall metaphor to label the space where people could post their thoughts and messages. This has now been replaced by a timeline, but many postings are still humorous.

There is a strong parallel between today's internet memes and graffiti. Indeed, between memes and joke cycles in general. However, graffiti are a more fitting comparison because, like internet memes, they are created to be seen and/or read, but as with all joke cycles, they are open to manipulation. A classic graffito reports two strikingly similar quotes:

> To do is to be – Rousseau
> To be is to do – Sartre

Beneath the two phrases we find a witty rejoinder which creates a new combination of "do" and "be" resulting in "Do be do be do" – Sinatra (Chiaro 1992: 72).

The cycle of "OK" graffiti also works on the alteration of an original frame ("Arsenal rules OK") to memetically become things like "Absolute zero rules 0°K°"; "French diplomacy rules, au quay", etc. Similarly, today an internet meme will generate numerous variants. The "We shall overcomb" meme that was popular just before the election of President Donald Trump exists in countless variants. In one meme, his combover is in the shape of the American eagle, in another the famous quiff contains a comb, while each image macro differs in colour or else in the President's pose. In other words, in these examples, the image macro changes rather than the words. On the other hand, many memes are of the same image macro framed with words that change with each meme. The "one does not simply [walk into Mordor]" meme featuring Sean Bean in the part of Boromir from the film version of *The Lord of the Rings* exemplifies the potential of a single image macro.[1] The original Tolkien quote, "One does not simply X into Mordor" is typically substituted with another verb which is often related to the subject of an image and "Mordor" with another location that has relevance to the situation depicted in the image.

Humour is extremely pervasive in Britain. The British are able to joke at times and in places where ludic behaviour would be inappropriate in other cultures. Joking comes to the British as second nature. From irony to understatement, we are unable to restrain ourselves from adding a sprinkling of wit in everyday discourse. More than our passion for gardening and discussing the weather, humour is an important value in UK culture. And possibly, the fact that the English language has become the world's most prominent language, the language of, amongst other things, the internet, may well be one of the reasons why the internet itself has become the stage for so much humour and silliness. After all, the step from using another language and appropriating the cultural values attached to that language is a small one. If that value involves a positive emotion such is humour, then long live global humour.

Finally, an important question remains unanswered. Is there such a thing as only joking? The sheer quantity of truth underlying the internet memes made by the people for the people reflects anger and a need to be heard. This rebellion is created with a smile on the faces of the thousands of people who generate the sea of politically based humorous content on line. But there is no "only joking" about it.

Note

1 For a variety of examples of this meme, see: www.google.it/search?q=trending+m eme&client=firefox-b-ab&source=lnms&tbm=isch&sa=X&ved=0ahUKEwj35_ Xu-tjTAhVMkRQKHV-qD_sQ_AUIBigB&biw=1147&bih=566#tbm=isch&q=one+do es+not+simply+meme. Retrieved 5 May 2017.

REFERENCES

Aarons, Debra. 2012. *Jokes and the Linguistic Mind*. New York: Routledge.
Adamic, Lada, Mike Develin and Udi Weinsberg. 2015. *Facebook Research*. "The not-so-universal language of laughter". Available at: https://research.fb.com/the-not-so-universal-language-of-laughter/#fn1. Retrieved 15 February 2016.
Alexander, Richard J. 1997. *Aspects of Verbal Humour in English*. Tübingen, Germany: Gunter Narr Verlag.
Apte, Terri. 2009. *What Do You Want from Me? Learning to Get Along with the In-Laws*. New York: W.W. Norton.
Aristotle. 1970. *Poetics*. (Translated by Gerald F. Else). Ann Arbor, MI: University of Michigan Press.
Attardo, Salvatore. 1994. *Linguistic Theories of Humor*. Berlin: De Gruyter.
Attardo, Salvatore and Victor Raskin. 1991. "Script theory (re)visited: Joke similarity and joke representation model". *Humor, International Journal of Humor Research* 4: 293–347.
Bateson, Gregory. 1953. "The position of humour in human communication". In Heinz von Foerster, Margaret Mead and Hans-Lukas Teuber (eds.) *Cybernetics, Circular, Casual and Feedback Mechanisms in Biological and Social Systems*. Transactions of the Ninth Conference. New York: Josiah Macey Jr. Foundation, 1–47.
Baym, Nancy. 1995. "The performance of humor in computer-mediated communication". *Journal of Computer-Mediated Communication* 1(2). Available at: http://onlinelibrary.wiley.com/journal/10.1111/(ISSN)1083-6101. Retrieved 9 October 2017.
Bergson, Henri. 1900. *Le rire. Essai sur la signification du comique*. Paris: Alcan.
Billig, Michael. 2005. *Laughter and Ridicule: Towards a Social Critique of Humour*. London: Sage.
Billingsley, Amy. 2016. "Humoring feminist philosophy: The politics of ameliorative and counter-ameliorative humorous wordplay". University of Oregon: Unpublished PhD.
Bing, Janet. 2007. "Liberated jokes: Sexual humor in all-female groups". *Humor, International Journal of Humor Research* 20(4): 337–66.
Bing, Janet and Joanne Scheibman. 2014. "Blended spaces as subversive feminist humor". In Delia Chiaro and Raffaella Baccolini (eds.) *Gender and Humor: Interdisciplinary and International Perspectives*. New York: Routledge, 13–29.

Bollettieri Bosinelli, Rosa Maria. 1994. "Film dubbing: Linguistic and cultural issues". *Il traduttore nuovo*, XLII(1): 7–28.
Brown, Callum G. 2006. *Religion and Society in Twentieth Century Britain*. Oxford, UK: Routledge.
Bucaria, Chiara. 2009. "Translation and censorship on Italian TV: An inevitable love affair?" *Vigo International Journal of Applied Linguistics* 6: 13–32.
Bucaria, Chiara. 2010. "Laughing to death: Dubbed and subtitled humour in six feet under". In Delia Chiaro (ed.) *Translation, Humour and the Media*. London: Bloomsbury, 222–37.
Bunch, Sonny. 2015. "Hillary Clinton's laugh is, objectively speaking, grating and awful". *The Editor's Blog*. 15 October. Available at: http://freebeacon.com/blog/never-laugh/. Retrieved 15 February 2016.
Butler, Judith. 1990. *Gender Trouble: Feminism and Subversion of Identity*. London: Routledge.
Chafe, Wallace. 2007. *The Importance of Not Being Earnest*. Amsterdam: John Benjamins.
Chiaro, Delia. 1992. *The Language of Jokes, Analysing Verbal Play*. London: Routledge.
Chiaro, Delia. 2004. "Translational and marketing communication: A comparison of print and web advertising of Italian agro-food products". In Beverly Adab and Cristina Valdés (eds.) *The Translator*. Special Issue. *Key Debates in the Translation of Advertising Material*. 10(2): 313–28.
Chiaro, Delia. 2008. "Verbally expressed humor and translation". In Victor Raskin (ed.) *The Primer of Humor Research*. Berlin: De Gruyter, 569–608.
Chiaro, Delia. 2009a. "Issues in audio visual translation". In Jeremy Munday (ed.) *The Routledge Companion to Translation Studies*. London: Routledge, 141–65.
Chiaro, Delia. 2009b. "The politics of screen translation". In Federico M. Federici (ed.) *Translating Regionalised Voices in Audiovisuals*. Rome: Aracne, 27–42.
Chiaro, Delia. 2010a. "Translation and humour, humour and translation". In Delia Chiaro (ed.) *Translation, Humour and Literature*. London: Bloomsbury, 1–29.
Chiaro, Delia. 2010b. "Translating humour in the media". In Delia Chiaro (ed.) *Translation, Humour and the Media*. London: Bloomsbury, 1–16.
Chiaro, Delia. 2013. "Passionate about food: Jamie and Nigella and the performance of food-talk". In Cornelia Gerhardt, Maximiliane Frobenius and Susanne Ley (eds.) *Culinary Linguistics: The Chef's Special*. Amsterdam: John Benjamins, 83–102.
Chiaro, Delia. 2016a. "Filthy viewing, dirty laughter". In Chiara Bucaria and Luca Barra (eds.) *Taboo Comedy: Television and Controversial Humour*. London: Palgrave.
Chiaro, Delia. 2016b. "Mimesis, reality and fictitious intermediation". In Rachele Antonini and Chiara Bucaria (eds.) *Non-Professional Interpreting and Translation in the Media*. Frankfurt, Germany: Peter Lang, 23–42.
Chiaro, Delia. 2017. "Humor and translation". In Salvatore Attardo (ed.) *The Routledge Handbook of the Linguistics of Humor*. New York: Routledge.
Cicero, M. Tullis. 1965. *De Oratore, Libri tres*. Heidesheim, Germany: Olm.
Coates, Jennifer. 2007. "Talk in a play frame: More on laughter and intimacy". *Journal of Pragmatics* 39(1): 29–49.
Coates, Jennifer. 2014. "Gender and humor in everyday conversation". In Delia Chiaro and Raffaella Baccolini (eds.) *Gender and Humor: Interdisciplinary and International Perspectives*. New York: Routledge, 147–64.
Critchley, Simon. 2002. *On Humour*. Routledge: London.
Cronin, Michael. 2004. *Translation Goes to the Movies*. London: Routledge.
Davies, Christie. 1990. *Ethnic Humour around the World: A Comparative Analysis*. Bloomington, IN: University of Indiana Press.

Davies, Christie. 1998. *Jokes and Their Relation to Society*. Berlin: Mouton de Gruyter.
Davies, Christie. 2002. *The Mirth of Nations*. New Brunswick, NJ: Transaction.
Davies, Christie. 2011. *Jokes and Their Targets*. Bloomington, IN: University of Indiana Press.
Davies, Christie. 2012. "The English mother-in-law joke and its missing relatives". *Israeli Journal of Humor Research*, 1(2). Available at: http://sfile.f-static.com/image/users/122789/ftp/my_files/International%201-2/1-Christie%20%20Davies%20mother%20in%20law.pdf?id=11369076. Retrieved 15 February 2016.
Dawkins, Richard. 1976. *The Selfish Gene*. Oxford, UK: Oxford University Press.
Delabastita, Dirk. 2005. "Cross language comedy in Shakespeare". *Humor: International Journal of Humor Research* 18(2): 161–84.
De Mooij, Marieke. 1998. *Global Marketing and Advertising, Understanding Cultural Paradoxes*. Thousand Oaks, CA: Sage.
Denton, John. 1994. "How a fish called Wanda became *Un pesce di nome Wanda*". *Il Traduttore nuovo* 42: 29–34.
Dworkin, Andrea. 2006 [1987]. *Intercourse*. New York: Simon and Schuster.
Egoyan, Atom and Ian Balfour (eds.). 2004. *Subtitles: On the Foreignness of Film*. Cambridge, MA: MIT Press.
Fauconnier, Gilles and Mark Turner. 2002. *The Way We Think: Conceptual Blending and the Mind's Hidden Complexities*. New York: Basic Books.
Franzini, Louis R. 1996. "Feminism and women's sense of humor". *Sex Roles* 11(12): 811–19.
Freud, Sigmund. 1977 [1905]. *Jokes and Their Relationship to the Subconscious*. Harmondsworth, UK: Penguin.
Fry, William F. 2010 [1963]. *Sweet Madness. A Study of Humor*. New Brunswick, NJ: Transaction.
Glenn, Phillip. 2003. *Laughter in Interaction*. Cambridge, UK: Cambridge University Press.
Glenn, Phillip and Elizabeth Holt (eds.) 2013. *Studies of Laughter in Interaction*. London: Bloomsbury.
Goffman, Erving. 1981. *Forms of Talk*. Philadelphia, PA: University of Pennsylvania Press.
Grice, Paul. 1975. "Logic and conversation". In Peter Cole and Jerry L. Morgan (eds.) *Syntax and Semantics 3: Speech Acts*. New York: Academic Press, 41–58.
Groch-Begley, Hannah. 2015. "Media return to deriding Hillary Clinton's laugh: 'The cackle', 'a record scratch', and other tired attacks from the debate". *Media Matters for America*, 14 October. Available at: http://mediamatters.org/blog/2015/10/14/media-return-to-deriding-hillary-clintons-laugh/206136. Retrieved 15 February 2016.
Gulas, Charles, S. and Marc G. Weinberg. 2010. "That's not funny here: Humorous advertising across boundaries". In Delia Chiaro (ed.) *Translation, Humour and the Media*. London: Bloomsbury, 17–33.
Hall, Jeffrey A. 2013. "Humor in long-term romantic relationships: The association of general humor styles and relationship-specific functions with relationship satisfaction". *Western Journal of Communication* 77(3): 272–92.
Hall, Jeffrey A. 2015. "Sexual selection and humor in courtship: A case for warmth and extroversion". *Evolutionary Psychology* 13: 1–10.
Highfield, Tom. 2015. "Memeology Festival 04. On hashtaggery and portmanteaugraphy: Memetic wordplay as social media practice". *Culture Digitally*, 5 November 2015. Available at: http://culturedigitally.org/2015/11/memeology-festival-04-on-hashtaggery-

and-portmanteaugraphy-memetic-wordplay-as-social-media-practice/. Retrieved 10 March 2016.
Hill, Amelia. 2008. "In-law tensions hit women hardest". *The Guardian*, 30 November. Available at: www.theguardian.com/lifeandstyle/2008/nov/30/women-family. Retrieved 16 June 2016.
Hobbes, Thomas. 1991. *Leviathan*. Richard Tuck (ed.). Cambridge, UK: Cambridge University Press.
Hockett, Charles. 1977. "Where the tongue slips there slip I". In: *To Honor Roman Jakobson. Essays on the Occasion of His 70th Birthday, 11 October 1966*, Volume 2. The Hague: Mouton, 910–36.
Hockett, Charles, F. 1977 [1960]. "Jokes". In: *The View from Language: Selected Essays 1948–1964*. Athens, GA: University of Georgia Press, 257–89.
Hoey, Michael. 2005. *Lexical Priming: A New Theory of Words and Language*. London: Routledge.
Holmes, Janet. 2006. "Sharing a laugh: Pragmatic aspects of humor and gender in the workplace". *Journal of Pragmatics* 38: 26–50.
Holmes, Janet and Meredith Marra. 2006. "Humor and leadership style". *Humor* 19(2): 119–38.
Holmes, Janet and Stephanie Schnurr. 2014. "Funny, feminine and flirtatious: Humor and gendered discourse norms at work". In Delia Chiaro and Raffaella Baccolini (eds.) *Gender and Humor: Interdisciplinary and International Perspectives*. New York: Routledge, 165–81.
Hurley, Matthew N., Daniel C. Dennett and Reginald B. Adams Jr. 2013. *Inside Jokes: Using Humor to Reverse-Engineer the Mind*. Cambridge, MA: MIT Press.
Jackobson, Roman. (1959/2004). "On linguistic aspects of translation". In L. Venuti (ed.) *The Translation Studies Reader*, 2nd ed. London: Routledge, 138–43.
Jardon, Ivor Hugh. 2014. *The Best of Sickipedia*. Print on demand. CreateSpace Independent Publishing Platform.
John, Nicholas A. 2012. "Sharing and Web 2.0: The emergence of a keyword". *New Media and Society* 15(2): 167–82.
Katan, David. 1999. *Translating Cultures: An Introduction for Translators, Interpreters and Mediators*. Manchester, UK: St. Jerome.
Kilroy, Roger. 1984. *The Scrawl of the Wild*. London: Corgi Books.
Kirchgaessner, Stephanie. 2016. "Five Star mayor of Turin to create Italy's first 'vegetarian city'". *The Guardian*, 20 July. Available at: www.theguardian.com/world/2016/jul/21/turin-mayor-italys-first-vegetarian-city-five-star. Retrieved 24 August 2017.
Koestler, Arthur. 1964. *The Art of Creation*. London: Hutchinson.
Kotthoff, Helga. 2006. "Gender and humour: The state of the art". *Journal of Pragmatics* 30(1): 4–25.
Kramer, Elise. 2011. "The playful is political: The metapragmatics of internet rape-joke arguments". *Language in Society* 40(2): 137–68.
Krefting, Rebecca. 2014. *All Joking Aside*. Baltimore, MD: Johns Hopkins.
Kuipers, Giselinde. 2006. *Good Humor, Bad Taste: A Sociology of the Joke*. Berlin: De Gruyter.
Kuipers, Giselinde and Barbara Van der Ent. 2016. "The seriousness of ethnic jokes: Ethnic humor and social change in the Netherlands, 1995–2012". *Humor International Journal of Humor Research* 29(4): 605–34.
Lakoff, Robin. 1975. *Language and Women's Place*. San Francisco, CA: Harper and Row.

Langer, John. 1981. "Television's 'personality system'". *Media, Culture and Society* 3(4): 351–65.
Lauer, Jeanette, C. and Robert H. Lauer. 1986. *'Til Death Do Us Part': How Couples Stay Together*. London: Haworth.
Lobrutto, Christina. 2015. "Facebook study on e-laughter says 'lol' is out, 'haha' is in". *Philly Voice*, 15 August. Available at: www.phillyvoice.com/facebook-study-e-laughter/. Retrieved 15 February 2017.
Martin, Rod M. 2007. *The Psychology of Humor: An Integrative Approach*. Burlington, MA: Elsevier Academic Press.
Martin, Rod M. 2014. "Humor and gender: An overview of psychological research". In Delia Chiaro and Raffaella Baccolini (eds.) *Gender and Humor: Interdisciplinary and International Perspectives*. New York: Routledge, 123–46.
McCrum, Robert, William Cran and Robert Macneil. 2002. *The Story of English*, revised edition. Harmondsworth, UK: Penguin.
McGhee, Paul, E. 1971. "Development of the humor response: A review of the literature", *Psychological Bulletin* 76: 328–48.
Mintz, Larry. 1998. *Humor in America: A Research Guide to Genres and Topics*. Westport, CT: Greenwood.
Nash, Walter. 1985. *The Language of Humour*. London: Longman.
Norrick, Neal R. 1993. *Conversational Joking: Humor in Everyday Talk*. Bloomington, IN: Indiana University Press.
Norrick, Neal R. 2000. *Conversational Narrative: Storytelling in Everyday Talk*. Amsterdam: John Benjamins.
Opie, Iona and Peter Opie. 1959. *The Language and Lore of Schoolchildren*. Oxford, UK: Oxford University Press.
Oring, Eliott. 1992. *Jokes and Their Relations*. Lexington, KY: University of Kentucky.
Orwell, George. 2000. "The art of Donald McGill". In Bernard Crick (ed.) *George Orwell Essays*. Harmondsworth, UK: Penguin.
Paolinelli, Mario and Eleonora di Fortunato. 2005. *Tradurre per il Doppiaggio*. Milan, Italy: Hoepli.
Phillips, Adam. 2001. *Promises, Promises: Essays on Literature and Psychoanalysis*. London: Faber and Faber.
Plato 1975. *Philebus*. In J. C. B. Gosling (ed.). Oxford, UK: Clarendon Press.
Provine, Robert R. 1996. "Laughter". *American Scientist* 84(1): 38–45.
Provine, Robert, R. 2000. *Laughter: A Scientific Investigation*. New York: Viking.
Raskin, Victor. 1984. *Semantic Mechanisms of Humor*. Dortrecht, The Netherlands: D. Reidel.
Redfern, Walter. 1984. *Puns*. Oxford, UK: Blackwell.
Ritchie, Graeme D. 2004. *The Linguistic Analysis of Jokes*. London: Routledge.
Rossato, Linda. 2009. "The discourse of British TV cookery". Unpublished PhD Thesis, University of Naples, Federico II.
Rowson, Martin. 2014. "Why the *Great British Bake Off* needs a sprinkling of smut". *The Guardian*, 8 October. Available at: www.theguardian.com/commentisfree/2014/oct/08/great-british-bake-off-sprinkling-smut-sexual-innuendo. Retrieved 10 August 2015.
Ruch, Willibald. 1993a. "Exhilaration and Humor". In M. Lewis and J. M. Haviland (eds.) *The Handbook of Emotion*. New York: Guilford Publications, 605–16.
Ruch, Willibald. 1993b. "Assessment of appreciation of humor: Studies with the 3 WD humor test". In J. N. Butcher and C. D. Spielberger (eds.) *Advances in Personality Assessment*. Hillsdale, NJ: Erlbaum, 27–75.
Sacks, Harvey. 1974. "An analysis of the course of a joke's telling in conversation". In Richard Bauman and Joel Sherzer (eds.) *Explorations in the Ethnography of Speaking*. Cambridge, UK: Cambridge University Press, 337–53.

Sacks, Harvey. 1978. "Some technical considerations of a dirty joke". In Jim Schenkein (ed.) *Studies in the Organization of Conversational Interaction*. New York: Academic Press, 249–75.
Sherzer, Joel. 2002. *Speech, Play and Verbal Art*. Austin, TX: University of Texas Press.
Shifman, Limor. 2007. "Humor in the age of digital reproduction: Continuity and change in internet-based comic texts". *International Journal of Communication* 1: 187–209.
Shifman, Limor. 2011. "An anatomy of a YouTube meme". *New Media and Society* 14(2): 187–203.
Shifman, Limor. 2013. "Memes in a digital world: Reconciling with a concept troublemaker". *Journal of Computer-Mediated Communication* 18: 362–77.
Shifman, Limor. 2014. *Memes in Digital Culture*. Cambridge, MA: MIT Press.
Shifman, Limor and Dafna Lemish. 2010. "Between feminism and fun(ny)mism: Analyzing gender in popular Internet humor". *Information, Communication and Society* 13(6): 870–91.
Shultz, Thomas R. and Robert Pilon. 1973. "Development of the ability to detect linguistic ambiguity". *Child Development* 44(4): 728–33.
Sommers, Jack. 2016. "Eddie Izzard hits out at Ian McEwan's 'uninformed' transgender comments". *The Huffington Post*, 5 April. Available at: www.huffingtonpost.co.uk/entry/eddie-izzard-ian-mcewan-transgender-comments_uk_57035dbbe4b069ef5c00a9ed. Retrieved 30 July 2016.
Sontag, Susan. 2004. "Performance art". In *PEN America Issue 5: Silences*, 92–96. New York: PEN American Centre.
Sternberg, Meier. 1981. "Polylingualism as reality and mimesis as mimesis". *Poetics Today* 2(4): 221–39.
Tannen, Debra. 1994. *Gender and Discourse*. Oxford, UK: Oxford University Press.
Tucker, Grant. 2012. *5,000 Great One-Liners*. London: Biteback.
Usborne, Simon. 2016. "Cereal offenders: The breakfast ads that turn out to be flakey", *The Guardian*, 20 July. Available at: www.theguardian.com/lifeandstyle/shortcuts/2016/jul/20/cereal-offenders-the-breakfast-ads-that-turn-out-to-be-flakey. Retrieved 24 August 2017.
Vennochi, Joan. 2007. "That Clinton cackle". *Boston News*, 30 September. Available at: www.boston.com/news/globe/editorial_opinion/oped/articles/2007/09/30/that_clinton_cackle/. Retrieved 9 February 2016.
Vine, Bernadette, Susan Kell, Meredith Marra and Janet Holmes. 2009. "Boundary marking humour: Institutional gender and ethnic demarcation". In Neal R. Norrick and Delia Chiaro (eds.) *Humor in Interaction*. Amsterdam: John Benjamins, 125–41.
Walker, Nancy. 1988. *A Very Serious Thing: Women's Humor and American Culture*. Minneapolis, MN: University of Minnesota Press.
Weaver, Simon. 2011. *The Rhetoric of Racist Humour: US, UK and Global Race Joking*. London: Routledge.
Weitz, Eric. 2016. "Editorial: 'Humour and social media'". *European Journal of Humour Research* 4(4): 1–4.
Weitz, Eric. 2017. "Online and internet humor". In Salvatore Attardo (ed.) *The Routledge Handbook of the Linguistics of Humor*. New York: Routledge.
Whaite, John. 2014. "Soggy bottoms and hot buns: Why *The Bake Off* thrives on innuendo". *The Telegraph*, 23 September. Available at: www.telegraph.co.uk/culture/tvandradio/11115090/Soggy-bottoms-and-hot-buns-why-the-Bake-Off-thrives-on-innuendo.html. Retrieved 10 August 2015.
Ziv, Anwar. 1988. "Humor's role in married life". *Humor* 1: 223–30.
Ziv, Anwar. 2010. "The social function of humor in interpersonal relationships". *Society* 47(1): 11–18.

INDEX

Aarons, Debra 6, 17, 85
accent 42, 49, 53–5, 58, 61–3, 67, 114, 117, 148
African-American Vernacular English 53
Alexander, Richard 6
alt.com 108
Aristotle 8, 23
Attardo 8, 15–16, 21, 32, 76, 94

banter 3, 12, 36, 38–40, 44–5, 58, 125, 131–35, 137
Bateson, Gregory 21, 32
Bean, Mr 4, 50–1, 56
Bergson, Henri 21
Billig, Michael 10, 45, 70, 77, 89
British National Corpus (BNC) 72, 75, 118
Brand, Jo 37, 43, 45, 98, 107–10
BTL (below the line) 2, 124, 127–28, 134
Bucaria, Chiara 53
Butler, Judith 70, 113

Carlin, George 96
Chafe, Walter 9, 14
Chaplin, Charlie 50, 65
Chiaro, Delia 8, 14, 17–18, 25, 39, 41, 47–8, 52, 62, 64, 67, 79, 125, 137, 139, 152, 156
Cho, Margaret 63, 109
Christie, Bridget 96, 98, 106, 110
chunking 49
class 25, 53, 55, 87

Clinton, Hillary 21, 74–6, 118
Coates, Jennifer 76, 86, 109
comedy 4, 23–4, 35, 37, 45, 49, 50–1, 53, 55–6, 64; scripted 37, 45, 48; slapstick 50; stand-up 10, 71, 93; unscripted 37–8, 42, 45
conceptual blending 16, 18, 117
countryballs 149, 150
Cowell, Simon 44–5
Critchley, Simon 14, 27, 32, 93, 151
Curtis, Tony 112

Davies, Christie 4, 8, 24–6, 30, 63, 76–8, 80, 84–7, 88–90, 92, 150
De Mooij, Marieke 37
dubbing 46–8, 54–5, 113

e-laughter 123
emoji 7, 123–24, 128
Evans, Annie Dr 75, 110
exhilaration 9

Facebook 10, 70, 100, 123–24, 126, 134, 137–40, 142
Far Side, The 27, 93
Freud, Sigmund 21, 23, 26, 64, 90, 151
Fry, William F. 21

gender bending 45, 112–18
General Theory of Verbal Humor (GTVH) 15–16, 21, 94, 105, 107, 109
globalization 4, 37

Goffman, Ervin 14, 51
Google 71, 78, 101, 144–45

hashtag 122, 135–38
Hobbes, Thomas 23
Hoffman, Dustin 112
humour, definitions of 8, 112
humour, theories of: bisociation 8, 21; incongruity 8; linguistic *see* GTVH; superiority 23
humour, types of: acoustic 51–2, 125; audiovisual 35–7, 48, 52–3, 57; charged 5, 70–1, 79, 99, 106, 109, 136; culture-specific 18–19, 25, 48–9, 52, 57–8, 65; non-verbal 2, 50–1; self-deprecatory 105; styles 38, 45–6, 50, 71, 75, 86, 93, 101, 103–5, 108, 116, 134; visual 2–3, 21, 48–53, 55–6, 59, 62, 102, 138, 143–44, 151

innuendo 26, 42, 45–6
image macro 122, 140, 144–45, 148, 157
Izzard, Eddie 115–16

jokes: about blondes 24, 30–2, 78, 86–90; canny 24–8, 30, 50, 64, 81, 83, 86, 90, 100; dirty 26–8, 77, 86–8, 89, 92; about disasters 3, 24, 31–2, 92; ethnic 16, 24, 52–3, 77, 89, 144–45, 149–50; feminist 32, 70, 77, 79, 89, 90, 96, 98–9, 111; marriage 77, 80–3; mother-in-law 16, 77–8, 83–6; about politics 4–5, 25, 78, 123, 130, 136; postfeminist 77, 99, 11; about rape 24, 81, 92–7, 119–20; about religion 17, 24, 30, 77, 123; about sex 17, 24, 26–31, 63–4; sexist 15, 74, 77–86, 105–6; stupidity 24–31, 52, 64, 77, 79, 80, 82, 86–9; underdogs 24, 50, 52, 76; wives 77, 80–3

Kafka, Franz 27, 93
Katan, David 49
Keaton, Buster 50
Kinky Boots 112–15
knowledge resource(s) (KR) 16
Koestler, Arthur 8, 21
Kothoff, Helga 86
Kramer, Elise 92
Kuipers, Giselinde 31, 76, 89

laughter 9–10, 21, 27, 40–1, 57, 64, 71–6, 88, 91, 92, 108–10, 115, 117, 123–25, 128, 142, 152; cackle 71, 74–5; giggle 71–5; guffaw 72, 74–6; "haha" 117, 123, 136
Laurel and Hardy 46–7, 50
Lemish, Dafna 70, 77, 79, 86, 98
Lemon, Jack 112, 114–15
LOL 75, 123, 136, 138, 150, 154
lolcats 139, 145, 150–51

Martin, Rod M. 8–10, 26, 76
Marx Brothers 50, 63, 65–6
McGhee, Paul E. 9
McGill, Donald 27, 34, 82
memes 2–5, 8, 10, 19, 122, 138–42, 143–51, 152–53, 156–57
Millican, Sarah 108–9
Mintz, Larry 144
mirth 9
Mrs Doubtfire 112, 113–14

Nash, Walter 6
Nigella Lawson 38–9
Norrick, Neal 14, 21–2, 122

Oliver, Jamie 38–9
Opie, Fiona and Peter 31
Orwell, George 27, 81–2, 93

Philomena 58–9
photobombing 142–43
photofad 142–43
ping-pong-punning 8, 11–13, 124–30, 132–33, 135
Plato 23
Provine, Robert, R. 9, 124, 137
puns 2–3, 8, 12–14, 17–18, 40, 42, 58, 63, 65, 93, 125–29, 131, 133–34, 154

rage comics 149
Ramsay, Gordon 124, 152–53
Raskin, Victor 15, 17, 21, 94
Redfern, Walter 6, 63
ridicule 2–3, 10, 24, 30, 32, 44–5, 61–3, 66, 74, 88
Rivers, Joan 86, 98, 105, 109
Roach, Hal 47
roast 124
RP (Received Pronunciation) 53
Ruch, Willibald 9

Sacks, Harvey 14, 27–8
Shifman, Limor 70, 77, 79, 98, 107, 141–42, 144, 149

Shrek 53, 55
Six Feet Under 57
Some Like It Hot 112, 114
Sonntag, Susan 29, 50, 60
stereotypes 54, 62, 78–9, 100, 115, 145
subtitling 47–8
Sopranos, The 59
Swift, Jonathan 3–5, 27, 93

taboo 17, 28, 43, 46, 49, 60–2, 64, 73, 76, 89, 97, 109
Tootsie 112, 114
translation 4, 12, 36–7, 46–61, 63–7, 154
tweets 3, 8, 19–20, 124, 134–38, 152
Twitter 1, 70, 124, 134–36, 138–39, 152

varieties of English 4, 54, 58, 65
verbally expressed humour 17, 21, 36, 48, 57, 71

Walliams, David
Wilder, Billy 112
Williams, Robin 112
Wood, Victoria 110
wordplay 2, 12–13, 19, 36, 42, 52, 57, 63–3, 130, 134–35, 151
World Wide Web 3–4, 7, 10, 78, 121–22; Web 2.0 10, 121, 124, 151

YouTube 10, 35, 61–2, 75, 98, 105, 110, 124, 142, 154

Zalone, Checco 53